The Cambridge Companion to
Modernist Culture

Modernism emerged alongside radical challenges to traditional belief systems, the reorganization of public and private spheres, new modes of visual display, and innovations in recreation and entertainment. This interdisciplinary collection focuses on the diverse inventions, products, pastimes, and creative forms that responded to and inspired American and European literature. It explores such wide-ranging subjects as religion, dance, and publishing, thus introducing readers to the diversity of modernist culture. The *Companion* serves as a valuable resource both for those undertaking the study of modernism for the first time and those seeking to expand their knowledge of modernism's cultural moment.

CELIA MARSHIK is Associate Professor of English at Stony Brook University. Her research focuses on British modernism, the relationship between modernism and the middlebrow, and the literature and culture of World War I. Marshik is the author of *British Modernism and Censorship*.

Cambridge Companions to Culture

The Cambridge Companion to
Modernist Culture

Edited by

CELIA MARSHIK
Stony Brook University

CAMBRIDGE
UNIVERSITY PRESS

32 Avenue of the Americas, New York, NY 10013-2473, USA

Cambridge University Press is part of the University of Cambridge.

It furthers the University's mission by disseminating knowledge in the pursuit of education, learning, and research at the highest international levels of excellence.

www.cambridge.org
Information on this title: www.cambridge.org/9781107627390

First published 2015

Printed in the United States of America

A catalog record for this publication is available from the British Library.

Library of Congress Cataloging in Publication data
Marshik, Celia, author.
The Cambridge Companion to Modernist Culture / Celia Marshik, Stony Brook University.
    pages   cm. – (Cambridge Companions to Culture)
ISBN 978-1-107-04926-0 (hardback) – ISBN 978-1-107-62739-0 (paperback)
1. Modernism (Literature)   2. Modernism (Aesthetics)   3. Modernism (Art)
4. Modernism (Music)   I. Title.
PN56.M54M37   2015
809'.9112–dc23   2014020983

ISBN 978-1-107-04926-0 Hardback
ISBN 978-1-107-62739-0 Paperback

Contents

Illustrations

Contributors

GEORGE BORNSTEIN, Patrides Professor of Literature, Emeritus, at the University of Michigan, Ann Arbor, is author or editor of twenty books on modernist literature, including most recently *The Colors of Zion: Blacks, Jews, and Irish 1845–1945* (2011) and a facsimile edition of W.B. Yeats's *The Winding Stair and Other Poems* (2011). He has held fellowships from the Guggenheim Foundation, National Endowment for the Humanities, American Council of Learned Societies, and others.

JESSICA BURSTEIN is the author of *Cold Modernism: Literature, Fashion, Art* (2012) and essays on Henri Gaudier-Brzeska, Dorothy Parker, and sophistication. A member of the editorial committee of the journal *Modernism/ modernity*, she teaches in the Department of English at the University of Washington.

HELEN CARR is Emeritus Professor in the Department of English and Comparative Literature, Goldsmiths, University of London. She has written widely on modernism, women writers, and postcolonial issues. Her most recent books are *The Verse Revolutionaries: Ezra Pound, H.D. and the Imagists* (2009) and the second edition of her critical study, *Jean Rhys* (2012). She is a founder and coeditor of the journal *Women: A Cultural Review*, now in its twenty-fifth year.

ALLEN GUTTMANN's first venture into sports studies, *From Ritual to Record* (1978), outlined a Weberian framework within which to understand the uniqueness of modern sports. Subsequent studies within this framework include *Sport Spectators* (1986), *A Whole New Ball Game* (1988), *Women's Sports* (1991), *Games and Empires* (1994), and *Japanese Sports* (with Lee Thompson, 2001). Guttmann has also published a history of the modern Olympic Games (1992), a biography of Avery Brundage (1984), and a venture in social psychology titled *The Erotic in Sports* (1996). His most recent publications are *Sports: The First Five Millennia* (2004) and *Sports and American Art* (2001). Among his awards is a prize from the International Olympic Committee.

Suzanne Hobson is Lecturer in Twentieth-Century Literature in the Department of English at Queen Mary University of London. She is the author of *Angels of Modernism: Religion, Culture, Aesthetics 1910–60* (2011) and the coeditor of *The Salt Companion to Mina Loy* (2010). She has published book chapters and articles on religious differences and (un)belief in modernist writing as well as on twentieth-century travel writing and guidebooks.

Celia Marshik is Associate Professor of English and faculty affiliate in Cultural Analysis and Theory at Stony Brook University. Her publications include *British Modernism and Censorship* (2006) as well as essays in *Modernism/modernity*, *Modern Fiction Studies*, *Modernism and Copyright* (2010), and *Cultures of Femininity in Modern Fashion* (2011). She is completing a book manuscript on garments in the literature and culture of Britain focusing on the evening gown, mackintosh, fancy-dress costume, and secondhand clothing.

Ulrika Maude is Senior Lecturer in Modernism and Twentieth-Century Literature at the University of Bristol. She is the author of *Beckett, Technology and the Body* (2009) and coeditor of *The Body and the Arts* (2009) and *Beckett and Phenomenology* (2009). She is currently completing a monograph on Beckett and medicine and coediting *The Cambridge Companion to the Body in Literature* (2015) and the *Bloomsbury Companion to Modernist Literature* (2015).

Susan McCabe is a Professor of English at USC, teaching modernist poetics, creative writing, and film. Her publications include two critical books, *Elizabeth Bishop: Her Poetics of Loss* (1994) and *Cinematic Modernism: Modern Poetry and Film* (2005), as well as two books of poetry, *Swirl* (2003) and *Descartes' Nightmare* (2008), which won the Agha Shahid Ali Prize. She was the president of the Modernist Studies Association and held the H.D. fellowship at Yale University's Beinecke Rare Book & Manuscript Room and in 2011 was a Fellow at the American Academy in Berlin. Currently, she is completing a literary biography of Bryher and a book of poems.

Elizabeth Outka is Associate Professor of English at the University of Richmond. She is the author of *Consuming Traditions: Modernity, Modernism, and the Commodified Authentic* (2009), which examines the creation and selling of authentic and nostalgic images in turn-of-the-century Britain, when writers, advertisers, and architects began to evoke an authentic cultural realm paradoxically considered outside the marketplace. Her articles have appeared in *Modernism/modernity*, *NOVEL*, and *Contemporary Literature*, and her current book project, *Raising the Dead: War, Plague, Magic, Modernism*, explores how the twin disasters of World War I and the 1918 influenza pandemic radically shifted perceptions of the corpse.

ILYA PARKINS is Associate Professor of Gender and Women's Studies at the University of British Columbia's Okanagan Campus. Ilya is a specialist in contemporary feminist cultural theories, early twentieth-century Western cultural formations, and fashion studies. She is the author of *Poiret, Dior and Schiaparelli: Fashion, Femininity and Modernity* (2012) and coeditor of *Cultures of Femininity in Modern Fashion* (2011). Her research has appeared in such periodicals as *Australian Feminist Studies*, *Time and Society*, *Women's Studies*, *Biography*, and *Feminist Review*. She is currently at work on a project that examines images of women as unknowable in early twentieth-century mass culture.

ALLISON PEASE is Professor of English at John Jay College, City University of New York. She is the author of *Modernism, Mass Culture, and the Aesthetics of Obscenity* (2000) and *Modernism, Feminism, and the Culture of Boredom* (2012) and the editor of the forthcoming *The Cambridge Companion to Virginia Woolf's To the Lighthouse*.

LEN PLATT is Professor of Modern Literatures at Goldsmiths, University of London. His research interests include modern European literature, James Joyce, popular musical theatre, and postmodern Scottish literature. His publications include *James Joyce: Texts and Contexts* (2011); *Modernism and Race* (ed. 2010); *Joyce, Race and "Finnegans Wake"* (2006); *Musical Comedy on the West End Stage, 1890–1939* (2004); and *Aristocracies of Fiction* (2003).

CARRIE J. PRESTON is an Associate Professor of English and women's, gender, and sexuality studies at Boston University. Her book, *Modernism's Mythic Pose: Gender, Genre, Solo Performance* (2011), was awarded the de la Torre Bueno Award for dance studies. Her essays on modernist culture and performance have appeared in *Modernism/modernity*, *Theatre Journal*, and *Twentieth-Century Literature*, among others. Her forthcoming book, *Learning to Kneel: Noh, Modernism, and the Pedagogies of Transnational Performance*, will examine the influence of noh drama on international modernist theater, poetry, and dance with chapters on W.B. Yeats, Ito Michio, Ezra Pound, Bertolt Brecht, Benjamin Britten, and Samuel Beckett.

ELLEN ROSS is Professor of History and Women's Studies at Ramapo College of New Jersey, where she teaches courses on modern Britain, World

War I, and twentieth-century Europe. She has published articles on London's poor in the nineteenth century and on Victorian and Edwardian women philanthropists and urban missionaries. Her books include *Love and Toil: Motherhood in Outcast London 1870–1918* (1993), *Slum Journeys: Lady Explorers "In Darkest London"* (anthology of collected original sources, 2007), and *Missionaries, Philanthropists, Warriors for Humanity: From Social Work to Global Activism in Britain, 1914–1950* (in progress).

JUDITH WALKOWITZ is a Professor of modern British history and women's history at Johns Hopkins University. Her research and writing have concentrated on nineteenth-century political culture and the cultural and social contests over sexuality. She is the author of *Prostitution and Victorian Society: Women, Class and the State* (1980) and *City of Dreadful Delight: Narratives of Sexual Danger in Late-Victorian London* (1992). Her recent book, *Nights Out: Life in Cosmopolitan London* (2012), recounts the cosmopolitan makeover of early twentieth-century Soho, a space of multiethnic settlement in London, renowned for its social diversity, raucous commerce, and disparate political loyalties.

Chronology

1874   The **First Impressionist Exhibition** (*Première Exposition de la Société Anonyme Coopérative des Artistes – Peintres, Sculpteurs, Graveurs, etc.*) held in Paris

1876   **Alexander Bell** patents the telephone; **John Wanamaker** starts to build his department stores, opening the Grand Depot in Philadelphia and quickly expanding to New York

1877   **Thomas Edison** invents the phonograph

1878   **Newton Heath** (later **Manchester United F.C.**) founded

1882   First neurology clinic in Europe inaugurated at the **Salpêtrière Hospital** in Paris

1885   **Louis Comfort Tiffany** establishes a glassmaking firm in New York City (renames it **Tiffany Studios** in 1902)

1887   **Marshall Field** opens a wholesale store in Chicago

1888   **Football League (soccer)** founded

1889   **Henri Bergson**, *Time and Free Will: An Essay on the Immediate Data of Consciousness*; British bodybuilder **Eugen Sandow** begins career and rise to fame; luxury hotel **The Savoy** opens in London

1890   Fall of Irish political leader **Charles Stuart Parnell**; **James George Frazer**, *The Golden Bough*; **William James**, *Principles of Psychology*; **Henrik Ibsen**, *Hedda Gabler*; **John Tiller** forms "Les Jolies Petites" (later the **Tiller Girls**) dancing troupe

1891   **Oscar Wilde**, *The Picture of Dorian Gray*; **Thomas Hardy**, *Tess of the d'Urbervilles*; **Arthur Conan Doyle**, *Sherlock Holmes* stories begin appearing in *Strand* magazine; **Dr. James Naismith** invents the game of basketball; **Loïe Fuller** starts a craze for skirt dancing

1892   *Vogue* fashion magazine founded in the United States

1893   **Gaiety Girls** begin to appear in shows produced by **George Edwardes**

1894   **Dreyfus Affair,** Jewish officer on the French General staff accused of treason (acquitted in 1906); **Claude Achille Debussy,** *Prélude à l'après-midi d'un faune;* first **major automobile race** sponsored by *Le Petit Journal*

1895   Founding of **London School of Economics; Guglielmo Marconi** invents telegraphy; **Wilhelm Röntgen** discovers **X-rays; Oscar Wilde,** *The Importance of Being Earnest* and trial/conviction; listing of "best-sellers" begins in *The Bookman* magazine in the United States; **Lumière brothers'** first projection of film to a paying audience in Paris; **William Morgan** invents the game of volleyball

1896   *The Daily Mail* (London) launched; **Giacomo Puccini,** *La Bohème;* first modern **Olympic Games** held in Athens; first production of *The Geisha,* a musical comedy that introduced a new craze in Japonaiserie, in London's West End. The show toured Europe and the Empire and went to Broadway

1897   **Havelock Ellis** and **John Addington Symonds,** *Sexual Inversion; Saturday Evening Post* redesigned; **Bram Stoker,** *Dracula*

1898   **Pierre and Marie Curie** discover radium and plutonium; **H.G. Wells,** *War of the Worlds;* **Thomas Hardy,** *Wessex Poems*

1899   Beginning of the **Second Anglo-Boer War** (1899–1902); **William Butler Yeats,** *The Wind among the Reeds;* **Kate Chopin,** *The Awakening;* **Sada Yacco** first performs in the United States

1900   **Boxer Rebellion** in China; **Max Planck** elaborates quantum theory; *Exposition Universelle* in Paris; **Sigmund Freud,** *The Interpretation of Dreams;* **Joseph Conrad,** *Lord Jim;* **Theodore Dreiser,** *Sister Carrie;* **German Soccer Federation** founded

1901   Death of **Queen Victoria,** accession of **Edward VII; Rudyard Kipling,** *Kim;* **Thomas Mann,** *Buddenbrooks;* **Frank Lloyd Wright** designs Willits House

1902   **Second Anglo-Boer War** ends; **Lenin,** *What Is to Be Done?;* **William James,** *Varieties of Religious Experience;* **Joseph Conrad,** *Heart of Darkness;* **André Gide,** *The Immoralist; Times Literary Supplement* founded; **Flatiron Building,** one of the first skyscrapers, completed in New York City; Georges Méliès, *A Trip to the Moon* (film) premieres; **Isadora Duncan** begins touring in

Europe; **Macy's** opens new department store at Herald Square in New York City

1903   **Emmeline Pankhurst** founds the **Women's Social and Political Union;** first successful flight of the **Wright Brothers; Samuel Butler,** *The Way of All Flesh;* **W.E.B. DuBois,** *The Souls of Black Folk;* **G.E. Moore,** *Principa Ethica;* **Henry James,** *The Ambassadors; Daily Mirror* (London) founded; *The Great Train Robbery* (film) premieres; **Henri Desgrange** launches **Tour de France;** first Major League Baseball **World Series**

1904   Outbreak of **Russo-Japanese War** (ends 1905); opening of Dublin's **Abbey Theatre; Anton Chekhov,** *The Cherry Orchard;* **Henry James,** *The Golden Bowl;* **Puccini,** *Madame Butterfly;* the Fédération Internationale de Football Association (**FIFA**) formed

1905   Founding of **Sinn Fein** in Dublin; **Albert Einstein,** "On the Electrodynamics of Moving Bodies" (later known as **Special Theory of Relativity**); **Edith Wharton,** *The House of Mirth;* **George Bernard Shaw,** *Major Barbara;* **Fauvist** exhibition in Paris; first **movie house** opens in **Philadelphia**

1906   **Upton Sinclair,** *The Jungle;* **Everyman's Library** founded; **Intercollegiate Athletic Association** (renamed National Collegiate Athletic Association in 1910) founded

1907   Prototype of the **transistor** patented; **Henri Bergson,** *Creative Evolution;* **Pablo Picasso,** *Les Demoiselles d'Avignon;* **Cubist exhibition** in Paris; Premiere of Franz Lehar's *The Merry Widow* in Vienna

1908   **Ford Madox Ford** founds *The English Review;* **Béla Bartók** first string quartet; **Jack Johnson** becomes first black heavyweight boxing champion

1909   **Henry Ford** perfects assembly-line technique for the Model T; **Sigmund Freud** lectures on psychoanalysis in the United States; **Marinetti,** *Futurist Manifesto;* **Sergei Pavlovich Diaghilev** presents Ballets Russes in France; **Gertrude Stein,** *Three Lives;* **Gustav Mahler,** *Symphony No. 9;* **Henri Matisse,** *The Dance;* **Ezra Pound,** *Personae;* **Gordon Selfridge** opens Selfridges in London

1910   **Japan** annexes **Korea;** Death of **Edward VII,** accession of **George V; Bertrand Russell** and **A.N. Whitehead,** *Principia*

Mathematica; **Post-Impressionist** exhibition in London; **E.M. Forster,** *Howard's End;* **National Collegiate Athletic Association** established

1911   **Frederick W. Taylor,** *The Principles of Scientific Management;* complete English translation of **Friedrich Nietzsche** available for first time

1912   Sinking of the *Titanic;* **Marcel Duchamp,** *Nude Descending a Staircase;* **Thomas Mann,** *Death in Venice;* **Poetry** magazine founded; **Vaslav Nijinsky** choreographs *Prélude à l'après-midi d'un faune;* James Thorpe star of 1912 **Olympic Games**

1913   **Edmund Husserl,** *Ideas: General Introduction to Pure Phenomenology;* **D.H. Lawrence,** *Sons and Lovers;* **Marcel Proust,** *Swann's Way;* **Vaslav Nijinsky** and **Igor Stravinsky,** *Le Sacre du Printemps;* **Armory Show** in New York displays Fauvists, Expressionists, Primitives, and Cubists; **Omega Workshops** established by members of the **Bloomsbury Group;** *Dress and Vanity Fair* (later *Vanity Fair*) society magazine founded; first **Far Eastern Games** in Manila, Philippine Islands

1914   Outbreak of **World War I; Margaret Sanger** coins the phrase **"birth control";** **James Joyce,** *Dubliners;* **Robert Frost,** *North of Boston;* **Des Imagistes** (anthology edited by **Ezra Pound**); founding of *Blast;* founding of *The Little Review* by **Margaret Anderson;** *The New Freewoman* becomes *The Egoist* (1914–1918); first **movie palace** in the United States, the **Mark Strand Theater,** opens in New York City

1915   **Albert Einstein,** *General Theory of Relativity;* first **transcontinental telephone** call from New York to San Francisco; **D.H. Lawrence,** *The Rainbow;* **Ford Madox Ford,** *The Good Soldier;* **Somerset Maugham,** *Of Human Bondage;* **D.W. Griffith,** *Birth of a Nation* (film); **Denishawn School of Dancing and the Related Arts** founded

1916   **Easter Rising** in Dublin; **Margaret Sanger** opens the first **birth control clinic** in Brooklyn, New York; **James Joyce,** *A Portrait of the Artist as a Young Man;* **W.B. Yeats,** *Responsibilities and Other Poems;* **H.D.** (Hilda Doolittle), *Sea Garden;* **Georg Lukács,** *The Theory of the Novel;* **Dada** begins in Zurich; **Oscar Asche,** *Chu Chin Chow* (musical comedy) premieres in London; *The Bing Boys Are Here* (musical revue) opens

1917   The United States enters the war on the Western Front; Bolsheviks take power in Russia; **Carl Jung,** *Two Essays on*

Analytical Psychology; **T.S. Eliot,** *Prufrock and Other Observations;* **Paul Valéry,** *La Jeune Parque;* **Amy Lowell,** *Tendencies in Modern American Poetry;* **Leonard** and **Virginia Woolf** found **Hogarth Press**

1918   **Armistice** signed between Allies and Germany on November 11; **Representation of the People Act** extends **vote to women** over thirty in Britain; **influenza pandemic** in Britain (1918–1919); **Marie Stopes,** *Married Love;* **Lytton Strachey,** *Eminent Victorians;* **Paul Klee,** *Gartenplan;* **Rebecca West,** *The Return of the Soldier;* **Willa Cather,** *My Ántonia;* **Wyndham Lewis,** *Tarr*

1919   **Treaty of Versailles,** end of **World War I; Eighteenth Amendment** to the U.S. constitution ratified, prohibiting manufacturing, distribution, and sales of alcohol; **famine** in Central Europe; **John Maynard Keynes,** *The Economic Consequences of Peace;* **Pablo Picasso,** *Pierrot and Harlequin;* **Virginia Woolf,** "Modern Novels" (revised and retitled as "Modern Fiction" in 1925); **Sherwood Anderson,** *Winesburg, Ohio;* **Bauhaus** founded at Weimar by **Walter Gropius**

1920   **Prohibition** goes into effect in the United States; American **women** achieve the **vote; League of Nations** holds its first meeting; **Mahatma Gandhi** wins control of Indian National Congress; **Sigmund Freud,** *Beyond the Pleasure Principle;* **D.H. Lawrence,** *Women in Love;* **Ezra Pound,** *Hugh Selwyn Mauberly;* **Edith Wharton,** *The Age of Innocence;* **Eugene O'Neill,** *The Emperor Jones;* **Robert Wiene,** *The Cabinet of Dr. Caligari* (film) premieres; New York City nightclub the Club Deluxe (later renamed the **Cotton Club**) opens in Harlem; **Negro National League** established; **National Football League** established

1921   Creation of the **Irish Free State** after ratification of the Anglo-Irish treaty; **Emergency Quota Act** restricts immigration to the United States from Europe; **Frederick Banting** and **Charles Best** discover **insulin; Luigi Pirandello,** *Six Characters in Search of an Author; The Little Review* prosecuted for obscenity over publication of *Ulysses;* **Charlie Chaplin,** *The Kid* (film) premieres; **Coco Chanel** releases her fragrance, **N° 5**

1922   **Mussolini** becomes Prime Minister of Italy; **BBC** founded; opening of **Tutankhamen's** tomb in Egypt; **Ludwig Wittgenstein,** *Tractatus Logico-Philosophicus;* **T.S. Eliot,** *The Waste Land;* **James Joyce,** *Ulysses;* **Virginia Woolf,** *Jacob's Room;*

founding of *The Criterion;* **Friedrich Murnau,** *Nosferatu* (film) premieres

1923 **Le Corbusier,** *Towards a New Architecture;* **Jean Toomer,** *Cane;* **William Carlos Williams,** *Spring and All;* **Cecil B. DeMille,** *The Ten Commandments* (film) premieres; the **Charleston** enters popular culture

1924 First **Labour** government in Britain; British Empire exhibition in London; **E.M. Forster,** *A Passage to India;* **Thomas Mann,** *The Magic Mountain;* London nightclub **Café de Paris** opens

1925 Launch of first miniature camera, the **Leica,** at Leipzig fair; **Adolf Hitler,** *Mein Kampf;* **Virginia Woolf,** *Mrs. Dalloway;* **Gertrude Stein,** *The Making of Americans;* **F. Scott Fitzgerald,** *The Great Gatsby;* **Theodore Dreiser,** *An American Tragedy;* **Franz Kafka,** *The Trial;* **Ezra Pound,** *A Draft of XVI Cantos;* **Pablo Picasso,** *Three Dancers;* **Condé Nast** begins publishing *The New Yorker;* **Sergei Eisenstein,** *Battleship Potemkin* (film) premieres; **Charlie Chaplin,** *The Gold Rush* (film) premieres

1926 **General Strike** throughout Britain; **T.E. Lawrence,** *The Seven Pillars of Wisdom;* **Ernest Hemingway,** *The Sun Also Rises;* **Dmitri Shostakovich,** *Symphony No. 1;* **Martha Graham** dance company founded

1927 **Charles Lindbergh's** first transatlantic solo flight; **Martin Heidegger,** *Being and Time;* **Sigmund Freud,** *The Future of an Illusion;* **Virginia Woolf,** *To the Lighthouse;* **Marcel Proust,** *Le Temps Retrouvé;* **Fritz Lang,** *Metropolis* (film) premieres; **Al Jolson** stars in the first successful "talkie," *The Jazz Singer;* **Elsa Schiaparelli** launches collection of knitwear **pour le Sport;** **Jerome Kern** and **Oscar Hammerstein,** *Show Boat* (musical) premieres

1928 **Alexander Fleming** discovers **penicillin;** **W.B. Yeats,** *The Tower;* **D.H. Lawrence,** *Lady Chatterley's Lover;* **Virginia Woolf,** *Orlando;* **Radclyffe Hall,** *The Well of Loneliness;* **Claude McKay,** *Home to Harlem;* **Bertolt Brecht,** *The Threepenny Opera;* the name of the **Lindy Hop** dance coined

1929 **New York Stock Market** collapses; **Ernest Hemingway,** *A Farewell to Arms;* **Virginia Woolf,** *A Room of One's Own;* **Museum of Modern Art, New York** opens; second **Surrealist** manifesto; **Alfred Hitchcock,** *Blackmail* (film) premieres; first **Marx Brothers** film, *The Cocoanuts,* released

1930   Beginning of global **Depression; Mahatma Gandhi** begins campaign of civil disobedience against British rule in India; **photo flashbulb** invented; **Charles Coughlin's** weekly, hour-long radio program picked up for national distribution in the United States; **F.R. Leavis,** *Mass Civilisation and Minority Culture;* **Sigmund Freud,** *Civilization and Its Discontents;* **Evelyn Waugh,** *Vile Bodies;* **W.H. Auden,** *Poems;* **John Dos Passos,** *U.S.A. Trilogy* (1930–1936); **Hart Crane,** *The Bridge;* **William Faulkner,** *As I Lay Dying;* **Mei Lanfang** tours North America; first FIFA-sponsored **Soccer Football World Cup;** first French professional soccer league

1931   **Scottsboro Boys** accused of rape in Alabama; **Karl Guthe Jansky** builds first **radio telescope; Ernst Ruska** and **Max Knoll** construct first **electron microscope; Virginia Woolf,** *The Waves;* **Salvador Dali,** *The Persistence of Memory;* **Henri Matisse,** *The Unfinished Dance;* **George and Ira Gershwin,** *Of Thee I Sing* (musical) premieres

1932   **Atom split** and **neutron** discovered in England; **Aldous Huxley,** *Brave New World;* **Elizabeth Bowen,** *To the North;* **Q.D. Leavis,** *Fiction and the Reading Public; Scrutiny* launched

1933   **Adolf Hitler** becomes Reich Chancellor in Germany; **André Malraux,** *La Condition humaine;* **Gertrude Stein,** *The Autobiography of Alice B. Toklas; Esquire* founded by the Hearst Corporation

1934   **Jean Rhys,** *Voyage in the Dark;* **Henry Miller,** *Tropic of Cancer*

1935   **Nuremburg Laws** enacted against Jews in Germany; **T.S. Eliot,** *Murder in the Cathedral;* **W.H. Auden** and **Christopher Isherwood,** *The Dog Beneath the Skin;* **Piet Mondrian,** *Composition C (No. III) with Red, Yellow, and Blue;* **George Gershwin,** *Porgy and Bess*

1936   **Spanish Civil War** begins (ends 1939); **George V** dies; **Edward VIII** reigns briefly before abdication crisis brings **George VI** to the throne; **BBC Television** first broadcasts; **John Maynard Keynes,** *General Theory of Employment, Interest, and Money;* **Dylan Thomas,** *Twenty-five Poems;* **William Faulkner,** *Absalom! Absalom!;* **Djuna Barnes,** *Nightwood;* **Stevie Smith,** *Novel on Yellow Paper;* **Charlie Chaplin,** *Modern Times* (film) premieres; games of the **11th Olympiad** celebrated in Berlin (**Jesse Owens** stars); **Shoriki Matsutaro** establishes **Japan Professional Baseball League**

1937   **Mass Observation** movement launched in Britain; **Zora Neale Hurston,** *Their Eyes Were Watching God;* **Pablo Picasso,** *Guernica*

1938   **Lewis Mumford,** *The Culture of Cities;* **Elizabeth Bowen,** *The Death of the Heart;* **Samuel Beckett,** *Murphy;* **Graham Greene,** *Brighton Rock;* **Béla Bartók,** *Violin Concerto No. 2;* **Orson Welles** radio broadcast of *War of the Worlds;* **Leni Riefenstahl,** *Olympia* (film) premieres

1939   Beginning of **World War II;** Hans von Ohain's **jet engine** first to fly successfully; Pan American Airlines begins **commercial flights** between the United States and Europe; **James Joyce,** *Finnegans Wake;* **John Steinbeck,** *The Grapes of Wrath;* **Christopher Isherwood,** *Goodbye to Berlin;* **Bertolt Brecht,** *Mother Courage and Her Children*

1940   Beginning of the **London Blitz; Charlie Chaplin,** *The Great Dictator* (film) premieres

1941   **Pearl Harbor** bombed and the United States enters **World War II; Virginia Woolf,** *Between the Acts*

1942   **Albert Camus,** *L'Etranger*

1944   **Invasion of Normandy** by the Western Allied forces; **Saul Bellow,** *Dangling Man*

1945   **Germany** surrenders and Allies liberate Auschwitz; America drops **atomic bombs** on Japanese cities **Hiroshima** and **Nagasaki;** Japan's surrender; **George Orwell,** *Animal Farm;* **Evelyn Waugh,** *Brideshead Revisited*

Introduction

Modernism emerged out of a historical moment ripe with cultural ferment. As painting, fiction, sculpture, poetry, film, and drama struggled to "make it new" in Ezra Pound's well-known imperative, writers were fascinated with the changes in culture that surrounded them.[1] Whether they lamented the passing of older forms of mass culture, as one finds in T.S. Eliot's paeans to the music hall performer Marie Lloyd, or enumerated the new possibilities opened by travel and industry, as one finds in *Blast*, modernist artists kept their eyes on both mass and high cultural forms and alluded to them in their work.[2]

In the past decade, scholars of modernism have become increasingly attuned to tracing modernist allusions to popular forms, and an interdisciplinary study of modernism has become the new norm. As Douglas Mao and Rebecca Walkowitz observed in their 2008 article "The New Modernist Studies," "*expansion*" has come to characterize the field over the last few decades.[3] A glance at the table of contents for any issue of *Modernism/modernity*, the field's premier journal, or a conference program for the annual meeting of the Modernist Studies Association demonstrates that articles and papers on modernist writers and artists are accompanied by pieces on designers of the period's *haute couture*, examinations of RAF air shows, and analyses of the revolving door, to name just a few.[4] Moreover, the founding in 2005 of the journal *Modernist Cultures*, which "seeks to ... examine the interdisciplinary contexts of modernism and modernity," demonstrates the hunger to understand the relationships among modernism, mass and visual cultures, forms of consumption and entertainment, and the movements of ideas and peoples around the globe. Such scholarship has increasingly moved away from a model based on a "great divide" – Andreas Huyssen's phrase for what he argues was instead a complicated relationship between modernism and mass culture[5] – to nuanced accounts of interpenetrating concerns and ongoing exchanges across cultural strata. Moreover, the new modernist studies has taken to heart the need to specify practices that might previously have been lumped under terms such as "culture" or "society," suggesting that, for example, the composition of Chanel N°5 might provide a better entrée into understanding modernist poetry than generalized accounts of advertising and consumption offer.[6]

While the interdisciplinary turn in modernist studies has produced volumes of exciting scholarship, it presents a high barrier to students and scholars, who are now expected not only to familiarize themselves with texts like *Ulysses* and *The Great Gatsby* and with movements such as Futurism, Symbolism, and the Harlem Renaissance but also to understand the significance of the Charleston, the gramophone, little magazines, "talkies," the bias cut, and numerous other cultural phenomena. Moreover, the relative ease of travel between the UK and the Continent (and between Europe and the United States), the circulation of media around the globe, and the international perspective adopted by many writers dictates that a national specialization – still the standard of many undergraduate and graduate programs – limits a student's awareness of the transnational culture of modernism. The field, once securely organized around a clear cohort of major writers, has exploded, not only in terms of the literary texts now considered worth examining but also in terms of the intertexts with which scholars are expected to be familiar.

This volume seeks to introduce readers to material and intellectual cultures that shaped the world in which modernist literature emerged. It focuses on the diverse inventions, products, ideas, entertainments, and creative forms that circulated roughly between 1890 and 1940 and constituted the culture that provoked and inspired modernist fiction, poetry, and drama.[7] *The Cambridge Companion to Modernist Culture* does not draw upon literature as its primary archive, although the fourteen essays collected here point to moments in which cultural phenomena cross-pollinated modernist work. Instead, the essays draw from a wide range of archives to answer a set of specific questions: What innovations in each field reshaped the material world and individuals' daily lives? To what extent did cultural phenomena work across national boundaries or categories of individual identity (such as gender, race, region, and class) and where did they remain distinctly local? What fields and forms other than the literary produced cultural innovations that might be thought of as modernist? And how might we understand the relationship between a historical moment ever receding from our own and the literature and art that we continue to study, teach, and enjoy?

The essays that follow answer these questions and others for readers beginning to study or hoping to expand their knowledge of modernism's cultural moment, offering lucid introductions to *some* of the venues that inspired and were themselves shaped by modernism. There are, of course, many additional subjects that might have been treated in a volume like this one; topics such as music, architecture, interior design, broadcasting, exhibition culture, pleasure parks, newspapers, and advertising, to name just a few, are largely outside the scope of the essays that follow. What readers will find, however, are essays that offer new and exciting approaches to significant social, political, cultural, and material forms that were themselves innovative and new and that inspired – and were themselves sometimes inspired by – modernism.

Part of what makes coming to grips with modernist culture – and with modernism itself – difficult is that the very category of the "modern" underwent constant change.[8] Perhaps nothing makes the evanescence of the modern clearer than a reminder of how early the term came into use: as the *Oxford English Dictionary* demonstrates, the word was printed as early as 1585 and was thereafter "often contrasted with *ancient* and hence in historical contexts taken as applying […] to the entire period following the fall of the Western Roman Empire."[9] While literary studies, art history, and other fields have reframed the term as a late-nineteenth- and twentieth-century phenomenon, it is important to remember that Western thought has long deployed the term "modern" as a way of understanding a break between the present and the past. This is not meant to evacuate the term of all meaning but rather to suggest we approach "modern" (and terms like "modernity" and "modernism") with some humility as well as the awareness that the qualities they describe are ephemeral. What counted as "modern" in a given year would scarcely be regarded as such ten or even five years later.

This claim is easy to substantiate by glancing at technology, which supplies a long history of innovations that were quickly outmoded by new developments. Wax cylinder recordings, for example, offered unprecedented opportunities to record music, important speeches, and even family gatherings; although this recording method had been invented in 1877, it was thought sufficiently important to receive a whole chapter in *Modern Inventions and Discoveries* (1904), where it was celebrated as a "wonder."[10] Yet within the next ten years, cylinder phonographs would fall out of favor as the gramophone came to dominate the marketplace.

Related examples could be repeated *ad infinitum* in registers ranging from fashion to transport to interior design; men and women who lived through the period came to take innovation (and rapid obsolescence) for granted. F. Scott Fitzgerald would lament that by 1923, "the flapper, upon whose activities the popularity of my first books was based, had become *passé*."[11] This sentiment is startling – Fitzgerald's first book, *This Side of Paradise*, had only been published in 1920, and few observers would have thought the flapper passé three years later – but similar attitudes were widespread. Noël Coward, the British actor, singer, playwright, and composer, expressed such a sentiment when asked to reflect on the 1920s, refusing to identify "[t]he latest dance from America" because "it will have become outmoded and been replaced in the short interval before these words get into print."[12] Coward's sense that the modern – the pursuit of the new, the "latest," and the modish – was such shifting ground that it wouldn't withstand transfer into print is reflected in many of the essays that follow, which demonstrate that the 1900s, the period of the Great War, the 1920s, and the 1930s each had their own version of the modern. The essays here are therefore attuned to historically specific versions of modernity – to not only *what* happened but also *when* and *where*.

If "modern" and "modernist" designate ever-shifting terrain, the term "culture" is equally protean. The twentieth century inherited a fairly constrained understanding of the term, one that was exemplified by Matthew Arnold's 1873 pronouncement that culture was "the best that has been known and said in the world." After the turn of the century, however, "culture" expanded through the use of modifiers: Arnold's successors might speak of a "high culture," but others widened its ambit by coining, for example, "corset culture," "warrior culture," and "popular culture."[13] The essays that follow address developments in long-standing cultural forms – visual art, for example, had a secure place – but they also take up innovations in material objects (pessaries, the automobile, printing presses); in public spaces (the cinema, night club, and department store); in newly organized and expanded forms of leisure (ranging from sport to travel to popular theater); and in ways of understanding the world through belief systems (such as religion) and attitudes toward the self (sexuality, the body). As the contributors to this volume demonstrate, modernism both responded to and took a shaping hand in this culture, and contributors gesture toward novels, poems, and plays that intervened in cultural formations.[14] For example, as Allison Pease's chapter on sexuality demonstrates, writers not only integrated aspects of new sexual theories into their works: authors like Radclyffe Hall would give readers powerful visions of sexual identities through their novels. Although our focus here is not on literature proper – we leave that work to other Cambridge Companions – these essays address dialogues between literature and culture.

A focus on examining different cultural phenomena in their own right offers insight into the twin roles of cultural translation and cultural value in the early twentieth century. No local or national culture evolved in a vacuum; as essays by Helen Carr ("Travel") and others that follow demonstrate, it is partly the rapidity with which things moved around the globe or up (and down) cultural strata that created the sense of a "modern" culture. By cultural translation, I indicate the ways in which practices, productions, types of knowledge, and commodities moved across national borders and around the globe; as Len Platt's essay on popular theater demonstrates, for example, a production like George Edwardes's *The Geisha* (1896) not only enjoyed a phenomenally long first run in London but then went to cities ranging from New York to Cape Town to Singapore to Mumbai. While this example might suggest that cultural transfer went one way – from the center of the Empire outward – the show's *japonaiserie* underlines the role of Asian culture (however imperfectly understood) in inspiring a theatrical production that circulated worldwide. In other cultural venues – including fashion, dance, and religion – the transfer of previously "foreign" motifs and ideas into a Western idiom underlined an increasing transnational experience of the world, whether that experience took the form of voyaging to a new country or continent, wearing a paisley shawl, watching dancers (in film and on stage) who styled their performance after Eastern art, or learning about Eastern religions proper or hybrid belief systems that sought to integrate East and West.[15]

Modern culture moved across national boundaries in the early twentieth century, and it was equally marked by the movement of ideas and practices across cultural strata: across the so-called lowbrow, middlebrow, and highbrow.[16] These terms come into being in the early twentieth century – according to the *Oxford English Dictionary*, "middlebrow" first surfaced in the 1920s – but the very act of attempting to demarcate the brows was a gesture against an increasingly untenable hierarchy of cultural value. Part of the generating force of modern culture, many contributors demonstrate, came from importing high cultural practices into mass forms of entertainment and vice versa. To take up just one example, Carrie J. Preston's chapter on dance explains that early film directors widely employed formally trained dancers, and they also encouraged actors and actresses to seek instruction from schools of dance, which offered techniques to express emotion physically. The movement of dance into and through cinema offers an example of a high cultural form providing inspiration for a genre that was both popular and avant-garde. If the early twentieth century witnessed a "battle of the brows," it was also a time of intense conversation within different forms and among the high, middle, and popular.

Often, of course, cultural transfer and the movement across cultural strata occurred simultaneously. As Judith Walkowitz writes in her chapter on urban pleasures, the Charleston – that dance that was to become so emblematic of modernism's cultural moment – began life in New York's Harlem nightclubs before moving "downtown" to the stages of Broadway. After crossing cultural strata on one side of the Atlantic, the dance was imported to London, and it ascended the cultural ladder through the auspices of the Prince of Wales, who learned the dance from a Café de Paris hostess. This complex synthesis of translation and what we might think of as cultural rehabilitation – turning what Walkowitz calls a "wild and vulgar" African-American dance into a step adopted by elites on both sides of the ocean – occurred through the actions of specific individuals (the Prince of Wales), nameless enthusiasts (the Café de Paris hostess, among others), and business owners looking to profit by promoting the latest, the most modern dance. Such crossing of national boundaries and cultural strata created the feeling of the modern not only through movement but also through a challenge to what had been considered appropriate or normal before.[17]

The essays in this volume are organized under three rough rubrics. The first section, "Shaping Worldviews," tackles large-scale systems of thought and belief that influenced daily life and individual identity for people around the globe. These essays, which address religion, science, sexuality, and internationalism, trace challenges to traditional understandings of the self as bounded by relation to a creator, a unique ontological experience as human, a biologically dictated sex drive, and an identification with one nation and people. Modernist culture, these essays demonstrate, meant not taking for granted one's identity or place in the world, offering optics like the X-ray and opportunities for travel such as the need for humanitarian relief workers; together, shaping worldviews offered modernists and their contemporaries the chance to see *themselves*, sometimes literally and sometimes figuratively, anew.

The next section of the collection, "Visual Culture," pays extensive tribute to what some critics have described as the period's "ocularcentrism": to seeing as *the* mode of perception and knowledge above all others.[18] Chapters on consumer culture, film and cinema, visual art, dance, and fashion explore some of the period's opportunities to delight and manipulate the eye – to show modern culture to itself in spectacular forms. Whether spectators could move through these venues as shoppers walked through the new department stores, observe them on a screen, canvas, or stage, or experience them bodily through dance or fashion, visual culture fueled the experience of the modern by circulating and representing the new.

The final section of the volume, "Entertainments," rounds out the collection by exploring twentieth-century developments in leisure activities ranging from social dance to reading. If some modernist writers prided themselves on making "no compromise with the public taste," as *The Little Review* motto famously stated, the public taste itself was less a static entity than in search of novelty and venues for self-expression and -improvement. The essays grouped here take up urban pleasures, sport, travel, popular theater, and publishing, areas of cultural practice that provided new venues for gratification and for cultural experience. If, as Laura Frost has recently argued, modernists were largely united in repudiating pleasure (or making pleasure difficult),[19] the culture in which they created was simultaneously offering increasing kinds and numbers of pleasurable experiences. Such entertainments were not, however, apolitical or unchallenging: as the essays in this final section indicate, pleasurable venues shaped understandings of race, class relations, the relationship between the so-called West and the rest, and (in some cases) provided access to modernism itself.

The Cambridge Companion to Modernist Culture does not assume that those who pick it up will necessarily read it from cover to cover. Like other Cambridge Companions, it allows the reader to dip in and out of individual essays, and yet those who read it through will discover intriguing

points of contact across disparate topics. For example, many contributors highlight the significance of what might be called new social and
cultural actors; women, Jews, African Americans, and other previously
marginalized groups took on significant roles as social and cultural producers in modernism's historical moment. In "Militarism, Pacifism, and
Internationalism," for instance, Ellen Ross examines the ways in which
women found new forms of public engagement through such venues
as policing, humanitarian work, and political advocacy. As Ross notes,
(white) men had long found in the military and national or international
politics an outlet for their talents and ambitions; what was genuinely
modern about these arenas in the twentieth century was that women
took traditionally feminine accomplishments (such as training in foreign languages) into decidedly untraditional directions. Allison Pease
("Sexuality"), Elizabeth Outka ("Consumer Culture"), and Ilya Parkins
("Fashion") similarly take up the newly important role of women as educators, social reformers, consumers, and designers in modern culture.
Such examples shed light on the complex relationship between women
and modernity, which (as Rita Felski has argued) was often thought of as
itself feminine (a gendering that could be complimentary or critical).[20]

Other essays look at ways in which different types of new social actors
networked; sometimes, the cultural aspirations of one group found an
accord with (or even facilitated) the ambitions of others. Walkowitz, for
example, notes how the practice and representation of female hedonism – of young, privileged women increasingly drawn to the nightclub
scene – twinned with the activities of black musicians, bandleaders, and
GIs to produce startling new images of interracial dancing. If images
in the *Picture Post* and elsewhere did not directly confront sexism and
racism, photographs of interracial couples highlighted the movement of
the "color question" onto the literal and figurative dance floor. Although
the offices of publishing houses might seem worlds away from shady
nightclubs, George Bornstein's essay echoes Walkowitz's analysis of the
intersecting cultural work of different social actors; as Bornstein writes,
women and Jewish men moved into publishing in the early twentieth
century, and their book lists often featured African-American, Irish, and
other authors who had previously struggled for entrée into print. While
these upstart publishers were not always appreciated by high modernist authors – Bornstein offers William Faulkner and T.S. Eliot as two
examples – they played a leading role in the dissemination of works of
the Harlem Renaissance as well as of British and Irish modernism in the

United States. As a whole, then, essays in this collection situate modern (and thus modernist) culture as a space in which groups that had previously been marginalized moved, however haltingly and unequally, into new prominence, sometimes in company with others.

In addition to collectively exploring the impact of changing social actors on modernist culture, many essays highlight what we might think of as an expanded model of consumerism. As venues for literal commodity exchange increased in number and size, they were accompanied by a consumerist reorientation to noncommodity items and experiences – or rather, a complication of the status of both material objects *and* ideas as commodities. Elizabeth Outka's essay sets the stage for this line of inquiry, noting that as consumer culture *became* a culture, marketers evoked "ideas of authenticity and the genuine artwork" and promised "that products were not tainted by commerce – and yet were the latest thing and might be easily purchased." Through such purchases, consumers were encouraged to remake their own gender and class identity, Outka argues, as though a persona or social standing might itself be available in the new stores. Ilya Parkins's analysis similarly explores the ways in which fashion put pressure on the perceptual "divides among art, industry, and commerce." As she writes, high fashion in particular "offered a vision of the ways that commerce impinged on the supposedly rarified sphere of art"; as other contributors demonstrate, modernist culture also witnessed commerce impinging upon foundational systems of identification and belief. Suzanne Hobson's essay on religion and spirituality, for example, argues that the experience of modern religion and faith was uniquely characterized by a range of options from which would-be adherents might select. Some faiths were themselves aware of the need to "market" their particular brand in the face of stiff competition; Hobson cites, in particular, the example of Christian Science. This development – the sense that an individual could "shop" for a congenial spiritual practice instead of worshipping in the footsteps of her fathers – points toward the qualified freedom offered by a thoroughly consumer culture, but as Hobson takes pains to demonstrate, it also generated a backlash that drove some people (including, famously, T.S. Eliot) into the arms of the Catholic and Anglican Churches. Modernist culture emerges through these essays and others as offering unprecedented choices but also the anxiety that many people felt in the face of their increased options.

Another thread that emerges from the essays as a whole is the development of what Jessica Burstein calls the "inter-arts": creative practices that merge multiple genres and forms. Burstein's immediate example is literary impressionism, but she also points to the deep relationships among painting, music, and poetry as well as to specific modernist productions that startlingly fuse, for example, sculpture and photography. As she writes, "Hans Bellmer made a doll but never showed it; it exists as a photograph." Similar examples recur across the collection. I have already mentioned Preston's attention to the interpenetration of dance and film; Susan McCabe's essay, on film and cinemas, points to silent film's borrowing from music and collage and concludes with a brief discussion of *Destino*, an animated short produced through the collaboration of Salvador Dali and Disney. Together, Preston's and McCabe's essays suggest that film's quintessential modernity stems not only from its emergence during the last decade of the nineteenth (and flourishing in the twentieth) century but also from its foundational conversations with other visual arts. The amalgamation of artistic and cultural forms these essays explore surfaces elsewhere in the volume, sometimes in surprising locations. Outka informs readers that not only did postimpressionist artists and others design advertisements for the new retail emporiums; early department stores also displayed original paintings and mounted art shows that were previously the purview of museums and galleries. This interchange of media and of genres of public space – art museum meets shopping center – points to a fundamental hybridity of modernist culture, which felt modern in part because of boundary crossings that challenged categorization of artistic products, forms of entertainment, and the organization of physical space.

The sense of modernity as boundary crossing, intersectional, and trans is perhaps nowhere more evident than in the emerging sense of alignment between the human body and the machine. As Ulrika Maude argues in her chapter on science, technology, and the body, modernist culture emerged at a moment when, in her words, there was a "newly discovered understanding of the human as itself biomechanical." Perhaps nothing captures the impact of this understanding better than "The Racing Reporter," Otto Umbehr's photograph of a hybrid man-machine that neatly represents the sense that modern humans, too, were more than *one* kind of substance. The ambivalence with which many artists, philosophers, and scientists regarded this biomechanical body did not prevent others from attempting to harness and "engineer" that body's properties for better performance. In his chapter on sport, Allen Guttmann demonstrates that ludic technology – new equipment and training – characterizes the development of both individual and team sports in the period. Guttmann offers a range of examples – including the development of purpose-built rowing shells, running hurdles, and even performance-enhancing drugs – that speak to the desire to extend and improve human physical capacity. As Guttmann notes, entire sports were created as part of the effort to fine-tune the human machine: the game of basketball developed to meet the express goal of creating opportunities to improve fitness while diminishing the chances of injury. The range of attitudes toward the body as machine points to its liberational promise – man might become better, stronger, faster, and more efficient – and to the fear that modernity would make humans nothing *but* machines, as McCabe's discussion of Charlie Chaplin's *Modern Times* illustrates.

Taken together, these essays shed light on a moment and movements that continue to attract scholars while also providing material for contemporary popular culture and literary fiction. Recent films based on specific authors and sites of modernist exchange, such as *Midnight in Paris* (2010), have portrayed a modernist "lifestyle" in compelling ways. Television series, such as Ken Burns's PBS documentary *Prohibition* (2011) and Julian Fellowes's drama *Downton Abbey* (2011–), have piqued viewers' interest in the culture of the period. On the stage, portrayals of modernist writers and their social circles, as well as theatrical versions of modernist texts like *Cabaret*, have kept modernism in the public mind. Finally, contemporary writers continue to set popular and critically acclaimed novels in the modernist period, thus figuring the early twentieth century as a persistent legacy.[21] If these productions often run the risk of a one-sided celebration of modernist culture as glamorous, increasingly egalitarian, and pleasurably dangerous, the essays here work to reestablish a period in which progress was experienced as Janus faced. The affect of modernist culture was a synthesis of pleasure *and* anxiety; *The Cambridge Companion to Modernist Culture* will assist scholars and students in orienting themselves to the variety and the unity of cultural formations that shaped and were shaped by modernism proper.

Notes

1   This slogan was the title of an essay collection Pound published in 1934: *Make It New* (London: Faber, 1934). The phrase later reappeared in his China Cantos.
2   T.S. Eliot, "London Letter," *The Dial* 73.6 (1922): 659–663; *Blast*, for its part, would celebrate ships, seafarers, and ports as well as the machinery that made ocean travel possible in its first issue.

3 Douglas Mao and Rebecca L. Walkowitz, "The New Modernist Studies," *PMLA* 123.3 (2008): 737. Emphasis original.

4 See Caroline Evans, "Jean Patou's American Mannequins: Early Fashion Shows and Modernism," *Modernism/modernity* 15.2 (2008): 243–263; Paul K. Saint-Amour, "On the Partiality of Total-War," *Critical Inquiry* 40.2 (2014): 420–449; and James Buzard, "Perpetual Revolution," *Modernism/modernity* 8.4 (2001): 559–581.

5 Andreas Huyssen, *After the Great Divide: Modernism, Mass Culture, Postmodernism* (Bloomington: Indiana University Press, 1987). See the conclusion of Elizabeth Outka's essay in this volume for discussion of the conversation Huyssen's book started.

6 See the first chapter of Judith Brown's *Glamour in Six Dimensions: Modernism and the Radiance of Form* (Ithaca, NY: Cornell University Press, 2009), which insightfully reads Wallace Stevens alongside the Chanel fragrance.

7 Modernist studies has certainly experienced what Mao and Walkowitz call a "temporal expansion" (738); scholars like Susan Stanford Friedman, Laura Doyle, and others have lengthened modernism's "when" far beyond the roughly fifty years this volume takes as its focus. I have adopted a more limited temporal ambit because, in the words of David James and Urmila Seshagiri, "Temporal contraction, or periodization, helpfully counterbalances the spatial expansiveness of the new modernist studies. Indeed, giving precision to modernism's place in time facilitates a more historically robust understanding of how it moved across cultures." See their "Metamodernism: Narratives of Continuity and Revolution," *PMLA* 129.1 (2014): 90.

8 Many scholars have taken up the definition of "modernism" as a critical question; Susan Stanford Friedman's "Definitional Excursions: The Meanings of Modern/ Modernity/Modernism" (*Modernism/modernity* 8 [2001]: 493–513) clearly traces the omissions caused by different methods of constructing the term.

9 The *OED* cites Thomas Washington's translation of Nicholas de Nicolay's *Nauigations Turkie* as the 1585 example.

10 Ray Stannard Baker, "The Story of the Phonograph," in *Modern Inventions and Discoveries* (New York: J.A. Hill, 1914), 1.

11 F. Scott Fitzgerald, *The Crack-Up*, ed. Edmund Wilson (New York: New Directions, 1956), 29.

12 Noël Coward, *The Letters of Noël Coward*, ed. Barry Day (New York: Vintage, 2009), 164.

13 The *OED* entry for "culture" includes Arnold's definition as well as the modified examples.

14 In this respect, the collection echoes Rita Felski's concerns that context may be invoked to explain away literature and art. As she observes, "Context is often wielded in punitive fashion to deprive the artwork of agency, to evacuate it of influence or impact, rendering it a puny, enfeebled, impoverished thing. We inflate context, in short, in order to deflate text" (582). The title of her piece, "Context Stinks!" (*New Literary History* 42.4 [2011]), indicates the need to reassess the relationship between culture and the artwork that evolves along with it (582).

15 Major art exhibitions over the last two decades underline the global development and transfer of modern artistic movements themselves; the 2003 *Art Deco* exhibition organized by the V & A documented the ways in which deco style drew upon Egyptian, Mexican, Asian, and African motifs and techniques and traced how artists in East Asia, India, Latin America, and South Africa (as well as Europe) adapted Art Deco to local tastes. See *Art Deco 1910–1939*, edited by Charlotte Benton, Tim Benton, and Ghislaine Wood (Boston: Bullfinch Press, 2003).

16 Mao and Walkowitz describe this development as a "vertical reconfiguration" unique to modernist studies since modernism itself was formerly understood as a movement of high against low culture (738).

17 What Jessica Berman describes as "trans-" – "not only a crossing of boundaries but also a challenge to the normative dimension of the original entity or space" – neatly captures the perceptual experience of modern culture I seek to capture here. See her *Modernist Commitments: Ethics, Politics, and Transnational Modernism* (New York: Columbia University Press, 2011), 10–11.

18 For an economic discussion of ocularcentrism, see Liz Conor's *The Spectacular Modern Woman: Feminine Visibility in the 1920s* (Bloomington: Indiana University Press, 2004), chapter 1 and particularly pp. 19–23.

19 See *The Problem with Pleasure: Modernism and Its Discontents* (New York: Columbia, 2013). Frost argues that "the fundamental goal of modernism is the redefinition of pleasure: specifically, exposing easily achieved and primarily somatic pleasures as facile, hollow, and false, and cultivating those that require more ambitious analytical work" (3). This collection does not challenge Frost's thesis but does seek to enrich a reader's understanding of the period's pleasures.

20 Felski explores how "the figure of the woman and the idea of the feminine" emerged as concepts to express ambivalences about modernity. See *The Gender of Modernity* (Cambridge: Harvard University Press, 1995), 210.

21 Contemporary novels set in and around modernism include Alan Hollinghurst's *The Stranger's Child* (2011), Paula McLain's *The Paris Wife* (2011), and Ellis Avery's *The Last Nude* (2012), but this list is inevitably partial. See James and Seshagiri for a discussion of additional writers who have been inspired by modernism's legacy.

Part I

Shaping Worldviews

1
—————

Religion and Spirituality

> Christianity and/or religion in the anglo-saxon world of our time
> has been something optional. Some of us went to church in our
> childhood and some didn't. – Ezra Pound, *Guide to Kulchur* (1952)[1]

Ezra Pound did attend church as a child. His parents were active
members of the Presbyterian church in Wyncote, Pennsylvania, and
Pound made his own Profession of Faith in March 1897. T.S. Eliot was
also raised in a prominent Protestant family. His parents belonged to
the Unitarian Church, a liberal and forward-thinking denomination
that Eliot definitively rejected when in 1927 he converted to Anglo-
Catholicism. H.D. grew up among members of a distinctive Pietist sect,
the Moravian Brethren, in Bethlehem, Pennsylvania, while Marianne
Moore, like Pound, was raised a Presbyterian and continued to attend
services for most of her life. In Britain and Ireland, the picture was just as
mixed. Virginia Woolf's father, Leslie Stephen, had famously become an
agnostic, giving up his Cambridge tutorship in order to do so. Woolf did
not, then, attend church as a child, although other members of her family held strong religious beliefs, including her Aunt Caroline Stephen, a
Quaker, from whom Woolf would inherit £2,500. Mina Loy had a non-
observant Jewish father and an Evangelical mother who, according to
Loy, had retained from Christianity only the idea that to suffer is to be
closer to God. Between the "unbelief," as Loy puts it, of her father and
the cruelty of her mother, the young Loy struggled to know which way
to turn: "'Be ashamed,' says the Christian / 'Think,' says the Jew."[2] James
Joyce was schooled by the Jesuits in Dublin and, although he famously
renounced his belief, he appreciated the standard of education his religion had afforded him.[3]

The Nineteenth-Century Background

The variety of religious and nonreligious childhoods seen among modernist writers is typical of the men and women of their generation, especially those who came from comfortable backgrounds and had similar levels of education. In England, although the Church of England remained the official (established) religion, the nineteenth century had seen a move toward greater tolerance and accommodation of other faiths. In 1829, the Catholic Relief Act removed the requirement for public officers to take Communion in the Anglican Church, effectively permitting not only Catholics but also Jews and Nonconformists to hold positions in public organizations. The Education Act of 1870, which made education compulsory for children aged between five and eleven, included a clause stipulating that instruction was to be nondenominational. While the curriculum was still broadly Christian in nature, educators were no longer permitted to favor the theology and practices of one Christian confession over another. This new spirit of tolerance was extended to those of no religion, too. In a famous case, the recently elected Member of Parliament Charles Bradlaugh applied to the courts for the right to take office without taking the Oath of Allegiance. Instead of swearing the oath to God, he asked to be permitted to "affirm" his loyalty. This privilege had already been extended to Quakers. Why not, Bradlaugh argued, extend it to the nonreligious, too?[4]

In the United States, religious freedom was and still is guaranteed by the First Amendment of the American Constitution. Alexis de Tocqueville, the French political theorist who traveled through America in 1831–32, explores the consequences of the separation of church and state in the second volume of *Democracy in America* (1840). Christianity had grown, he remarks, even though religious observance and practice might seem to run counter to the thoroughly modern and democratic spirit with which America had been founded. When religion strays into politics, he continues, it inevitably attracts controversy and argument as seen in the literature and philosophy of his own country. In America, by contrast, religion has been insulated from politics, and under these conditions, Christianity has grown and diversified:

> In America, religion has, so to speak, set its own limits; the realm
> of religion has remained entirely distinct from the realm of
> politics, so that it has been possible to alter the ancient laws easily
> without shaking previously held beliefs. Christianity has therefore

maintained a strong sway over the American mind and – something I wish to note above all – it rules not only like a philosophy taken up after evaluation but like a religion believed without discussion. In the United States, Christian sects are infinitely varied and are endlessly modified, while Christianity itself is an established and unassailable fact which no one undertakes either to attack or defend.[5]

De Tocqueville's view of American religion as politically disinterested does not stand up to scrutiny and, as this chapter goes on to explain, politics and religion are very much entwined in the modern era. But the question de Tocqueville attempts to answer by these means *is* a crucial part of the discussion of religion in this period: How could belief in God as the ultimate source of moral law be reconciled with modern standards in public life such as democratic representation, independence of mind and conscience, and evidential standards of proof?

Religion, Spirituality, and Secularism

Although Pound is right, then, to suggest that in his generation religion had increasingly become an "option," it does not necessarily follow that religion was easily adopted or that it was easier to believe in God than it had been in previous generations. On the contrary, as Pound goes on to suggest in *Guide to Kulchur*, to profess a hard-line belief in God had become altogether more difficult in his own time than to opt for unbelief or the softer alternatives of agnosticism or spirituality: "'Belief' as the pious once used the term is alien to our age. We may have a respect for the unknown. We may have a wide sense of possibility."[6] As recent studies of secularism have pointed out, the problem for religion in a secular age is not just that belief has become an option but that unbelief has become the default option. To believe in God requires more effort than it used to do, not least because the believer is very likely to encounter stiff resistance to his or her views. On discovering that T.S. Eliot had converted to Anglo-Catholicism, for instance, Virginia Woolf was famously aghast: "I mean there's something obscene in a living person sitting by the fire and believing in God."[7] G.K. Chesterton, who styled himself as an unfashionable spokesperson for the Christian cause, suggested that it was no longer considered decent even to mention the subject of religion in a public place. Chesterton's novel, *The Ball and the Cross* (1905), contains a scene in which a magistrate upbraids a plaintiff for daring to bring a religious dispute into his courtroom: "'Be quiet,' said the magistrate angrily, 'it is most undesirable that things of that sort should be spoken about – a – in public, and in an ordinary Court of Justice [...] to talk in a public place about one's most sacred and private sentiments – well, I call it bad taste.'"[8] The magistrate is self-evidently a caricature, but his words are symptomatic of what Chesterton takes to be the prevailing indifference to, even revulsion from, Christianity in his times: "It is still bad taste to be an avowed atheist . . . it is equally bad taste to be an avowed Christian."[9]

What, then, of the alternatives to which Pound alludes in the phrase "respect for the unknown and a wide sense of possibility"? In one sense, he might be taken to mean the commonsense understanding of the difference between religion and spirituality in which to be spiritual means to commit to the "inner truth" of religion rather than its external or social forms ("practices, symbols and beliefs played out in a collective setting"). As the introduction to *Religions in the Modern World* points out, this difference is both approximate and entirely relational so that "spirituality" entails an understanding of and conscious rejection of "religion" in the sense outlined earlier.[10] Giselle Vincent and Linda Woodhead add that this meaning is already implicit in the early use of the term "spirituality" to describe the mystical stream within Christian, Jewish, and Islamic faiths. The mystic withdraws from the world and, by extension, the worldly aspects of religion such as church officials and collective worship in search of a more immediate experience of the divine.[11]

During Pound's lifetime, religion was subject to new methods of investigation, which produced, on the one hand, generic and transcultural definitions of religion, as in the religious/spiritual distinction seen earlier and, on the other, more fine-grained analysis of the different ways in which religion might be understood and practiced. Anthropologists, for example, often studied so-called primitive religions for clues as to the premodern origins of Western beliefs and traditions. Psychologists looked at the effect of religion on the mind and, on occasion, suggested that belief had an organic or material cause, while sociologists sought to explain religion in terms of the function it played in the wider social context. One of the general results of this study was to further separate spirituality from religion (understood in the manner described previously) so that spirituality increasingly floated free from tradition of any kind while religion, conversely, was more tightly bound into its social forms.

The psychologist and philosopher William James, for example, makes a sharp distinction between religion as an inherited set of conventions and traditions and religious feeling as it is experienced firsthand. For

James, philosophy and theology are second-order phenomena built on a feeling that is irreducible to system or reason: "I do believe that religious feeling is the deeper source of religion and that philosophical and theological formulas are secondary products, like translations of a text into another tongue."[12] James's study, *The Varieties of Religious Experience* (1902), privileges the testimony of converts and the founders of new religions, especially Protestant confessions, over that of churchmen and -women. This method is, of course, altogether consistent with James's theory, but it conveniently ignores the very people who might speak for the strength and felt intensity of religious beliefs, even, or perhaps especially, when they are shared with family, church, or community.

The priorities are reversed, however, in the works of social scientists such as Max Weber and Emile Durkheim. Like James, Durkheim attempts a general definition of religion, which is capacious enough to include even nontheistic religions (Buddhism, for example) while excluding magic on the grounds of the contempt in which magic is held by most churches. Durkheim departs from his contemporary, however, in making inherited group behavior the determining factor in his definition:

> We arrive thus at the following definition: *A religion is a unified system of beliefs and practices relative to sacred things, that is to say, things set apart and forbidden – beliefs and practices which unite into one single moral community called a Church, all those who adhere to them*. The second element thus holds a place in my definition that is no less essential than the first: In showing that the idea of religion is inseparable from the idea of the Church, it conveys the notion that religion must be an eminently collective thing.[13]

needs definition as not a 'truth' anymore

The need to *define* religion is itself particular to the modern age. While disputes over theology and liturgy have long been part of the history of religions, the question as to what religion means *per se* only arises when there are viable alternatives such as secularism or agnosticism. In fact, both James and Durkheim thought of themselves as contributing to an incipient "science of religions." The origins of this science lay in the late-nineteenth-century comparative studies of myths undertaken by E.B. Tylor, Max Müller, and G.S. Fraser. The influence of these studies on *The Waste Land* is well known. But the science of religion permeates modernist cultures in other ways, too; it lends support to the claim that spirituality rather than tradition is religion degree zero *and* to the idea that community rather than good works or individual salvation is its ultimate end. On the one hand, John Middleton Murry can legitimately claim to be "religious" without affiliation with any one particular Church: "I am not Christian . . . I have been forced to the conclusion that I am religious."[14] On the other, writers such as D.H. Lawrence and H.D. can plausibly imagine a new religion, one in which belief would be lived rather than preached. H.D. herself featured in Lawrence's plans to found a new community, which would be religious in ethos without, that is, having the structure or organization of a church as conventionally understood:

> I hold this the most sacred duty – the gathering together of a number of people who shall so agree to live by the *best* they know. The ideal, the religion, must now be *lived practiced*. We will have no more *churches*.[15]

An Education in Unbelief

The reasons that unbelief and/or "spirituality" seemed to have overtaken the church as the default option for the modern man and woman are complex and have variously been seen to involve increased levels of migration (especially into cities, which put strain on the parish system as it had operated in England), the declining status of the ministry as compared to other professions, and the gradual erosion of the church's visibility in and influence over public life. There were powerful intellectual reasons to opt for unbelief, too, although, as historians of the period point out, it is difficult to gauge their impact outside the relatively small circles in which they were discussed. Nonetheless, the idea of a burgeoning literature of unbelief is regularly rehearsed in modernist novels. This literature includes not only explicitly antireligious works but also a variety of books, both fact and fiction, that were thought to suggest the godless nature of the times. Modernist authors and fictional characters are frequently recorded as reading these books, and even when, as is often the case, they later reject skepticism in favor of belief, there remains a strong sense that to believe in God is to swim against a powerful tide. Many of D.H. Lawrence's characters, for example, are, like Lawrence himself, well read in nineteenth-century evolutionary science and psychology, French naturalism and realism, and pessimistic German philosophy. In an early story, "A Modern Lover" (written

1909–10), the young writer Cyril Vane recalls the books he shared with his adolescent sweetheart, Muriel:

> He smiled as he traced the graph onwards plotting the points with Carlyle and Ruskin, Schopenhauer and Darwin and [T.H.] Huxley, Omar Khayyam, the Russians, Ibsen and Balzac; then Guy de Maupassant and "Madame Bovary." They had parted in the midst of Madame Bovary. Since then had come only Nietzsche and William James.[16]

Huxley was a biologist and major public advocate of Darwin and evolutionary theory. He coined the word "agnosticism" and said famously of *The Origin of Species*: "Extinguished theologians lie about the cradle of every science as the strangled snakes besides that of Hercules."[17] Omar Khayyam was the twelfth-century Persian author of the *Rubaiyat* translated in the nineteenth century by Edward FitzGerald. The poem contains elements of Sufi mysticism and fed the growing appetite for Eastern philosophy and thought in this period. Nietzsche, who was read piecemeal until the first full English translation of his works appeared in 1913, was championed for his aristocratic morality, which turned the Christian understanding of good and evil on its head. Virginia Woolf echoes Nietzsche's post-Christian message at the end of "Not Knowing Greek." Woolf recommends the unforgiving cosmology of the Greeks as a tonic for those who are "sick of the vagueness, of the confusion, of the Christianity and its consolations, of our own age."[18] William James, as described earlier, subjected religion to psychological investigation and, although he was careful not to explain religion away as the product of physiological or pathological processes, others would come much closer to doing so. Henry Maudsley, for example, one of the leading psychiatrists in late-nineteenth-century England, argued that belief in spirits of all kinds is determined by organic causes. In the specific case of belief in "supernatural Providence" (in other words, the Christian God), he gives as explanation the "instinctive" need to compensate for the harsh realities of life.[19]

American fiction supplies some additional names to the list of radical and skeptical authors. Carol Kennicott in Sinclair Lewis's *Main Street* (1920) reads: "young American sociologists, young English realists, Russian horrorists, Anatole France, Rolland, Nexo, Wells, Shaw, Key, Edgar Lee Masters, Theodore Dreiser, Sherwood Anderson, Henry Menken and all the other subversive philosophers."[20] Again, the list suggests a crash course in socialist and skeptical thinking: Anatole France was a well-known French novelist and atheist; Mencken had introduced America to the work of Nietzsche, much, in fact, as H.G. Wells, George Bernard Shaw, and their colleagues at various London-based journals had done in Britain; Dreiser and Anderson were novelists noted for their bleak and godless portraits of contemporary American life. Dreiser himself reported to Menken that in "1894 – I discovered Herbert Spencer and Huxley and Tyndall. They shifted my point of view tremendously, confirmed my worst suspicions and destroyed the last remaining traces of Catholicism which I now detest as a political organization or otherwise."[21] As Charles Ryder explains in Evelyn Waugh's *Brideshead Revisited* (1945), there could only be one outcome of an education of this kind:

> I had no religion ... The view implicit in my education was that the basic narrative of Christianity had long been exposed as a myth, and that opinion was now divided as to whether its ethical teaching was of present value, a division in which the main weight went against it; religion was a hobby which some people professed and some people did not.[22]

Ryder alludes to two further powerful currents in nineteenth-century scholarship and thought: first, a discipline known as Higher Criticism that offered historical arguments against the existence of Jesus and the events described in the Bible; and second, the scientific proof against the existence of God. He echoes Pound's sense that religion has lost prestige and conviction and further downgrades its status from an option to a mere hobby, on a par, presumably, with golf or sketching.

Exoteric and Esoteric Religion

Although belief in God was no longer the default option, religion had by no means disappeared from the modern world. On the contrary, the chances of finding a religion to suit a modern lifestyle and to satisfy an enquiring mind had increased. Both the late nineteenth and early twentieth century were remarkably creative periods in terms of new and alternative beliefs, and modernist writers frequently opted for these new religions in preference to the churches in which they had been raised. The phrase "new religion" is perhaps misleading because some groups did not strictly identify themselves as religions at all, preferring, as does Pound in the example cited, to speak in terms of "wide possibilities" and "spirituality" rather than a hard-line belief in God. Even so, they often had many of the characteristics that sociologists now associate with new religions, including global communities of believers, charismatic leaders, strictly controlled messages, and claims to ancient origins as a means of establishing authority and legitimacy in what was rapidly becoming a crowded market.[23]

"Theosophy," for example, describes a religion, or more accurately "a philosophy, a science, and a religion" devoted to the recovery and guardianship of hidden ("esoteric") knowledge.[24] This endeavor was hardly new, but it assumed a new institutional form in the guise of the Theosophical Society founded in the 1880s by Madame Blavatsky and Henry Steele Olcott. Blavatsky was a Russian aristocrat who had supposedly undertaken a course of instruction with immortals living in the Himalayas. Olcott was an American colonel selected by Blavatsky (following the direction of her spirit guides) as her collaborator. The aim of the Theosophical Society was to derive the secret of all religions. At its most conservative, the method involved the study of texts and traditions from a bewildering range of sources (classical texts in Greek and Sanskrit, banned Jewish and Christian texts, Eastern philosophies and literatures) and, at its wilder fringes, the revival of magical practices as seen in Elizabethan magicians and alchemists such as John Dee. Frequently, however, the ethos and message of theosophy seemed altogether more current than these sources would suggest. Annie Besant, for example, begins the *Introduction to Theosophy* (1895) by giving the precise details of the society's origins: "in New York City in the year 1875, the day recognized as its official birthday being November 17th." This was an opportune moment, Besant continues, for the foundation of a new religion because the old church had reached an impasse in its struggle against the implacable reason of science. What the times needed, she argued, was a reconciliation of the two:

> [A]lready the cry was being raised that between Rome and Atheism there was no sure or defensible standing-ground, and that the battle of the near future was between a Religion devoid of all Science and a Science devoid of all Religion. It was at this crisis that the great guardians of spiritual truth stepped forward, and sent into the arena a new combatant, the Esoteric Philosophy.[25]

The word "esoteric" appears appended to all kinds of movements in this period, signaling, in a conveniently vague way, an opposition between religion as outwardly manifest in buildings, rituals, and congregations (*exoteric* religion) and something like an essence or mystery that escapes containment within these material forms. (One of the most popular theosophical books in this period was A.P. Sinnett's *Esoteric Buddhism* [1883].) Theosophy answered, then, to the felt need for a "third way" between the seemingly all-or-nothing alternatives of religion *or* science. Furthermore, it had an inclusive message that exoteric religion, often embedded within national traditions and cultures, struggled to match: the object of theosophy, Besant continues, is "to form a nucleus of a universal brotherhood with no distinction of race, creed, sex or colour."[26] Theosophy did, in fact, attract an international following in Europe, India, and the United States, including, among some of its better-known enthusiasts, the poets W.B. Yeats and George William Russell (A.E.) and the artists Wassily Kandinsky and Piet Mondrian.

The occult was not the only option for those looking for an alternative to the religion of their childhood. The mainstream religions produced alternatives, too. Christian Science, for example, dates to 1866, when Mary Baker Eddy discovered the system of mind-healing to which she gave that name. Eddy claimed the Bible as the source of her method, but the means by which she disseminated and defended her method suggests she had a strong grasp of the rational planning needed to survive in the modern marketplace, too. As Bryan Wilson points out, Christian Science made (and still makes) use of mass circulation and "salesmanlike techniques"[27] to ensure the brand remained strong even in the face of imitations:

> Any theory of Christian Science, which departs from what has already been stated and proved to be true, affords no foundation upon which to establish a genuine school of this Science. Also, if any so-called new school claims to be Christian Science, and yet uses another author's discoveries without giving that author proper credit, such a school is erroneous, for it inculcates a breach of that divine commandment in the Hebrew Decalogue, "Thou shalt not steal."[28]

Mina Loy and Mabel Dodge were both converts to Christian Science. Loy's unpublished notes suggest that she had found in Eddy's method a religion that spoke directly to her concerns as a woman and a parent. Eddy's mind-healing refused to recognize the reality of disease and might assuage, therefore, a mother's fears for her children: "Homey and comforting her contribution – was particularly adapted to erase the incalculable anxiety of raising a family."[29]

Religious Modernism and Its Critics

The need to keep pace with changing times and changing attitudes to belief had long been recognized by elements within the major monotheisms. Within Judaism, for example, reformers had long since challenged the separatism inherent in the foundation of the religion (the idea of the Jews as God's chosen people). Saul Ascher's *Leviathan* (1792), described in *Religions of the Modern World* as perhaps the "philosophical cornerstone" of Reform Judaism, had argued that the essence of Judaism was its religious faith rather than its legal and political constitution.[30] This cleared the way, so far as circumstances allowed, for Judaism to become one religion among others, to take its place, in other words, in the pluralist context to which Pound refers in the passage quoted at the beginning of this chapter. The new situation received dramatic treatment and became firmly associated with the phrase used in the play's title, in Israel Zangwill's *The Melting Pot*, which was first performed in New York in 1908 and published in New York and London a year later. Jewish immigration to America had increased exponentially in the years leading up to this date so that by 1910, Jews from Russia represented the largest group of immigrants in New York. By 1917, the city had more than 1.4 million Jewish inhabitants.[31] For Loy, drawing on the phrase made popular by Zangwill's play, these circumstances created the perfect conditions for the growth of a new modernist idiom: "Out of the welter of this unclassifiable speech, while professors of Harvard and Oxford laboured to preserve 'God's English,' the muse of modern literature arose, and her tongue had been loosened in the melting pot."[32]

In Europe, the situation of the Jewish population varied enormously. In some areas, notably Tsarist Russia, Jews were subject to persecution and violence throughout the nineteenth and early decades of the twentieth century. In the West, however, the tendency among Jewish communities over the same period was toward greater contact with the non-Jewish world. Kafka's grandfather, for example, had been a *schechita* (an official responsible for the ritual slaughter of animals) in a predominantly Jewish village in the present-day Czech Republic. His son, Kafka's father, brought the family to Prague, where he established a successful clothing firm and mixed with the predominantly German-speaking bourgeoisie. Kafka himself attended a German- and Czech-speaking school and only rarely went to the synagogue. In a famous letter to Max Brod, Kafka depicted his generation as stranded between two worlds, neither of which could provide a solid foundation: "[W]ith their posterior legs they were still glued to their fathers' Jewishness and with their waving anterior legs they found no new ground. The ensuing despair became their inspiration."[33] Loy's family story, as told in the poem "Anglo-Mongrels and the Rose," is also one of migration and assimilation, this time by means of her Hungarian father's marriage to an English bride. Like Kafka, Loy finds herself stranded between two worlds, and, again like him, she represents this predicament in physical terms akin to those of the naturalist. In "Anglo-Mongrels and the Rose," for example, the cross-breeding of Albion and Israel is seen to produce a very peculiar flower indeed: "the rose / that grows / from the red flowing / from the flank of Christ / thorned with the computations / of the old / Jehovah's gender."[34] Loy ironizes the rhetoric of contemporary raciologies that reduced the Jews and other national, ethnic, and social minorities to a list of unenviable physiological and psychological facts.

On the one hand, then, assimilation was seen to bring the social and material benefits of modernity within the reach of the Jewish community. On the other, it was seen to come at the cost of a distinctive Jewish culture, and it did so without any guarantee of acceptance into European society or an end to persecution. Looking back on the period of Kafka and Loy's youth, for example, Hannah Arendt remarks on the rise of anti-Semitic parties across Europe. This development had less to do, she argues, with Christian prejudice – "the old religious Jew-hatred" – than with an economic situation in which Jewish businesspeople and financiers were supposed to have even sovereign governments under their control.[35] Such ideas would resurface among totalitarian politicians and intellectuals of the 1930s who exploited fears of a Jewish world conspiracy, in part, to justify their own supranational projects. The consequences of these policies would be seen in World War II and the death camps of the Third Reich.

The churches to which Pound's and Eliot's parents belonged were in the vanguard of liberal Protestantism in America. These churches had no difficulty accepting the findings of modern history and science and took a humanistic approach to Christianity, which emphasized the need for ethical concern and activism. Pound's parents, for example, volunteered in the Italian Settlement in the slums of South Philadelphia. Meanwhile,

Charles William Eliot, a distant relative of T.S. Eliot, had used his position as president of Harvard to promote a more socially responsible form of Unitarianism: "The object," he said, "will not be the personal welfare or safety of the individual in this world or the other … but … service to others, and contributions to the common good."[36] The Catholic Church was more resistant to reform, and although it gave birth to its own modernizing movement (known as "modernism" long before the word was appropriated to describe experimental tendencies in literature), this was condemned by Pope Pius X in 1907 as "The compendium and the poison of all heresies."[37] It was not until the Second Vatican Council in 1962–63 that modernization (*aggiornamento*) gained the official support of the Vatican (under Pope John XII).

For some modernist artists and writers, however, it was precisely Catholicism's resistance to reform, its stance against modernity, that constituted its appeal. In a secular age, to commit (and especially to convert) to Rome could be and frequently was cast as *anti*establishment, especially when the establishment was itself painted as morally bankrupt, spiritually dissolute, and in league with sinister financial interests. In 1930s America, for example, believers rallied around the figure of Charles Coughlin, a Catholic priest based at the Shrine of the Little Flower in Royal Oak, Michigan. Coughlin achieved remarkable listening figures for his radio broadcasts, which frequently took the ills of contemporary society and politics as their topic. In particular, Coughlin railed against the New Deal policies of Franklin Delano Roosevelt and the evils of "international financiers" (i.e., the Jews), whom he held directly responsible for the stock market crash of 1929. Coughlin attempted, although ultimately unsuccessfully, to leverage his grassroots popularity into a political career. For a brief time in the early 1930s, he was confidant to Roosevelt and Joe Kennedy, and he cofounded the National Union for Social Justice, which aimed to be the third party in America's two-party state. Coughlin's fame, like his message, was international. During the 1930s, he received visits from Chesterton and Pound; all three men had longstanding interests in the economic theories of Major C.H. Douglas known as Social Credit.[38] Catholicism did not, of course, entail these extreme political views, and not all converts in this period (Graham Greene, David Jones, and Edith Sitwell are some of the best known) were so quick to combine religion and politics. But for Pound and Eliot, among others, religion still had a part to play in public conversation and policy even if this meant reversing the trend that, since the Reformation, had seen religion increasingly pushed back into the private sphere.

Pound did not convert to Catholicism, although he did find in the Roman Church and Catholic theology much with which to sympathize. In fact, *Guide to Kulchur*, for all that it seems at times pluralist in attitude, reserves particular praise for Christianity in the supposedly pure form that survived in Italy. In Italy, Pound argues, Christianity has been preserved both from Protestantism with its tendency to schism and to "sectarian snobbism" and from the Hebrew influence that had diverted Christianity from its classical and pagan roots.[39] Like Coughlin, Pound saw a future for Christianity, if only it would return to the unadulterated form in which it existed in the past and especially, in Pound's case, to the economic theories found in the medieval Catholic Church. These theories took a hard line against usury (money lending at a very high rate of interest) and chimed therefore with Pound's own sense that the system of credit was at the root of modern social and political ills. Eliot too thought that the future of Christianity lay in the amelioration of the sorry state of affairs that prevailed in Europe in the 1930s. In books of social criticism such as *The Idea of a Christian Society* (1939) and *Notes Towards the Definition of Culture* (1948), he envisages the transformation of English culture. This would not be achieved by a wholesale conversion of the skeptical but instead by nurturing the Christian religion that Eliot thought formed an organic and lived part of English culture as a whole along with "Derby Day, Henley Regatta, Cowes, the twelfth of August, a cup final, the dog races, the pin table, the dart board, Wensleydale cheese, boiled cabbage cut into sections, beetroot in vinegar, nineteenth-century Gothic churches and the music of Elgar."[40] Eliot belonged to a discussion group, the Moot, established by J.H. Oldham in 1939 in order to discuss possible Christian solutions to the failure of democracy (as seen in World War II) and the threat of state socialism. And although he was never quite convinced, either by the Moot's message or by its methods, Eliot was in accord with the idea that Christianity was the solution to an urgent problem.

Eliot resisted some of the very changes that, this chapter has argued, made religion modern. He wanted to make whole again a culture that had splintered along many more fault lines than the secular/religious divide that has sometimes been permitted to overshadow all the others. Religion had adapted relatively well to modern conditions, and it had done so often by increasing choice and accessibility: by offering new options, some of which, Christian Science and theosophy, for example, were specifically designed to travel across national and cultural boundaries; by taking advantage of advanced methods of distribution and transmission (Coughlin's radio broadcasts or the Christian newsletter published by the Moot); or by splitting off practice from belief, which meant that an individual could take the spirituality without the collective behavior and/or the community without the doctrine. For Pound's generation, therefore, questions of religion and spirituality went far beyond the question of whether to attend church. That particular decision was often just the beginning of an individual's journey along the many byways of religion in the twentieth century.

Notes

1 Ezra Pound, *Guide to Kulchur* (Norfolk, CT: New Directions, 1952), 26.
2 Mina Loy, "Goy Israels," Mina Loy Papers, Yale Collection of American Literature, Beinecke Rare Book and Manuscript Library, MSS 6, fol. 28, 64.
3 See Richard Ellmann, *James Joyce* (New York: Oxford University Press, 1982), 27, and for a more recent view of Joyce's "unbelief," see Geert Lernout, *Help My Unbelief: James Joyce and Religion* (London: Continuum, 2010).
4 See Brian Sudlow, *Catholic Literature and Secularization* (Manchester: Manchester University Press, 2011), 56.
5 Alexis de Tocqueville, *Democracy in America and Two Essays on America* (London: Penguin, 2003), 497.
6 Pound, 26.
7 Virginia Woolf to Vanessa Bell, 11 February 1928, *The Letters of Virginia Woolf*, ed. Nigel Nicolson and Joanne Trautmann, Vol. 3 (San Diego: Harcourt Brace Jovanovich, 1975–1980), 458.
8 G.K. Chesterton, *The Ball and the Cross* (New York: Dover, 1995), 18.
9 G.K. Chesterton, *Heretics* (London: Bodley Head, 1919), 15.
10 Linda Woodhead, introduction to *Religions in the Modern World: Traditions and Transformations*, ed. Linda Woodhead, Hiroko Karwanami, and Christopher Partridge, 2nd edn (London: Routledge, 2001), 11.
11 Giselle Vincent and Linda Woodhead, "Spirituality," in *Religions in the Modern World*, 319.
12 William James, *Varieties of Religious Experience* (London: Longman, 1929), 431.
13 Emile Durkheim, *The Elementary Forms of Religious Life*, translated by Karen E. Fields (New York: The Free Press, 1995), 44.
14 Murry as quoted by Alex Owen, "'The Religious Sense' in a Post-War Secular Age," *Past and Present* 1 (2006): 159.
15 D.H. Lawrence to Ottoline Morrell, 1 February 1915, *Letters*, Vol. 2, *June 1913–October 1916*, ed. James T. Boulton (Cambridge: Cambridge University Press, 1981), 272.
16 D.H. Lawrence, "A Modern Lover," in *A Modern Lover and Other Stories*, ed. Antony Atkins (Oxford: Oxford University Press, 1995), 20.
17 T.H. Huxley. "The Origin of Species," in *Darwiniana*, Vol. 2, *Collected Essays* (London: Macmillan, 1893), 53.

18 Virginia Woolf, "On Not Knowing Greek," in *The Common Reader*, 2nd edn (London: Hogarth, 1925), 59.

19 Henry Maudsley, *Natural Causes and Supernatural Seemings* (London: Kegan Paul, Trench, 1886), 358.

20 Sinclair Lewis, *Main Street* (New York: Barnes and Noble, 2003), 306.

21 Dreiser to Mencken, 13 May, 1916, *Letters of Theodore Dreiser: A Selection*, Vol. 1, ed. Robert H. Elias (Philadelphia: University of Pennsylvania Press, 1959), 211.

22 Evelyn Waugh, *Brideshead Revisited* (London: Penguin, 2000), 69.

23 See Bryan Wilson, "Old Sects and New Religions in Europe," in *New Religions and the New Europe* (Aarhus: Aarhus University Press, 1995), 11–31.

24 Annie Besant, "Introduction," to Walter S. Old, *What Is Theosophy? A Handbook for Inquirers into the Wisdom-Religion* (London: Nisbet, 1891), 6.

25 Annie Besant, *An Introduction to Theosophy* (Benares, London, Madras: Theosophical Publishing Society, 1895), 1–2.

26 Besant, *An Introduction*, 5.

27 Wilson, 19.

28 Mary Baker Eddy, *Science and Health* WITH *Key to the Scriptures* (Boston, MA: Allison V. Stewart, 1912), 112.

29 Mina Loy, "History of Religion and Eros," n.d., Mina Loy Papers, YCAL MSS 6, fol. 159.

30 Seth D. Kunin, "Judaism," in *Religions in the Modern World*, 181.

31 Frederick M. Binder and David M. Reimers, *All the Nations Under Heaven: An Ethnic and Racial History of New York City* (New York: Columbia, 1995), 115.

32 Mina Loy, "Modern Poetry," in *The Lost Lunar Baedeker*, ed. Roger Conover (New York: Farrar, Straus and Giroux, 1996), 159.

33 Kafka to Max Brod, June 1921, in *Letters to Friends, Family and Editors*, translated by Richard and Clara Winston (London: Calder, 1978), 289.

34 Mina Loy, "Anglo-Mongrels and the Rose," in *The Last Lunar Baedeker*, ed. Roger Conover (Highlands: North Carolina, 1982), 132.

35 Hannah Arendt, *The Origins of Totalitarianism* (Orlando: Harvest, 1968), 7.

36 Barry Spurr, *Anglo-Catholic in Religion: T.S. Eliot and Christianity* (Cambridge: Lutterworth Press, 2011), 5.

37 Pope Pius X speech on April 17, 1907, as quoted in *The Catholic Modernists: A Study of the Religious Reform Movement 1864–1907*, by Michele Ranchetti, translated by Isabel Quigly (London: Oxford University Press, 1969), 195.

38 See Donald Warren, *Radio Priest: Charles Coughlin, the Father of Hate Radio* (New York: The Free Press, 1996).

39 Pound, *Guide to Kulchur*, 30, 191.

40 T.S. Eliot, *Notes Towards the Definition of Culture* (London: Faber, 1948), 32.

2

Science, Technology, and the Body

The Modernist period has often been described as the age of disenchantment. This is the view, for instance, of the German sociologist Max Weber (1864–1920), who argued that modern societies are "characterized by rationalization and intellectualization and, above all, by the 'disenchantment of the world.'"[1] The new technologies that proliferated in the Modernist period, however, triggered sensations of Aristotelian wonder and, I will argue, reenchantment among the moderns. They enhanced our ability to see, hear, travel, discover, and comprehend, and in the process, they reconfigured our understanding of the self. One need only think of the advent of telephony, the X-ray, cinematography, and aviation, which at their inception appeared like forms of modern magic: to speak to a person in a different city from the comfort of one's home, to peer inside the human body without cutting it open, to capture image and movement on celluloid formaldehyde, and to fly across the continent in a matter of hours figured among the transformative inventions of the turn of the century, whether experienced vicariously by the masses or first hand by the privileged few.

New technologies functioned as markers of human ingenuity. They multiplied manyfold our sensory and motor capacities and, by proxy, our potential for further discovery and innovation. In the second half of the nineteenth century, for instance, advances in lens technology led to more powerful microscopes, which in turn inaugurated the study of bacteriology, with dramatic improvements in health care and food hygiene. The process of pasteurization, still in use today, has its origins in Louis Pasteur's (1822–1895) bacteriological research. Pasteur also contributed to the development of immunization through vaccination, which worked by triggering the body's own immune mechanism. The technological and scientific discoveries of the period seemed to point to and draw on analogies rather than discrepancies between the human organism and technology. Darwinian thought, experimental psychology, and Freud's theory of the unconscious drew attention to the essentially automatic functions of the human body, which operated outside of the realm of agency and free will and gradually led to the emergence of a new conception of the self. These innovations raised anxieties about the limits of the human and paved the way to a posthumanist conception of the self.

Technological innovations, as Sigmund Freud argued, are modeled on the human body and its functions. Early telephone technology, for instance, used the "vibrations of a tympanum to induce a variable current which [was] then converted back to sound," while sound-recording devices were compared by the French philosopher Jean-Marie Guyau (1854–1888) to memory traces in "brain cells" and "nerve streams."[2] Such technologies operate as extensions of the central nervous system, and they both mimic and extend its abilities. They enhance the sensory and muscular powers of the human body or, alternatively, supplement its deficiencies; Alexander Bell's invention of telephony, for instance, had its origins in his attempts to teach the hearing-impaired to speak. The telephone augments the sensory range of the human ear, while typewriters were originally designed to enable the blind to write. In his seminal essay *Civilization and Its Discontents*, first published in 1929, Freud argued that

> With every tool man is perfecting his own organs, whether motor or sensory, or is removing the limits to their functioning. Motor power places gigantic forces at his disposal, which, like his muscles, he can employ in any direction; thanks to ships and aircraft neither water nor air can hinder his movements; by means of spectacles he corrects defects in the lens of his own eye; by means of the telescope he sees into the far distance; and by means of the microscope he overcomes the limits of visibility set by the structure of his retina. In the photographic camera he has created an instrument which retains the fleeting visual impressions, just as a gramophone disc retains the equally fleeting auditory ones; both are at bottom materializations of the power he possesses of recollection, his memory. With the help of the telephone he can hear at distances which would be respected as unattainable even in a fairy tale.[3]

Freud foregrounds the prosthetic nature of technology and evokes its magical quality to underscore both the pragmatic and the wondrous dimensions of modern technology. This sense of fascination, however, is accompanied in the period by an anxiety over the perceived and, more often than not, very real dangers technological innovations entailed. This is epitomized, for instance, in advances in technologies of transport. During the interwar years, the travel industry began to thrive. Improvements in mass production had brought down the cost of motorcars, and during World War I, many soldiers had learned to drive. The annual holiday became an entitlement for most of Britain's working population, and there was a proliferation of commercial airlines and travel agencies. However, in the early days of the automobile, roads were poor and accident rates alarmingly high.[4] The speed-loving Anglo-Irish novelist Elizabeth Bowen observed that

> About motor cars and their off-spring motor-bikes, there continued, for longer than may be realised now, to be something mythical and phenomenal – even hostile? "Flying machines," at the start were less ill-seen: few and freakish, they constituted a threat only to aeronauts who took off in them. Motor-cars, which spawned at a greater rate, looked at once Martian and caddish. Their colour spectrum and flashing fittings of brass were themselves offensive.[5]

One thinks of F. Scott Fitzgerald's novel, *The Great Gatsby* (1925), in which Tom Buchanan, Gatsby's antagonist, refers to his yellow-and-chrome car as a "circus wagon."[6] It is no coincidence that it is the "big yellow car [...] going faster'n forty. Going fifty, sixty" that kills Buchanan's lover, Myrtle Wilson.[7]

Aviation, however, also raised serious concerns. Zeppelins or airships frequently exploded, as in the case of the *Hindenburg* in 1937, and aeroplanes crashed to the ground with alarming regularity. Airships, after all, "received [their] lift from 70,000 cubic meters of highly inflammable hydrogen gas, which could be ignited by a tiny spark," while accounts of aeroplane crashes "focused on the physical appearance of the wrecks themselves to emphasize the havoc that the accidents had wreaked on erstwhile stable structures."[8] There were descriptions in newspapers of "'a shapeless mass' of debris or a 'heap of wildly tangled tubes' that bore no resemblance whatever to flying machines."[9] The simultaneous thrill and anxiety of an early flight from London to Paris is captured in Bowen's novel *To the North* (1932), where the plane's precarious landing in Paris is described in nail-biting terms:

> Markie's fingers tightened, blood roared in his ears as the plane with engines shut off, with a frightening cessation of sound plunged

downward in that arrival that always appears disastrous. Tipped
on one wing, they appeared to spin over Le Bourget in indecision; a
glaring plan of the suburb tilted and reeled; now roofless buildings
gaped up at them; no one, however, looked up. Earth rejoined
the wheels quietly and they raced round the bleached aerodrome
in a whirr of arrival. Then, grasping their small baggage, tipped
like grain from a shovel, they all stepped, incredulous, out of the
quivering plane.[10]

To be modern in Bowen's novel is to live fast and to embrace risk. It is
to be wired into the many technological innovations of modernity, to be
electrified and at times overcharged by a heightened nervous energy. The
glamor associated with aeroplane pilots has its origins in this period: not
only did they brave frequent and devastating accidents, but they were
also seen as an elite that possessed the exceptional characteristics needed
to fly a plane successfully. They were heroes who mediated between the
technological complexity of aeroplanes and the lay passengers for whom
such intricacy was beyond conception. Indeed, as Bernhard Rieger has
argued, "the iconography of the solo pilot promoted aviation not so
much despite, as because of, its risks."[11]

The experience of ever-greater speed, entailed by advances in transport and communication technology, was seen both as a rousing novelty
and as fundamentally detrimental to the nervous system. *To the North*,
a novel obsessed with speed, locomotion, and various communication
systems – cars, taxis, trains, aeroplanes, telegrams, and telephones –
simultaneously captures the exhilaration, anxiety, nervous exhaustion,
and somatic discomfort of the technological innovations that characterize
modernity. Cecilia, one of the novel's protagonists, experiences a series
of striking somatic symptoms on a train journey from Italy to London:
"On a long journey, the heart hangs dull in the shaken body, nerves ache,
senses quicken, the brain like a horrified cat leaps clawing from object
to object, the earth whisked by at such speed looks ephemeral, trashy: if
one is not sad one is bored."[12] Cecilia's symptoms are those of neurasthe-
nia, a buzzword of the turn of the century. The sensory overload speed
and motion induce has a detrimental effect on the perceptual faculties
and emotions, and Bowen, herself a compulsive traveler, describes these
effects in great detail:

[T]hey blinked in and out of minor tunnels; suffocation and boredom
came to their climax and lessened; one was in Switzerland, where
dusk fell in sheets of rain. Unwilling, Celia could not avert her

> eyes from all that magnificence in wet cardboard: ravines, profuse
> torrents, crag, pine and snow-smeared precipice, chalets upon their
> brackets of hanging meadow.[13]

Nature itself undergoes a metamorphosis, which turns the natural beauty of the landscape into a profusion of technologically mediated images, as if the mechanics of train travel had infected the scenery itself. The train window is transformed into a film screen, and the splendor of the Swiss landscape is reduced to a set made of "wet cardboard."[14]

Even something as seemingly innocuous as going to the cinema offered vicarious thrills while also posing serious risks to the nervous constitution of the spectator. Films were perceived to play "tricks on the imagination by 'fooling' human perceptive faculties." The illusion of movement, after all, was generated by presenting the spectator with a succession of still images. Films therefore presented what was perceived to be a morally problematic "deception of consciousness."[15] In 1937, Bowen remarked with fascination on film's unique medium: "fluid pattern, variation of light, speed." But she went on to complain that "Mechanics, the immense technical knowledge needed, have kept the art, as an art, unnaturally esoteric; its technical progress (more and more discoveries: sound, now colour) moves counter to its spiritual progress."[16] The technology of modern newspaper journalism posed yet another kind of threat. By bringing the world too close, it was feared, the daily press threatened the modern subject with an excess of sensory and cognitive stimuli that had the potential to harm the reader's nervous constitution. In *Degeneration* (*Entartung*, 1892; trans. 1895), Max Nordau speculated that only at the end of the twentieth century would we witness "a generation to whom it will not be injurious to read a dozen square yards of newspapers daily, to be constantly called to the telephone, to be thinking simultaneously of the five continents of the world, to live half their time in a railway carriage or in a flying machine, and to satisfy the demands of a circle of ten thousand acquaintances, associates, and friends."[17] The modern pace of life, Nordau argued, required "nerves of gigantic vigour."[18] The simultaneous fascination and anxiety generated by new technologies is captured in Freud's observation in *Civilization and Its Discontents* that

> Man has, as it were, become a kind of prosthetic God. When he puts on all his auxiliary organs he is truly magnificent; but those organs have not grown on to him and they still give him much trouble at times.[19]

FIGURE 1 Otto Umbehr, *Der Rasende Reporter (The Racing Reporter)* (Egon Erwin Kisch), 1926. © Phyllis Umbehr/Galerie Kicken Berlin/ DACS 2013

Otto Umbehr's 1926 photograph, *The Racing Reporter (Egon Erwin Kisch)* (Figure 1), captures (*avant la lettre*) Freud's sense of modern man as a "prosthetic God": the reporter's speed is enhanced by the aeroplane and motorcar that replace his right leg and left foot; one eye is improved by a camera and both ears contain auditory devices that augment his hearing, while the gramophone commits the auditory data to memory (the verb "to record" comes from the Latin *recordare*, "to commit to memory; to learn by heart"). The Reporter's trunk consists of a typewriter and a printing press, while his right hand is replaced by a fountain pen, highlighting the way in which writing itself is always already a technology. The background blends a mountainous landscape with a cityscape to emphasize the speed at which the modern reporter roves as he hovers high above the city and its crowds in the manner of a bionic man. That the technological prostheses are incorporated with such ease points to the newly-discovered understanding of the human body as itself biomechanical.

The new and enhanced methods of transport and communication transformed notions of time and space. As the world grew faster, it also shrank and became more crowded as its spatial and temporal parameters were reconfigured by technologies such as the telephone, patented by Alexander Bell (1847–1922) in 1876, and wireless transmission, which had its early successes in Guglielmo Marconi's (1874–1937) experiments of 1895. In Western culture, voice has been associated with unmediated presence, as Jacques Derrida has argued. The spoken word has been invested with agency and immediacy and has therefore been perceived as "authentic" and "uncorrupted," while the written word, according to this received bias, had been taken out of its original context and further "contaminated" by rhetoric. Early auditory technologies, such as the telephone and the radio, however, took advantage of sound's transgressive qualities by exploiting the principle of spatial transport offered by voice and sound. Sound possesses a peculiar "strength that light cannot rival: it can penetrate solid walls, boom through the depths of the ocean, go round corners, shatter delicate glasses, or force its way through the earth."[20] As the French philosopher Michel Serres has remarked, one can "put the ear on the other side of the window, projecting it great distances, holding it at a great distance from the body."[21] Telephony extended the already-expansive range of the human ear. It took advantage of sound's ability to travel and to transport us. Physical presence was now no longer a condition of speech. Furthermore, the technologically enhanced transmission of sound could transport the listener to the site of major world events, but now without the inconvenience of travel. Auditory innovations, therefore, allowed the listener to occupy two sound-spaces at once. In April 1912, after the sinking of the *Titanic*, *The Times* commented on the "expanded range of experience made possible by the wireless": "We recognise with a sense near to awe that we have been almost witness of a great ship in her death agonies."[22]

New technologies also triggered a yearning for times past. The disembodied voices on the telephone, the phonograph – invented by Thomas Edison (1847–1931) in 1877 – and later the wireless, prompted close associations between technology and the spirit world in a period that witnessed rapid secularization and a simultaneous yearning for new forms of spirituality.[23] Friedrich Kittler has observed that the spirit world seemed to mirror and mimic developments in communication technology. He has noted, for instance, that

> [T]he tapping specters of the spiritualistic séances with their messages from the realm of the dead, appeared quite promptly at the moment of the invention of the Morse alphabet in 1837.

> Promptly, photographic plates – even and especially with the camera
> shutter closed – provided images of ghosts or specters which in
> their black and white fuzziness, only emphasized the moments of
> resemblance.[24]

The phonograph and other inscription methods for recording sound, in
turn, "parallel the automatic writing and 'direct writing' practiced by
mediums during this period."[25]

The invention of the phonograph and early experiments in magnetic
recording in the 1890s turned the fleeting and ephemeral quality of sound
into a form of inscription. The transitory nature of sound, here and then
gone, was materialized and made tangible on clay and, later, vinyl discs.
It now became possible to relisten to a sound event and to travel back in
time: "Our power to transport ourselves with sound [became] reinforced
by the power to transport sound itself."[26] In the age of inscription technologies, Steven Connor remarks,

> Our world is a world of multiple times; of variable, manufactured
> nows. This is largely because our world is a world of recordings,
> replications and action replays; and above all, a world of replicable
> sounds. Such a world is characterised by multiple rhythms, durations
> and temporalities; by temporal comings, goings and crossings, of
> rifts and loops and pleats in the fabric of linear time.[27]

One of the most crucial consequences of inscription technologies was the
manner in which they distanced sound from the conceit of interiority,
"the necessity of human agency and metaphysical presence."[28] A humorous instance of this occurs in the Hades episode of James Joyce's great
novel *Ulysses* (1922), in which the protagonist, Leopold Bloom, attends
his friend Paddy Dignam's funeral and fantasizes about placing a gramophone in every grave to commemorate the dead:

> [H]ow could you remember everybody? Eyes, walk, voice. Well,
> the voice, yes: gramophone. Have a gramophone in every grave
> or keep it in the house. After dinner on a Sunday. Put on poor old
> greatgrandfather Kraahraark! Hellohellohello amawfullyglad kraark
> awfullygladaseeragain hellohello amarawf kopthsth. Remind you of
> the voice like the photograph reminds you of the face.[29]

Bloom's thoughts, in fact, mirror Edison's own suggestion that the
gramophone be used to preserve the last words of the dying. After
Paddy Dignam's body has been lowered into the ground, the dread of

premature internment crosses Bloom's mind: "They ought to have some law to pierce the heart and make sure or an electric clock or a telephone in the coffin and some kind of a canvas airhole."[30] Bloom's association of both the gramophone and the telephone with thoughts of death and the afterlife is in tune with the wider reassessment of notions of presence and absence these technologies triggered. The telephone, after all, enabled the interlocutor to be present in his spatial absence, while the gramophone allowed him to continue speaking, even after death.

Telephony, in fact, can be thought of as a technologically-mediated form of telepathy. Pamela Thurswell has investigated the ways in which psychical research at the *fin de siècle* contributed to the wider reassessment of the boundaries of individual consciousness brought about by inventions such as telegraphy, telephony, and medical therapies such as hypnosis.[31] Nicholas Royle points out that "'telepathy' is historically linked to numerous other tele-phenomena: it is part of the establishment of tele-culture in general. It is necessarily related to other nineteenth-century forms of communication from a distance through new and often invisible channels, including the railway, telegraphy, photography, the telephone and gramophone."[32]

A visual counterpart to the inscription of sound can be found in stop-motion photography, chronophotography, and film. Like the inscription of sound, all three media are ways of capturing time and movement on film and, in the process, of enhancing the perceptual powers of the human eye. In the late nineteenth century, these technologies were "designed to chart, explore, and record sensory phenomena that [it] had never before been possible to perceive." Étienne-Jules Marey's stop-motion photographs of flying birds and galloping horses turned physiological action invisible to the human eye into visual records and data.[33] Early photographic techniques had not been refined enough to record moving subjects and, due to long exposure times, any movement produced blur on the silver plate. To study the flight of birds, Marey invented a camera, the *fusil photographique*, which resembled a "small portable rifle that took twelve pictures [...] at intervals of 1/720 of a second."[34] The images could then be combined to represent movement. This 1882 invention was followed by Marey's chronophotographs, consisting of multiple exposures on single glass plates using a rotating slotted-disk shutter. With the arrival in France in 1888 of George Eastman's photographic paper, Marey was able further to improve his invention.[35] Chronophotography had an important impact both on science (for instance, studies of muscle function) and on the arts (for example, twentieth-century photography and painting); many even consider Marey the real inventor of motion film. In 1894, Marey adapted the motion-picture camera to the microscope and subsequently inaugurated microscopic film. It is no coincidence that Marey was a physician by training, for a great number of the most important innovations of the twentieth century originated precisely in medical research.

The year 1895 saw the development of another ground-breaking visual technology, namely Wilhelm Röntgen's (1845–1923) X-ray, which exposed the human skeleton and other organs within the *living* body. This device, which for the first time turned the body inside out without surgical intervention, enhanced our sense of embodiment by revealing physiological processes and detailed anatomical information previously unavailable in living subjects. X-rays, furthermore, collapsed the distinction not only between the inside and the outside of the body but also between "public and private; specialized knowledge and popular fantasy; and scientific discourse, high art, and popular culture."[36] The earliest X-ray photograph of the human body, an image of Röntgen's wife Bertha's hand, taken in 1896, attests to some of the cultural ramifications of the invention. The photograph was circulated around the world and reprinted in at least 1,100 publications as proof of the wondrous new invention. It triggered a fashion among New York women, who had "X-rays taken of their hands covered with jewelry" to prove that beauty was not only skin deep but resided in bone structure.[37] Women gifted the X-ray photographs to their fiancés and husbands, and they were placed on the mantelpiece or sideboard for display. The X-ray also triggered fantasies and fears of X-ray spectacles, which might, it was dreaded, enable their wearer to see through clothing and hence induce a new form of voyeurism.

The novel that best captures the sense of wonder triggered by X-ray technology is Thomas Mann's *The Magic Mountain* (1924). It is set in a sanatorium in the Swiss Alps, and when its protagonist, Hans Castorp, first witnesses his cousin Joachim have an X-ray, he is taken, baffled even, at the sight of "something like a bag, a strange, animal shape, darkly visible behind the middle column, or more on the right side of it – the spectator's right. It expanded and contracted regularly, a little after the fashion of a swimming jelly-fish."[38] What Hans Castorp sees, of course, is his cousin Joachim's heart, and the experience is so strange and intimate that he feels apologetic and mildly embarrassed about peering into the inside of his companion's body. The narrator goes on to say that "Hans Castorp gazed without wearying at Joachim's graveyard shape and bony tenement, this lean *memento mori*, this scaffolding for mortal flesh to hang on."[39] Fascinated, Castorp then requests that an X-ray be taken of his own hand. The impact of the image is striking:

> Hans Castorp saw exactly what he should have expected to see, but which no man was ever intended to see and which he himself had never presumed he would be able to see: he saw his own grave. Under that light, he saw the process of corruption anticipated, saw the flesh in which he moved decomposed, expunged, dissolved into airy nothingness – and inside was the delicately turned skeleton of his right hand and around the last joint of the ring finger, dangling black and loose, the signet ring his grandfather had bequeathed him [...] With the eyes of his Tienappel forebear – penetrating, clairvoyant eyes – he beheld a familiar part of his body, and for the first time in his life he understood that he would die.[40]

Thomas Mann's novel, whose opening is set in 1910, captures the way in which medical advances of the turn of the twentieth century began to transform our conception of the self. Particularly significant had been the neurological discoveries of the second half of the nineteenth century, such as the Spanish histologist Santiago Ramón y Cajal's (1853–1934) discovery of synapses and neural pathways, which he unveiled in his desire to determine the "material course of thought and will."[41] The French aphasiologist Paul Broca (1824–1880), in turn, identified the vetroposterior region of the frontal lobes as the part of the brain governing language, now known as Broca's area. In the process, he revealed that language was not the transcendental or metaphysical performance of the self that guaranteed the human its hierarchical position among species but an embodied process that could easily be impaired by a lesion in the brain.

In 1862, Jean-Martin Charcot (1825–1893) had been appointed head physician at the Salpêtrière Hospital in Paris. Under his directorship, the hospital underwent numerous reforms, including the laicization of its nursing staff, an increase in the number of beds, "better salaries for ancillary staff, improved bathing facilities, as well as laboratories, a museum, a new lecture hall" and, from 1882, a *Service des hommes*. By the second half of the 1870s, Charcot's famous Tuesday lectures had become crowd magnets; they "were an essential part of Parisian intellectual life."[42] At the lectures, Charcot exhibited his patients and developed his case studies before an admiring public. In 1882, he inaugurated the first neurology clinic in Europe. At his clinic, Charcot and his many eminent students, among them Sigmund Freud and William James, made important discoveries in the understanding of conditions of the nervous system such as Parkinson's disease, epilepsy, Tourette's syndrome, and hysteria. These conditions were brought to public attention at the Tuesday lectures and in the many journals founded in the Third Republic, such as *Le Progrès médical,* in which Charcot published a number of his lectures. *La Nouvelle Iconographie de la Salpêtrière* (1888–1918), the hospital's own publication, distributed images of epileptics, hysterics, and sufferers of other neurological conditions. Knowledge of Charcot's discoveries entered even the popular newspapers and magazines, and a number of Charcot's patients became celebrities in their own right. So pervasive was Charcot's work and so profound its impact on the popular imagination that it rapidly influenced the performance style of the Parisian cabaret and vaudeville "with a new repertoire of movements, grimaces, tics and gestures," which mimicked the comportment and disposition of the Salpêtrière patients.[43] Comedians in particular sported convulsive and marionette-like gaits and movements, and mime troupes and singers followed suit in performances that seemed to cast doubt over received notions of the body's functioning and, by implication, the wider questions of agency and free will. Many cabaret and music hall performers went on to have successful careers in silent film, which, as a genre, adopted the frenetic, convulsive, and automatic performance style of vaudeville and cabaret. As Rae Beth Gordon writes: "There is a continuous line and directing force running from the cabaret and café-concert performances of the last quarter of the nineteenth century, through the films of Méliès and the musicals of Ernst Lubitsch [. . .]. The uniting element is hysterical gesture and gait."[44] Henri Bergson's *Laughter: An Essay on the Meaning of the Comic,* first published in 1899, was itself centered around the notion of "automatic gesture and word," and one can trace a direct genealogy between Charcot's work, the popular culture of the period, and Bergson's theory of comedy.[45] So fashionable and intriguing did hysteria and neurological disorders prove around the turn of the century that they generated, besides a new performance style, a number of songs and literary works, such as Guy de Maupassant's 1884 short story "Le Tic" ("The Spasm") or, to give an Anglo-American example, T.S. Eliot's 1915 poem "Hysteria."

Bergson's *Laughter* was anxiously indebted to neurological discoveries and especially the dyskinesia and the various automatisms that presented in neurological disorders and that figured so prominently in the performance culture of the period. Bergson argued in his book that "The attitudes, gestures and movements of the human body are laughable in exact proportion as that body reminds us of a mere machine."[46] Humor, Bergson reiterated, arises from "Something mechanical encrusted on the living," for "a comic character is generally comic in proportion to his ignorance of himself."[47] This makes the subject appear as if deprived of his or her essential freedom:

> The soul imparts a portion of its winged lightness to the body it animates: the immateriality which thus passes into matter is what is called gracefulness. Matter, however, is obstinate and resists. It draws to itself the ever-alert activity of this higher principle, would fain convert it to its own inertia and cause it to revert to mere automatism. It would fain immobilise the intelligently varied movements of the body in stupidly contracted grooves, stereotype in permanent grimaces the fleeting expressions of the face, in short imprint on the whole person such an attitude as to make it appear immersed and absorbed in the materiality of some mechanical occupation instead of ceaselessly renewing its vitality by keeping in touch with a living ideal. Where matter thus succeeds in dulling the outward life of the soul, in petrifying its movements and thwarting its gracefulness, it achieves, at the expense of the body, an effect that is comic.[48]

What neurological conditions such as Parkinson's disease, Tourette's syndrome, and epilepsy had in common, and what was seen as a source of black humor in cabaret and early cinema, was the body's seemingly mechanical capacity to act outside of the realm of conscious control. Neurological disorders that informed the performance style of music hall, vaudeville, cabaret, and film, and as a consequence, Bergson's work questioned notions of agency and intentionality and hence cast serious doubt over received notions of subjectivity, suggesting that the mechanical, the automatic, and the involuntary were in fact integral to the self. These pathologies, after all, "raised serious questions about the philosophical viability of the doctrine of free will," something that Charcot and his students suggested was a mere metaphysical construct. Such conclusions doubtless reflect Charcot's and his students' anticlericalism, which permeated not only their political views but also their research.[49]

The question of free will is a central concern in Bergson's work, as the title of his doctoral thesis and his first published book, *Time and Free Will: An Essay on the Immediate Data of Consciousness*, from 1889, reveals. It is central, for instance, to his notion of duration (*durée*), whose flow is constantly threatened by habit, repetition, and automatism. Bergson in fact at times appears overly determined to defend the faculty of free will, to the point where his work frequently unveils a deep-rooted anxiety over its limitations. In his essay *Laughter*, habitual, mechanical, ossified comportment, as we have seen, appears as a source of humor, but it is also a locus of intense anxiety, which persists throughout Bergson's writing. In the essay, laughter is designed to function as "a bursting out of life and elasticity in the face of the intolerable stiffening of life into automatic or repeated gestures."[50] However, as Bergson himself often acknowledges, laughter itself can function "as a kind of machinery": as an involuntary somatic reaction beyond intentional control.[51] Steven Connor writes:

> [I]n laughing at what is inhumanly inelastic, we actually mirror the condition that is said to be comic. This confusion between stimulus and response, or between the laughable and the laugh, runs through Bergson's account. "[I]nvoluntarily I laugh," he writes; and when he asserts that "it is really a kind of automatism that makes us laugh [une espèce d'automatisme qui nous fait rire]," it is not certain whether he means that we laugh at automatism or that we laugh as an instance of it.[52]

In the late nineteenth century, Darwinian thought postulated that the mind was a function of the body and its various organic processes. Neurological discoveries cast further doubt over traditional conceptions of agency as the basis of selfhood. This was also subsequently questioned in Sigmund's Freud's insistence on the primacy of the unconscious. What these and other medical and scientific discoveries revealed to the moderns was that the mind was not its own entity, independent of the body, but itself embodied and that its functioning depended on and could radically be limited by the body, which often functioned unpredictably and was conditioned at least as much by biomechanical processes as by agency and will. If the great question in nineteenth-century literature and culture had been "Who am I?," Modernist culture characteristically poses the perhaps even more fundamental question of what it means to *be* an "I," to *have* a self, in the first place. These discoveries were followed by John B. Watson's development of behaviorism in the first decades of the twentieth century. Behaviorism received a great impetus from Russian objectivism and Ivan Pavlov's stimulus-response experiments with dogs, and Watson declared in 1913 that "The behaviourist, in his efforts to get a unitary scheme of animal response, recognized no dividing line between man and brute."[53] The impetus Pavlov's experiments gave to behaviorism is precisely the conviction that all behavior is acquired through conditioning and learning and that even emotions are trigged by changes in the visceral and glandular systems. In his 1925 book *Behaviourism*, Watson argues that "Probably many of the tears of the infant – of the hardened theatre fan, of the criminal, and the malingering invalid – are true examples of conditioning."[54] In short, Darwinian thought, neurology, behaviorism, and even some aspects of psychoanalysis pointed to a biomechanical conception of the self.

The scientific discoveries and new technologies that proliferated in the Modernist period unveiled to us the marvelous nature of the everyday. These technologies were closely modeled on the human body, at least in part because the body and the mind were themselves seen in newly biomechanical terms. This new conception of the self is captured in Otto Umbehr's photograph (Figure 1), which attests as much to the prosthetic nature of technology as to the body's own mechanical functioning. The great Victorian question "Who am I?" evolved in the Modernist period into the more stark consideration: "*What* am I?" Modernist culture responds with a reconceptualized sense of self, one that persists to the present day – and still causes us much trouble at times.

Notes

1 Max Weber, *From Max Weber: Essays in Sociology*, trans. and ed. H.H. Gerth and C. Wright Mills (London: Routledge, 1997), 155.

2 Steven Connor, "The Modern Auditory I," in *Rewriting the Self: Histories from the Renaissance to the Present*, ed. Roy Porter (London and New York: Routledge, 1997), 203–23, 207.

3 Sigmund Freud, "Civilization and its Discontents," in *Civilization, Society and Religion: Group Psychology, Civilization and Its Discontents and other Works*, The Penguin Freud Library, Vol. 12, trans. James Strachey, ed. Albert Dickson (Harmondsworth: Penguin, 1991), 251–340, 279.

4 See Sean O'Connell, *The Motor Car in British Popular Culture* (Manchester: Manchester University Press, 1998), 112–49.

5 Elizabeth Bowen, *Pictures and Conversations: Chapters of an Autobiography* (London: Allen Lane, 1975), 43.

6 F. Scott Fitzgerald, *The Great Gatsby* (Harmondsworth: Penguin, 1950), 115.

7 Fitzgerald, *The Great Gatsby*, 133.

8 Bernhard Rieger, *Technology and the Culture of Modernity in Britain and Germany 1890–1945* (Cambridge: Cambridge University Press, 2005), 54, 56.

9 Ibid., 56.

10 Elizabeth Bowen, *To the North* (London: Vintage, 1999), 139.

11 Rieger, *Technology and the Culture of Modernity*, 277.

12 Bowen, *To the North*, 10.

13 Ibid., 6.

14 Ibid.

15 Rieger, *Technology and the Culture of Modernity*, 30.

16 Elizabeth Bowen, "Why I Go to the Cinema," in *Broadcasts, Speeches, and Interviews by Elizabeth Bowen*, ed. Allan Hepburn (Edinburgh: Edinburgh University Press, 2010), pp. 192–202, 202.

17 Max Nordau, *Degeneration* (Lincoln and London: University of Nebraska Press, 1993), 541.

18 Nordau, *Degeneration*, 541.

19 Freud, "Civilization and Its Discontents," 280.

20 Jonathan Rée, *I See a Voice: A Philosophical History of Language, Deafness and the Senses* (London: HarperCollins, 1999), 38.

21 Cited in Steven Connor, "Michel Serres's *Les Cinq Sens*," in *Mapping Michel Serres*, ed. Niran Abbas (Ann Arbor: University of Michigan Press, 2005), 153–69, 161.

22 Cited in Stephen Kern, *The Culture of Time and Space: 1880–1918* (Cambridge, MA: Harvard University Press, 2003), 67.

23 See Suzanne Hobson's essay in this volume, "Religion and Spirituality," for an extended analysis.

24 Friedrich Kittler, "Gramophone, Film, Typewriter," *October* 41 (1987): 101–18, 111.

25 Steven Connor, *Dumbstruck: A Cultural History of Ventriloquism* (Oxford: Oxford University Press, 2000), 354.

26 *Noise*, radio program, by Steven Connor, prod. Tim Dee, five episodes (BBC Radio 3, February 24–28, 1997).

27 Ibid.

28 Douglas Kahn, "Introduction: Histories of Sound Once Removed," in *Wireless Imagination: Sound, Radio, and the Avant-Garde*, ed. Douglas Kahn and Gregory Whitehead (Cambridge: MIT Press, 1992), 1–29, 18.

29 James Joyce, *Ulysses* (Harmondsworth: Penguin, 1992), 144.

30 Ibid., 140–41.

31 Pamela Thurswell, *Literature, Technology and Magical Thinking, 1880–1920* (Cambridge: Cambridge University Press, 2001).

32 Nicholas Royle, *Telepathy and Literature: Essays on the Reading Mind* (Oxford: Basil Blackwell, 1991), 5.

33 Sara Danius, *The Senses in Modernism: Technology, Perception, and Aesthetics* (Ithaca and London: Cornell University Press, 2002), 19.

34 Marta Braun, *Picturing Time: The Work of Étienne-Jules Marey (1830–1904)* (Chicago: Chicago University Press, 1994), 57.

35 Ibid., 147.

36 Lisa Cartwright, *Screening the Body: Tracing Medicine's Visual Culture* (Minneapolis: University of Minnesota Press, 1995), 107.

37 Ibid., 115.

38 Thomas Mann, *The Magic Mountain*, trans. H.T. Lowe-Porter (London: Vintage: 1999), 217.

39 Ibid., 218.

40 Thomas Mann, *The Magic Mountain*, trans. John E. Woods (New York: Vintage International 1995), 215–16. This translation captures the mood of the original passage more forcefully than Lowe-Porter's translation does.

41 Cited in Roy Porter, *The Greatest Benefit to Mankind: A Medical History of Humanity from Antiquity to the Present* (London: Fontana, 1999), 536.

42 Ruth Harris, "Introduction," in Jean-Marin Charcot, *Clinical Lectures on Diseases of the Nervous System*, ed. Ruth Harris (London: Tavistock/Routledge), ix–lxvii, xix, xviii.

43 Rae Beth Gordon, "From Charcot to Charlot: Unconscious Imitation and Spectatorship in French Cabaret and Early Cinema," *The Mind of Modernism*, ed. Mark S. Micale (Stanford, CA: Stanford University Press, 2004), 93–124, 93.

44 Ibid., 111.

45 Ibid., 109.

46 Henri Bergson, *Laughter: An Essay on the Meaning of the Comic*, trans. Cloudesley Brereton and Fred Rothwell (New York: Macmillan, 1911), 29.

47 Ibid., 37, 16.

48 Ibid., 28–29.

49 Harris, "Introduction," xvii, xix.

50 Steven Connor, "Elan Mortel: Life, Death and Laughter." stevenconnor.com/elanmortel/, accessed October 30, 2013.

51 Ibid.

52 Ibid.

53 John B. Watson, "Psychology as the Behaviourist Views It," *Psychological Review* 20 (1913): 158–77, 158.

54 John B. Watson, *Behaviourism* (London: Kegan Paul, Trench, Trubner & Co., 1925), 30–31.

3

Sexuality

Sexuality in the early twentieth century was shaped by two competing explanations that described and assigned values to sex: the increasingly influential discourse of science and the decreasingly influential discourse of Christianity. The rise of science to regulate sexuality is epitomized by the first conference of the World League for Sexual Reform (WLSR) in Copenhagen in 1928. Under the leadership of its three physician presidents, the League announced that its goal was "to encourage the development of a sexual sociology and a sexual ethic, based on sexual biology and sexual psychology, rather than, as in the past, on theology."[1] In framing sexuality through the new sciences of sociology, biology, and psychology, the WLSR advocated for marriage as a "living comradeship between two people," access to and education about birth control, racial improvement through the application of eugenics, the prevention of prostitution and venereal disease, and tolerance for all consensual, adult sexual behaviors, including homosexuality.[2] These proposed reforms represent the most marked transformations in the ways that those living in Western countries came to express their sexuality during the modernist period.

The World League for Sexual Reform had 190,000 members and a list of supporters that reads like a "who's who" of modernism, but it also had a short life, petering out in 1935 after the death of its Nazi-exiled leader, Magnus Hirschfeld.[3] That it existed at all points to the multiple and sometimes coordinated efforts of many during the modernist period to use science to detail sexual behaviors, develop methods for and disseminate means of contraception, alter reproductive patterns for what was termed "racial improvement," detect and prevent the spread of venereal disease, and, in separating sexual intercourse from reproduction, create an entire ethic and industry around sex for pleasure.

Yet while science was used to endorse sexual pleasure as a biological necessity, Christianity was marshaled in defense of public morality. Legal codes that impinged on sexual behavior proliferated in the early twentieth century, including laws that prohibited the dissemination of obscene literature, criminalized abortion in Britain and the United States, further circumscribed prostitution in imperial countries and their colonies, and increased the legal repression of homosexuality.[4] Behind both scientific and moral purity attitudes toward sexuality was a relatively new voice clamoring to be heard: that of women. Feminism used both scientific and Christian arguments to dispute traditional masculine attitudes that considered women the sexual property of men. Transatlantic feminists of socialist and medical backgrounds advocated a woman's right to active sexual pleasure. In contrast, British feminist Cicely Hamilton's 1909 polemic, *Marriage as a Trade*, argued in favor of female celibacy as a way to defeat patriarchy.

From the mass marketing of birth control to the first public health campaigns about venereal disease to the growth of the sex advice industry and homosexual identity, sexuality was reinvented during the modernist period as a public and scientific endeavor, and the effects of this shift are still being felt today.

The Science of Sexology and the Birth of Sexuality as Identity

Charles Darwin's 1870s claims that biological success depends on sexual selection created a new and legitimate scientific interest in exploring sexual behavior. Beginning with the publication of Richard von Kraft Ebbing's 1886 study of the sexually abnormal, *Psychopathia Sexualis*, a new genre of what was classified as medical literature blossomed in the 1890s and early 1900s. This work catalogued sexual behaviors and attitudes and circulated the idea that sexuality is central to individual identity and social behavior. As the most prominent sexologist in England, Havelock Ellis, wrote in the opening pages of *The Psychology of Sex* (1933), "Sex penetrates the whole person."[5] And yet, sexologists such as Ellis and the German "Einstein of Sex" Magnus Hirschfeld claimed that most people remained in ignorance about sex. By observing behaviors, collecting first-person accounts of sexual experiences and feelings, and classifying this information, sexologists hoped to contribute to society by providing a scientific view of what sexuality is and how it might best be channeled.

One of the first topics about which Havelock Ellis and Magnus Hirschfeld wrote was homosexuality, alternatively called sexual inversion, the third or intermediate sex, or those who had contrary sexual sensations. Ellis's *Sexual Inversion* (published first in German in 1896 because Germany was considered the center of sexual research, and then in English in 1897) and Hirschfeld's *Die Transvestiten* (1910) and *De Homosexualität des Mannes und des Weibes* (1914) argued that homosexuality was a natural and innate characteristic, an identity that defined an individual's self-concept. This notion was furthered by the literary and mystical treatment given to homosexuals by Edward Carpenter in his 1896 book *Love's Coming of Age* and his 1908 book *The Intermediate Sex: A Study of Some Transitional Types of Men and Women*, which was the first generally available book in English to frame homosexuality positively rather than as a moral or medical problem. This essentialist approach was in contrast to a legal history that had criminalized sodomy as an act that could encompass male-female oral-genital and anal-genital contact but not homosexuality as an identity in itself.[6] Sexual acts had heretofore not correlated to sexual identities. In *Sexual Inversion*, for instance, Ellis says, "In England, I am told, the soldier often has little or no objection to prostitute himself to the 'swell' who pays him, although for pleasure he prefers to go to women; and Hyde Park is spoken of as a center of male prostitution."[7] There were plenty of men who had sex with men in the early twentieth century and who did not see themselves as homosexuals, either because it was seen as a normal part of boyhood (as some men commented of life in the single-sex public schools) or it was a useful way to "ply a lively trade" for working-class men. Similarly, in the United States, female same-sex romances at the turn of the twentieth century were not necessarily understood as homosexual. Boarding school- and college-educated women formed romantic partnerships openly and "developed crushes, fell madly in love, courted, wrote love notes, and exchanged presents"; popular stories in magazines wrote about such characters in an overtly sexualized way.[8] The children's magazine *St. Nicholas*, for instance, published a 1908 story in which "with a rush like a mountain gale, Carol came in, caught Jean, whirled her around, pulled her down on a cot, and gave her a warm kiss."[9] As in other stories about young women in romantic relationships, these girls were not labeled, nor did they self-identify as inverts, tribads, or sapphists, the terms used at the time to denote lesbians.

Ellis observes in *Sexual Inversion* that "the importance of a clear conception of inversion" was critical to one's self-identification as an invert, a notion corroborated by the number of firsthand accounts in Ellis's book that speak of Oscar Wilde's 1895 public scandal involving same-sex liaisons as the event that helped them to crystallize their own inchoate feelings.[10] Similarly, Radclyffe Hall's 1929 novel *The Well of Loneliness* and the publicity surrounding its obscenity trial brought lesbian identity into the middle-class parlors of the English-speaking world, and generations of lesbians in the twentieth century referred to *Well* as the novel that helped them find their lesbian identity. That later men and women were able to self-identify as a uranian or a tribad is a direct result of the labeling and categorizing work performed not just by media-generated sex scandals or popular novels but also by the publication of sexological works, including those by Ellis and Hirschfeld as well as other continental authors such as Iwan Bloch, Auguste Forel, Charles Féré, Albert Moll, and, of course, that other scientist who preferred to create systems of thought rather than empirical studies, Sigmund Freud.[11] All of these men, trained physicians who more often than not did not practice medicine, knew of and cited one another's work in their own.

More than any of the other sexologists of his time, Sigmund Freud disseminated the idea that sexuality is at the core of human personality, and, as with other sexologists, he brought sexuality into the realm of science and medicine by approaching it as an observable and treatable aspect of human behavior. Like Ellis and Hirschfeld, Freud argued that all humans are bisexual and either develop or choose singular inclinations. However, unlike the sexologists who argued that sexual characteristics were innate, Freud insisted that adult sexuality was affected by experiences in early childhood that could alter the path of one's sexuality. He viewed humans as sexually malleable, finding pleasure in a range of bodily sensations, but saw social stricture and the forces of civilization as those that necessarily but sometimes pathologically constricted individual sexual behavior. Freud's views on female sexuality were at odds with some of the other sexological and popular scientific writing about women's sexuality in the modernist period: he argued that women had "penis envy" because the penis was the most sexual and important organ, and he disavowed the clitoris as the site of mature sexual pleasure for women, a notion that Ellis ridiculed.

Women's sexuality was a topic of interest and curiosity for sexologists, Freud famously calling it a "dark continent" and Ellis finding it "elusive."[12] For all of their prognosticating, there is a lot of extant evidence about women's sexuality in the early decades of the twentieth

ı from empirical studies of the time as well as from the birth
ments in England and the United States, which were led by
h to reveal the sexual experiences of women.

ırth Control and Eugenics

A small study of 2,200 middle-class American women, sponsored by the Bureau of Social Hygiene in 1929, provides a useful snapshot of their sexual experiences toward the end of the modernist period. Of those women, 74 percent practiced some form of contraception, 85 percent thought married people justified in having sexual intercourse for purposes other than procreation, 64 percent of unmarried women acknowledged masturbating, and 71 percent believed abortion was justified; only 7 percent engaged in premarital intercourse. Of the same group, 25 percent had had intense emotional ties to another woman that involved a physical component recognized as sexual; another 25 percent had emotional attachments to women that involved kissing and hugging.[13] Women's sex lives were no longer the taboo subjects they had been in the nineteenth century but rather a central focus of the early twentieth century.

To trace the evolution of the birth control movement is to witness the increasing jurisdiction women gained over their lives in the early twentieth century. Where the first two decades of the twentieth century were spent with social purity activists and "population control" advocates in the United States and United Kingdom in battle over whether and where one could disseminate information about contraception, after World War I, the newly termed "birth control movement" gained momentum, and men and women had unprecedented access to birth control information and products. The new cultural focus on contraception rather than abstinence indicated and afforded female sexual expression before and after marriage, decoupled sexual intercourse from procreation, and in doing so significantly altered the meaning of marriage. Though there were no laws against using fertility control in the nineteenth century, the topic was culturally taboo, and print laws in England and the Comstock Laws in the United States outlawed distributing such information or selling contraceptive devices through the mail. In spite of such laws, birth rates in both countries declined in the nineteenth century, and there is evidence that, with the exception of the diaphragm, every form of birth control available in the mid-twentieth century was also available one-hundred years prior. Women were advised to douche with quinine, alum, or bicarbonate of soda, vinegar, and salt water, to insert vaginal sponges or plugs, and, once the manufacturing of rubber was perfected in the 1850s, to insert pessaries.[14] Condoms, in contrast, were developed as prophylactics against venereal disease, not as a form of contraception, and because of their association with prostitution were rarely used by married couples until after World War I.[15] Further, until the 1920s, the price of "French rubber goods," manufactured across Europe and the United States, was beyond the financial reach of working-class men.[16] Though contraceptives were available and even mass marketed, they were not labeled as such in order to avoid antiobscenity laws. Instead, one had to look for "marital aids" or "hygienic" devices.

If withdrawal or any of the above methods failed, there were a number of known abortifacients. Folklore recipes, quack doctors, and druggists facile with euphemisms when a woman found herself "obstructed" were able to supply poisonous drinks or pills containing quinine, pennyroyal, yew, juniper, bitter aloes, lemon balm, castor bean oil, or mustard baths, and many pills sold as laxatives in the early twentieth century doubled as abortifacients when taken in specific doses.[17] In *Family Limitation*, the 1916 pamphlet that Margaret Sanger distributed illegally before fleeing the United States for a year in order to avoid prosecution, she advises "Beechams Pills. Two of these taken night and morning, four days before menstruation, will give a good cleansing of the bowels, and assist with the menstrual flow." Notably, even Sanger's language is indirect, addressing menstrual regularity rather than pregnancy, thus showing the range of euphemisms that were so common as to appear clear to her audience. Sanger stresses, "If a woman will give herself attention BEFORE the menstrual period arrives, she will almost never have any trouble, but if she neglects herself and waits to see if she 'comes around,' she is likely to have difficulty."[18] Advertisements for pills claiming to treat women's "troubles" and "obstructions," such as Widow Welch's Female Pills and Dr. Patterson's Famous Female Pills, were widely available and marketed using a language that would have been recognized by girls "in trouble" or married women who were "caught" and looking for abortifacients.

Strikingly, abortion was by far the most common form of birth control and was popularly considered far less immoral than mechanical or chemical contraception. Where contraception required planning ahead and making the mental decision to engage in sexual intercourse without risking pregnancy, abortions and abortifacients were interpreted as restoring a woman's health by "bringing back the monthlies."[19] Though women tried to give themselves abortions, and some middle- and upper-class doctors in urban centers would perform them, there were also known destinations for abortion tourism. Englishwomen went to Paris as well as to Geneva, Naples, and Constantinople, where there were hospitals that routinely performed abortions. In Geneva in the first two decades of the twentieth century, there were approximately fifty dilation and curettage procedures a day.[20] While those with financial means could procure an abortion, the working classes had far less access. In New York in the 1930s, Margaret Sanger remarked, "On Saturday nights I have seen groups of from fifty to one hundred [women] with their shawls over their heads waiting outside the office of a five-dollar abortionist."[21] Such scenes in large part drove the likes of Sanger in the United States and Marie Stopes in the United Kingdom to develop the first birth control clinics in their countries, in 1916 and 1921, respectively.

There were multiple impulses behind the birth control movement, also referred to in England as conscious or voluntary motherhood. One influential group was the Neo-Malthusians, who, following Thomas Malthus's contention that the rate of population would continue to rise exponentially because of the human sex drive, looked to contraception to control population growth. Formed in 1877 and dissolved in 1927, the Malthusian League had two aims: to stop legal proscriptions against public discussion of contraception and to educate the public about the importance of family planning. When Margaret Sanger coined the term "birth control" in the first issue of her 1914 magazine, *The Woman Rebel*, she argued that prostitutes and women of the upper middle class "have all available knowledge and implements to prevent conception. The woman of the lower middle class is struggling for this knowledge" and left to "blood-sucking men with M.D. after their names who perform operations for the price of so-and-so."[22] After a brief stint as a nurse in the tenements of New York's Lower East Side, Sanger was distressed at the many working-class women who were ignorant about methods of birth prevention and for whom "pregnancy was a chronic condition."[23] She was motivated, certainly at first, by a strong social conscience for equality of opportunity for all women. Her belief that "woman is enslaved by the world machine, by sex conventions, by motherhood and its present necessary child-rearing, by wage-slavery, by middle class morality, by customs, laws, and superstitions"[24] led her first to disseminate information about contraception via pamphlets. On her tour through Europe while avoiding prosecution at home, Sanger visited a Dutch clinic that used the diaphragm (invented in 1882) and was convinced that a doctor-fitted device would be the best method of birth control. She opened her first birth control clinic in Brownsville, a working-class Brooklyn neighborhood, where women could be advised on contraceptive options and fitted for diaphragms.

Similarly, Marie Stopes's first clinic was located in Holloway, a working-class district in north London. Stopes held a PhD in paleobotany and always published as Dr. Marie Carmichael Stopes. This use of her title was perhaps misleading in that the popular marriage and birth control manuals she published, *Married Love* (1918) and *Wise Parenthood: A Book for Married People* (1919), may have appeared to represent advice from a medical doctor. After Sanger's clinic in Brooklyn was legally forced to close, Sanger talked with Stopes about opening a clinic in London. Though Sanger did not follow through, Stopes did, resigning from her lectureship at the University of London in 1920 and opening the Mothers' Clinic for married women in 1921, which was run by midwives with visiting doctors. The clinic offered birth control advice and taught women how to use the cervical cap. According to Stopes, eight years after the opening of the clinic, its midwives and nurses had taught ten thousand female patients the use of birth control appliances; by 1937, this number had increased to twenty-six thousand "individual poor women."[25] Both Sanger and Stopes led the efforts to build networks of clinics across Britain and the United States during the 1930s and 1940s.

Birth control advocates exploited the logic and popularity of eugenic ideas to defend family planning as a moral project. Eugenics, promulgated by Charles Darwin's cousin Francis Galton, was the science of improving racial characteristics by promoting early marriage of the fit. The Eugenics Education Society was founded in 1907 and included prominent literary, intellectual, and political figures.[26] Placed within a eugenics framework, birth control avoided its association with sexuality and instead became a benchmark of so-called racial progress. Marie Stopes marketed her birth control cervical caps, sponges, and pessaries under the name "Prorace" (see Figure 2) and prefaced the fifth edition of her book on birth control, *Wise Parenthood*, by saying, "I sincerely trust that this little book will help to improve our race."[27] Through her friendship with Havelock Ellis, Margaret Sanger learned about eugenics and adopted its arguments to advocate family planning. When Sanger founded the American Birth Control League in 1922, their official

FIGURE 2 Cervical cap, Marie Stopes; John Bell and Croyden Limited (1915–25). Science Museum / Science & Society Picture Library

statement of "Principles and Aims" made the case that birth control was essential because:

> Everywhere we see poverty and large families going hand in hand. Those least fit to carry on the race are increasing most rapidly. People who cannot support their own offspring are encouraged by Church and State to produce large families. Many of the children thus begotten are diseased and feeble-minded; many become criminals. The burden of supporting these unwanted types has to be borne by the healthy elements of the nation. Funds that should be used to raise the standard of our civilization are diverted to the maintenance of those who should never have been born. To create a race of well-born children it is essential that the functions of motherhood should be elevated to a position of dignity, and this is impossible as long as conception remains a matter of chance.[28]

Sanger's racialist and Darwinian arguments, which have long clouded her legacy, participate in a larger discourse of class and race superiority that epitomize the 1920s and 1930s and reached their apotheosis in World War II. But they formed just one part of the arguments forwarded on behalf of making birth control accessible to all. Over the modernist period, advocates argued that mass access to birth control information and birth control proper would reduce infant and maternal mortality; improve women's health and free women from "enforced motherhood"; limit abortion; prevent the male and female neuroses and sexual dysfunction that many physicians attributed to withdrawal and prolonged abstinence; strengthen marriage; space births; control population; limit disease and defect; improve the quality of the human race, and enhance sexual pleasure for all. Such arguments were necessary because at the turn of the twentieth century, government, medicine, and public opinion jointly supported state suppression of contraception.[29]

Venereal Disease, the Great War, and the Decline of Prostitution

Inasmuch as there was a small group of liberal-minded sexologists, eugenicists, and feminist reformers advocating for greater access to birth control and greater tolerance of sexual activity, there were also antivice crusaders and feminists committed to what was called "social purity" in the late nineteenth century. They advocated abstinence and male sexual continence through Christian morality as well as self-restraint in order to eradicate the "social evil" of prostitution, which was a normalized aspect of men's sexual lives of all classes. Social purity later turned into the social hygiene movement in the early twentieth century, which advocated self-restraint but also engineered public health campaigns to eradicate venereal disease and, with it, prostitution (Figure 3). In Europe and North America, suppressing sexuality had the effect of exercising control over the lower classes or at least encouraging them to adapt to middle-class sexual mores. In the United States, this was most obvious in the social hygiene movements' targeting of immigrant populations in the urbanized North and blacks in the rural South.[30] In England, feminists promoted social purity in the late nineteenth and early twentieth centuries in order to abolish prostitution, targeting not just the women who could be medically examined or incarcerated simply for walking down a street alone but also the men assumed to form their clientele and who were thought to have animal-like appetites. Throughout the British Empire, colonial officials saw prostitution as a routine part of life and "living evidence of native disorder."[31] Colonial authorities employed a variety of regulatory systems that controlled female prostitutes. In Britain's Southeast Asian colonies, for instance, women who worked in the brothels had to carry identity cards and were classed into brothels based on their lineage.[32]

FIGURE 3 "Will you be a free man or chained?" (1918) United States Army, Social Hygiene Division

In 1918, the United States Public Health Service joined with the Young Men's Christian Association (YMCA) to develop the nation's first sex-education program, targeted at boys between fourteen and twenty-one years of age. Available as exhibit and pamphlet, *Keeping Fit* linked boys' athletic fitness to their sexual health and advocated self-control as the highest value; the program implied that physical and moral health were linked. *Keeping Fit* discussed neither reproduction nor sexually transmitted diseases explicitly; instead, it consistently reiterated the idea that "lack of control leads to disease, decay, and ultimately, death."[33] This message had a robust life during the modernist period and was a direct result of a venereal disease crisis in Europe, North America, and the British colonies, with rates of infection estimated between 10 to 15 percent of the total population. The spread of venereal disease was made more obvious and problematic by the mobilization of thousands of young men into armies during World War I.[34]

War brought with it an array of sexual violence. Not only did rape, gang rape, and genital mutilation occur, but sexual violence (and images thereof) against a nation's women were also used as propaganda to encourage men to enlist as soldiers. The largest sex-related issue promulgated by the war, however, was the spread of syphilis ("pox"), gonorrhea ("clap"), and chancroid ("soft chancre"). Where the German military approached venereal diseases from a medical-scientific point of view, distributing condoms to its soldiers and administering prophylactic injections of antiseptic liquids into the penis before and after encounters with prostitutes, the British and American armies approached venereal disease as a moral issue to be prevented by abstinence, as the American military poster in Figure 3 reinforces. The US government instated civilian quarantines from soldiers and incarcerated and treated those women suspected as venereal disease carriers, apprehending a total of 30,000 American women between 1918 and 1920 and institutionalizing half of them for treatment.[35] This somewhat hysterical response was as much a backlash against women's growing sexual autonomy as an approach to contain the medical danger. The Allied troops are reputed to have contracted 1.5 million cases of gonorrhea and syphilis during World War I.[36]

In response to such rates of infection, the 1920s and 1930s saw a great increase in the use and distribution of condoms. Where in Britain, couples in 1912 used condoms about 10 percent of the time, by 1921, couples used condoms 40 percent of the time.[37] Condom machines were popularized and could be found not just in gentlemen's clubs or nightclubs but on public streets, often outside chemist's shops in Britain in the 1930s. By 1938, American birth control industry sales were estimated to be more than $250 million per year, just a bit less than the jewelry business.[38]

With increased access to birth control and public awareness campaigns against the dangers of sexually transmitted diseases, sexual behaviors of working-class and middle-class men changed significantly in the 1920s and 1930s. Where for middle-class men in the first decade of the twentieth century, sex with prostitutes and abstinence at home would have been the norm, by the 1920s, the companionate, erotic marriage became a new ideal, with one's wife as consistent sexual partner not just for procreation but for pleasure, intimacy, and emotional health.

Eroticizing Marriage

Dagmar Herzog contends that "One of the great dramas of the early twentieth century, [is] the effort to eroticize marriage itself and the related effort to make women's sexual agency and experience be understood as a positive good, rather than a source of shame and dishonor."[39] Such effort could be seen at the First American Birth Control Conference in 1921, when Margaret Sanger pronounced, "I contend that it is just as sacred and just as beautiful for two people to express their love when they have no intention whatsoever of being parents."[40] It can also be seen in some of the best-selling sex and marriage manuals of the time: Ellen Key's *Love and Marriage* (1911), Marie Stopes's *Married Love* (1918), Joseph Collins's *The Doctor Looks at Love and Life* (1926), and Theo Van de Velde's *Ideal Marriage: Its Physiology and Technique* (1926). Both Stopes's and Van de Velde's books were best sellers. *Married Love* sold 17,000 copies in its first year, far outperforming the best-selling fiction of the era. By 1925, it had sold more than 500,000 copies. *Ideal Marriage* was reprinted forty-six times in its first edition, and as it was written for and endorsed by the medical profession, it played a profound role in shaping modern ideas about "healthy" sexuality. Both Stopes and Van de Velde were explicit in arguing that shared sexual pleasure was one of the primary aims of marriage, with mutual orgasm a stated goal. Van de Velde's text encourages men not to think that their wives were above or made dirty by sexual exploration lest this leads men to look for sex outside of marriage, which, he argued, was "real debauchery." Instead, Van de Velde's text advocates a new moral discipline of making the marital bed a place of spiritual and physical union.[41] The currency of such ideas is encapsulated in the mutual orgasms that have a privileged place in D.H. Lawrence's 1928 *Lady Chatterley's Lover*.

The effects of the increased access to birth control and the sexually companionate marriage may possibly be measured through Alfred Kinsey's pioneering study on female sexuality (1953), which interviewed women who reached sexual maturity in the first decades of the twentieth century. The studies found a steady increase in the number of women reaching orgasm during intercourse.[42] But even as the 1920s and 1930s liberalized sexual behaviors in various arenas, there was a counterforce. Openness with regard to contraception and abortion, which were part of women's growing equality, coupled with the increasing visibility of male and female homosexuality, created the grounds for a backlash against the rights of individual sexual expression and formed the sexual politics of German Nazism, Vichy France, and the fascist regimes of Italy and Spain.[43] Throughout the 1930s, openness about women's rights, sexual expression, and homosexuality were increasingly curtailed in these countries. Director of Nazi propaganda Joseph Goebbels pronounced, "the mission of women is to be beautiful and to bring children into the world."[44] Homosexuals were among the groups targeted by the Nazis for destruction and were immediately exterminated in the camps.

Where the dissemination of birth control and the sexually companion-ate marriage persisted beyond World War II, tolerance for homosexuality did not, and eugenics reached its destructive apotheosis in the racist policies and actions of Nazi Germany. The original impulse behind sexual reform of the period, science, persisted as a dominant organizing principle behind modern sexuality in North America and Europe.

Notes

1 Pamphlet produced by the World League for Sexual Reform, 1928. SA/EDG/D.250: Box 54. Wellcome Library Archives and Manuscripts.
2 Ibid.
3 The Third International Congress of the WLSR held in London (1929) lists among its supporters Clive Bell, Arnold Bennett, Vera Brittain, Jonathan Cape, Hugh de Selincourt, E.M. Forster, Vyvyan Holland, Aldous Huxley, Julian Huxley, J. Maynard Keynes, D.H. Lawrence, Vernon Lee, Horace Liveright, W. Somerset Maugham, Francis Meynell, Sylvia Pankhurst, H.B. Priestley, Dorothy M. Richardson, Bertrand Russell, Vita Sackville-West, Bernard Shaw, Upton Sinclair, Adrian Stephen, Marie Stophes, Lytton Strachey, Frank Swinnerton, Hugh Walpole, H.G. Wells, Rebecca West, Leonard Woolf, and many more. Ibid.
4 Mary E. Odem, *Delinquent Daughters: Protecting and Policing Adolescent Female Sexuality in the United States, 1885–1920* (Chapel Hill: University of North Carolina Press, 1995), 2.
5 Havelock Ellis, *The Psychology of Sex* (London: Heinemann, 1933), 3.
6 Annette F. Timm and Joshua A. Sanborn, *Gender, Sex and the Shaping of Modern Europe* (New York: Berg, 2007), 31.
7 Havelock Ellis, *Sexual Inversion* (Philadelphia: F.A. Davis Co, 1915), 21.
8 John D'Emilio and Estelle B. Freedman, *Intimate Matters: A History of Sexuality in America*, 2nd ed. (Chicago: University of Chicago Press, 1997), 190–01.
9 Mary Constance DuBoise, "The Lass of the Silver Sword," *St. Nicholas* 36.2 (1908): 700.
10 Ellis, *Sexual Inversion*, p. 196.
11 In addition to those cited by Havelock Ellis and Magnus Hirschfeld, significant works include Iwan Bloch, *Beitrage zur Aetiologie der Psychopathia Sexualis*, 2 vols. (Dresden: H.R. Dohm, 1902–03); Charles Féré, *L'Instinct sexuel: Evolution et dissolution* (Paris: Felix Alcan, 1899); Albert Moll, *Die Konträre Sexualempfindung* (Berlin: Fischer's MedicinischeBuchhandlung, 1891); *Handbuch der Sexualwissenschaften* (Berlin: Voge, 1912); August Forel, *La Question Sexuelle* (Paris: Steinheil,1905); and Sigmund Freud, *Drei Abhandlungen zur Sexualtheorie* (Leipzig und Wein: Franz Deuticke, 1905).
12 Sigmund Freud, *The Standard Edition of the Complete Psychological Works of Sigmund Freud*, 24 vols., trans. & ed. James Strachey (London: The Hogarth Press & The Institute of Psychoanalysis, 1953–74), 212; Havelock Ellis, *Analysis of the Sexual Impulse, Love and Pain, The Sexual Impulse in Women* [1903] 2nd ed. (Philadelphia: F.A. Davis, 1925), 189.
13 Katharine Bement Davis, *Factors in the Sex Life of Twenty-Two Hundred Women* (New York: Harper, 1929).

14 Peter C. Engelman, *A History of the Birth Control Movement in America* (Santa Barbara, CA: Praeger, 2011), 4; Dagmar Herzog, *Sexuality in Europe: A Twentieth-Century History* (New York: Cambridge University Press, 2011), 20–21.

15 Peter C. Engelman, *A History of the Birth Control Movement in America* (Santa Barbara, CA: Praeger, 2011), 4.

16 Annette F. Timm and Joshua A. Sanborn, *Gender, Sex and the Shaping of Modern Europe* (New York: Berg, 2007), 182.

17 Herzog, pp. 20–21.

18 Margaret Sanger, *Family Limitation*, The Public Writings and Papers of Margaret Sanger, http://www.nyu.edu/projects/sanger/

19 Herzog, p. 20.

20 Timm and Sanborn, p. 23.

21 Margaret Sanger, *An Autobiography* (New York: W.W. Norton and Co., 1938), 92

22 Margaret Sanger, "The Prevention of Conception," *The Woman Rebel*, 1.1 (March 1914): 8.

23 Sanger, *An Autobiography*, p. 92.

24 Sanger, "Why Women Rebel?" *The Woman Rebel*, 1.1 (March 1914): 8.

25 Alexander C.T. Geppert, "Divine Sex, Happy Marriage, Regenerated Nation: Marie Stopes's Marital *Married Love* and the Making of a Best Seller, 1918–1955," *Journal of the History of Sexuality* 8.3 (Jan 1998): 400.

26 Lucy Bland and Lesley A. Hall, "Eugenics in Britain: The View from the Metropole," in *Oxford Handbook of Eugenics*, eds. Alison Bashford and Philippa Levine (Oxford: Oxford University Press, 2010), 15.

27 Marie Stopes, *Wise Parenthood: A Practical Sequel to* MARRIED LOVE. Sixth Edition. (London: G.P. Putnam's Sons, 1920), viii.

28 Qtd. in Engelman, p. 130.

29 Engelman, p. 20.

30 John D'Emilio and Estelle B. Freedman, *Intimate Matters: A History of Sexuality in America*. 2nd ed. (Chicago: University of Chicago Press, 1997), 203.

31 Philippa Levine, 'A Multitude of Unchaste Women': Prostitution in the British Empire," *Journal of Women's History* 15.4 (Winter 2004): 159.

32 *Ibid.*, pp. 160–61.

33 Alexandra Lord, *Condom Nation: The U.S. Government's Sex Education Campaign from World War I to the Internet* (Baltimore: Johns Hopkins University Press, 2009), 36–39, 39.

34 Estimates of rates of infection in the U.S. at 10 percent can be found in John H. Stokes, *The Third Great Plague: A Discussion of Syphilis for Everyday People* (Philadelphia: W.B. Saunders Company, 1920), 26. Estimates of a 15 percent infection rate in the United States can be found in Elie Metchnikoff, *The New Hygiene: Three Lectures on the Prevention of Infectious Disease* (Chicago: W.T. Keener and Company, 1907), 77. In Britain, the Contagious Diseases Acts of 1864, 1866, and 1869 had provided for the compulsory medical examination of prostitutes in order to check for venereal diseases, and by the early twentieth century, rates of infection were just under 10 percent. As Hera Cook argues, "Both the support for the Acts and the campaign against them can be thought of as publicity that raised people's awareness of the dangers of venereal diseases and of the high rates of infection." *The Long Sexual Revolution: English Women, Sex, and Contraception, 1800–1975* (New York: Oxford University Press, 2004), 94. Where rates of admission to military hospitals for British troops with venereal disease were about 5 percent, they were consistently higher for Canadians, Australians, and New

Zealanders, at about 10 percent. Philippa Levine, *Prostitution, Race, and Politics: Policing Venereal Disease in the British Empire* (Hove: Psychology Press, 2003), 146.

35 Wendy Kline, *Building a Better Race: Gender, Sexuality, and Eugenics from the Turn of the Century to the Baby Boom* (Berkeley: University of California Press, 2001), 47; John Parascandola, *Sex, Sin, and Science: A History of Syphilis in America* (Westport, CT: Praeger, 2008), 57.

36 John V.H. Dippell, *War and Sex: A Brief History of Men's Urge for Battle* (Amherst, NY: Prometheus Books, 2010), 370, *n*220.

37 Engelman, p. 109.

38 Engelman, p. 167.

39 Herzog, p. 18.

40 Engelman, p. 127.

41 Theodore Van de Velde, *Ideal Marriage: Its Physiology and Technique* [1926] (Santa Barbara, CA: Praeger, 1980), 9.

42 Engelman, p. 144.

43 Timm and Sanborn, p. 60.

44 Ibid., p. 154.

4

Militarism, Pacifism, and Internationalism

Both pacifism and militarism were major constituents of the interwar political and cultural world. Militarism could refer, in the immediate postwar years, to advocates of holding Germany strictly to the Versailles terms or to hawks on the Irish question. Supporters of Italian, German, and eventually Spanish fascism form another category of militarists who in Britain would be particularly visible in blackshirt form. A fixation on uniforms, parading, and drilling, "the love of medals and decorations," as Virginia Woolf put it,[1] is another brand of militarism, one encouraged by the militarization of the entire society during 1914 through 1918 and which had special resonances for many women in this period. Pacifism and internationalism – particularly in the form of League of Nations support and massive peace mobilizations – were extraordinarily popular causes among Liberals, Labour, and the thousands of former suffrage supporters for whom war was the inevitable result of patriarchal power. Both women and men were of course drawn to international action in the 1920s and 1930s, but educated men had routinely and for generations incorporated the international into their domain. What is distinctly modern is the political creativity, international contacts, and energetic mobilizations among the newly enfranchised women of Britain who will be my subject here. Women's earlier entrance into the public sphere through higher education and employment now extended to international movements and causes; the formal grant of a vote was a factor in the creation of modern women who situated themselves as both national and global citizens.

The 1920s and 1930s are decades of paradoxes in women's history – uncomfortable blends of the Victorian and the modern. The younger women of the era had been schooled in the radicalism of the suffrage movement or of Bolshevism, yet family traditions and connections continued to structure the lives of many. In these decades of across-the-board religious decline, Christ was the inspiration for some of the boldest women of these decades. Finally, some of those who struggled for women's political rights before 1914 became supporters of Mussolini's or Hitler's dictatorship two decades later.

This essay begins with a brief survey of women's massive and remarkable efforts to achieve collective security and peace during these two decades. Three case studies will follow, representative of different internationalist positions in relation to the modern. (1) Mary Allen (1878–1964) was a wealthy former suffrage militant who helped to open police forces to women and who became a high-ranking member of Oswald Mosley's British Union of Fascists; she is an exemplar of female militarism but also of creativity in shaping the modern female body and extending women's authority over public space. (2) Francesca Wilson (1888–1981) was a multilingual, Quaker-connected humanitarian aid worker from 1916 through 1947 who extended philanthropy into a global internationalist politics and lived the life of an independent self-supporting woman. (3) The third figure, antifascist internationalist Winifred Holtby (1898–1935), was a sharp-witted political journalist; before her death at age thirty-seven, she had become increasingly involved in anticolonial efforts through print journalism, fiction, friendships, and more formal political connections.

Women and Peace Activism

Women's traditional role as guardian of religious feeling offered a paradoxical point of entry into twentieth-century peace activism; strong religious belief was close to a common denominator among peace advocates from 1914 to 1939. Of those who attempted to get to the 1915 women's Hague conference that pressed for a negotiated peace, as many as a quarter were practicing Quakers. One of the conference organizers, Theodora Wilson, a tireless peace campaigner for decades, felt she had been called by Jesus "to a life-service for the enthronement of Love in personal, social, commercial, and national life."[2] The writer and activist Evelyn Sharp was a former Anglican who found as an adult that the "teaching of Christ suddenly seemed to shine out like a diamond from a dust-heap."[3] To take one more example, the enormously successful (in terms of members) Peace Pledge Union arose in the mid-1930s out of a series of meetings of Christian pacifist groups of several denominations and coalesced in 1935 under the Anglican minister Samuel Sheppard, vicar of St. Martin-in-the-Fields.

The suffrage movement, too, proved to be a crucible of interwar women's internationalism. Feminists' dedication to peace was based on a range of thinking, from a divine call like that of Wilson's to a new confidence in women's political voice to the maternalist certainty that female nurturance had to shape the political realm. The organic connection between militarism and the subordination of women explored in so many ways by feminist authors through 1939 was forcefully enunciated in a 1915 book designed to coincide with the convening of The Hague conference. Its probable authors were pacifist editor Charles Ogden and artist Mary Sargant Florence, and their book was aptly titled *Militarism versus Feminism: An Enquiry and a Policy Demonstrating that Militarism Involves the Subjection of Women*. Most of the nearly three hundred British women who applied for exit permits to travel to The Hague or who publicly supported it had been connected to the suffrage cause. After 1918, the suffragists were involved not only in feminist causes but also in the new women's sections of the Labour Party, League of Nations support, and the Women's International League for Peace and Freedom (WILPF, called WIL in Britain), which formed after the war among Hague delegates. In 1919, ex-suffragists could be found demanding the end of Britain's naval blockade of the Central Powers, which played a role in the near starvation of thousands in central Europe. Women's organizations attempted to get a place at the treaty negotiations in 1919 and were rebuffed.

The sheer scale of the Continent's postwar famine and destitution challenged activists to disentangle political engagement from philanthropy, the modern woman from the Victorian. WILPF defined itself as a *political* organization, which would shape policy permanently through pressure on state governments and on the League of Nations. Emily Greene Balch, the American educator who was the first post-World War I International Secretary, crisply stated that the organization was "not primarily a humanitarian one."[4] As Quakers organized feeding for Austrian preschool children, WILPF's 1919 resolution plainly demanded that the diplomats in Paris immediately end the naval blockade. Political and philanthropic activism could not easily be separated in any case. One longtime peace campaigner defined her own relief work in Vienna, Poland, and elsewhere in the 1920s as a statement against the harm done by war. The imbrication of humanitarian aid and "political" intervention is obvious in the efforts of non-Spanish nationals to aid the hungry and sick of the Spanish Republic being battered by Francisco Franco's armies. Relief was offered by Quakers – who allegedly maintained a strictly neutral position – by Communists, by rescue workers representing Save the Children, and by volunteers like the unaffiliated nurse who simply hoped that "I could perhaps help in some small way." Any aid to the Spanish Republic was, in fact, a statement against the British government's so-called neutrality policy.[5]

Women's political action promoting disarmament and arbitration of international disputes was intense between 1925 and 1935, a significant element in the era's political history. Campaigns were often coordinated with issues being considered by the League of Nations. Just after the General Strike, the WIL joined with twenty-eight women's organizations in an "Arbitration Pilgrimage," marching across Britain from several sites and then converging in London's Hyde Park for an enormous rally – demonstrating the power of "the flapper voter," as the *Evening Standard* put it. The meeting of the World Disarmament Conference in 1932 – just after the Japanese invasion of China, a League member – was another massive focus of women's international efforts. An enormous global coalition, including such mainstream groups as the World YWCA, circulated a disarmament petition that garnered eight million signatures. It was delivered with pageantry reminiscent of early suffrage parades by two long columns of women in national costume. The Conference itself, controlled by politicians, was a heartbreaking anticlimax. Another instance of mass support for collective security is the colossal Peace Ballot in Britain – officially called the National Declaration on the League of Nations and Armaments – organized by the League of Nations Union in 1934 and 1935. It asked for an all-around reduction of armaments and military equipment and the prohibition of their sale. This was not a women-led movement, but WIL was one of the most active of the thirty-eight organizations gathering responses. Half a million voluntary canvassers collected eleven and a half million replies from all over the British Isles, representing about 40 percent of the national electorate.

The three lives briefly narrated next illustrate a range of female performances of modernity along differing axes of the yearning for peace, security, and justice. Two of the women were part of the peace movement. All three subjects demonstrate the creative implementation of new concepts of women's work, citizenship, sexuality, and the body. Theirs was a modernity that pulled away from the local to connect with wider worlds: international fascism for Mary Allen; several sites of starvation and suffering in central Europe for Francesca Wilson; and – via travel, ties of friendship, and print media – Africa for Winifred Holtby.

Three Case Studies in Militarism, Pacifism, and Internationalism

Mary Allen was one of the cluster of former suffragists, almost all from the increasingly authoritarian Women's Social and Political Union (WSPU), who eventually became fascists. Immediately upon her recruitment, Allen became a staunch WSPU cadre; she had three imprisonments to her credit, one for throwing a brick – along with thirteen others – through a Home Office window. Much of her activism was funded by an allowance from her father, a railroad manager. Allen had certainly discovered her militarist strand in the suffrage movement and displayed many elements of an authoritarian personality. While so many other suffragists were stunned by the outbreak of war in 1914, Allen, following the Pankhursts' lead, supported the war effort with great enthusiasm from the very beginning. The war generated a range of new kinds of uniformed women in military auxiliaries or service organizations that offered women new status and bodily freedom, but Allen was attracted to domestic policing. She teamed up with Margaret Damer Dawson, a wealthy and well-connected Londoner and former animal rights and antivice crusader, and early in 1915 they took over an existing organization that they renamed the Women Police Service (WPS).

Although Allen and Damer Dawson, who lived together as lovers until the latter's sudden death in 1920, were innovators, they built on what Allen had taken away from her suffrage years: a fascination with discipline, an interest in spectacle, and an identification with her former jailers. While the suffrage cause for most participants meant justice, social equality, and horizontal ties with women throughout the world, Allen and her associates read hierarchy and order. Damer Dawson designed a police uniform in 1915 – Allen was apparently never seen out of hers – that endorsed military and class hierarchy but simultaneously made a statement about women's bodily freedom; it included heavy boots and trousers, the latter somewhat disguised by a long dress-like greatcoat. Top WPS officers' uniforms were both more military and more masculine than those of lower ranks: more brass buttons, extra military insignia, and leather accouterments; many of the officers had closely cropped hair. But their Women's Police Service members, who operated in many towns throughout the United Kingdom, were usually not official police and in fact were sued in 1921 by the Metropolitan Police for impersonating their own female police officers. At its peak, the WPS had perhaps a thousand members; its top leadership were mainly lesbians, scholars now agree. These volunteers functioned mostly as social purity activists who, as gentlewomen, claimed the job of supervising the behavior of young women in garrison towns and elsewhere, asserting their own public presence as they zipped around on motor bikes with sidecars. Allen did this so energetically that she was awarded the Order of the British Empire in 1917, Damer Dawson the following year. Though the WPS lost its official backing after 1918, Allen continued her police career, travelling to Germany, Poland, Egypt, Brazil, and the United States to train or promote women police. In the early 1930s, Allen founded a Women's Reserve of several hundred social-purity women that was antilabor and anti-Communist, though not affiliated with Oswald Mosley's fascists. Members received instruction in civil defense and in a variety of firearms and wore handsome double-breasted blue overcoats.

Mosley's fascism resonated with Allen's form of modernism. She and several former WSPU members became associated with his British Union of Fascists (BUF) in 1933 or 1934, though Allen did not formally join the party until 1939. Despite its hostility to "spinsters," Mosley's party made an effort to be particularly welcoming to women, even those with "feminist attitudes." Former suffragette Norah Elam likened Mosley to WSPU cofounder Christabel Pankhurst and claimed that the suffrage and fascist movements had a great deal in common: both were disciplined, followed a leader, and supported important material changes that would benefit women and men. Another former suffragette, Mary Richardson, saw in fascism the "courage, the action, [and] the loyalty" she had encountered in the suffrage movement.[6]

Women, nearly full party participants, made up about a quarter of the total BUF membership (about forty thousand in 1934) before the violence of the Olympia rally, which cost it so many supporters. To be sure, fascist women were sometimes relegated to serving tea to men returning from "active duty" – there were Fascist Teas, for example, every Saturday in Hull in 1934. The party, however, ran a few women for political office, and its policy was to support employment opportunities and equal pay for women and to include women as speakers at rallies, thus forming a "fascist feminism," as some historians name it. Scholars have begun to recognize the central place of the body in the self-representation of the

British Union of Fascists; fascist women seem to have relished embodying modern strength and confidence. In black uniforms and not wearing
lipstick or makeup, BUF women trained in the martial arts and marched
in formation. World War I women's auxiliary military experience (the
Women's Auxiliary Army, the Women's Royal Naval Service, and so on)
was very common among them. A black-shirted Woman's Propaganda
March in May 1936 paraded with band accompaniment from Bethnal
Green to Victoria Park "in perfect step with commendable order."[7]

Allen was one of a handful of British women to be welcomed by Adolf
Hitler and Hermann Goering (in two visits in 1934 and 1936) and became
a convert to the German brand of fascism. She demonstrated this by wearing jackboots thereafter. She had considerable stature within the Axis, for
early in 1937 and several times thereafter, Franco personally invited her to
visit, and it is possible that she was engaged in establishing ties between
the Spanish Falange and Britain's far right. Though not interned after
the outbreak of war in 1939, she was put under a kind of house arrest,
which was slightly adjusted when she appealed her sentence.

Francesca M. Wilson exemplifies the marriage of internationalism,
philanthropy, religion, and the modern career woman. Wilson came
from Newcastle; she was born into a middle-class family that had been
Quaker for generations. Her father was a traditional Quaker, a faithful
workhouse visitor whose mother had been a social reformer. He hated
war and jingoism and insisted on publicly speaking German during
World War I. Wilson's mother, however, became a Plymouth Brethren
convert, bringing her children to church meetings. Wilson rejected bap-
tism as a teenager and, to judge from her adult friendships and associations, it was her father's religion that had left more traces.

The Friends' tradition of respect for women went into constructing
Wilson's cheerful, confident subjectivity and her commitment to human
creativity and well-being. Friends at Newnham College had been suffragists, and she came to share their position but displayed no sign of any
zeal for that cause. Despite her privileged background, Francesca needed
to earn her living. In an unpublished autobiography, Wilson admitted
that she "had no particular desire to teach, no sense of vocation," but
those of her generation of university-educated women who joined the
workforce were channeled wholesale into teaching.[8] World War I provided Wilson an alternative. In October of 1914, coming from her school
at Gravesend on the opposite side of the Thames, she met bewildered
and weary Belgian refugees disembarking at Tilbury and daily came

to converse with them in her excellent French. Facility in European languages was a skill that well-off women traditionally cultivated at school or through governesses, and Wilson was a particularly talented linguist, the number of whose languages grew as she went from crisis to crisis. At Tilbury, Wilson discovered her true calling, assisting the lost and dispossessed. "I had tasted blood," she said, and applied to house two Belgian young women.[9]

Like Mary Allen, Wilson was adventuresome. In 1916, having been disappointed by aid assignments in France and Holland, work that she found insufficiently exciting, she became involved in a joint Quaker and Serbian Relief Fund project headed by her brother Maurice. Arriving after the work had begun, Wilson cared for wounded and shell-shocked Serbian troops who had been evacuated across the Adriatic to Corsica and Tunisia when their country was overrun by the Austrians. In 1919, she served as an interpreter in Vienna, where Quakers and the Save the Children fund were organizing the feeding of preschool children. Next, in 1922 and 1923, she joined a famine relief program the Friends had established at a base in the Southern Ural Mountains, where hundreds of thousands were dying due to massive crop failures and civil war.

Wilson used print as well as public lectures, travel, and friendships to establish a modern and cosmopolitan female identity. In the three books she wrote that dealt with her aid work, Wilson refused the Victorian discourse of compassion for the unfortunate and positioned herself as a modern international-minded career woman whose main motives were a search for adventure, travel, and work that was "interesting and stimulating" or "important."[10] Her altruism was no greater than average, she insisted. Brief allusions to lovers enhanced her claim to modernity. She insisted that relief work was a trade, most of it "humdrum emergency stuff; salvaging the destitute means organizing children's breakfasts, milk canteens, soup-kitchens, distributing dry rations, and clothing the naked out of cast-off wardrobes of Britain and America." Nonetheless, some moments transcended the routine: "Occasionally one has the chance of doing something more creative, of throwing into the void some new things, of bringing some castle down from the air on to the solid earth." Relief workers were not especially saintly, but Wilson was glad that nearly all of her humanitarian work was with Quakers, who, unlike many others, "do not seek personal glory from their service."[11] She later marveled at her lack of training and credentials for the demanding relief work she began with. The international by-products of war – refugees, the wounded, the hungry – provided Wilson and her pioneering peers with opportunities to forge modern identities.

In Spain in the late 1930s, Wilson used her now extensive relief skills to serve a political cause that she passionately supported. Acutely aware of the rise of fascism in Germany and in Eastern Europe, Wilson had lectured extensively on this threat. Support for the struggling democratic Spanish Republic and its defense after Franco's invasion in 1936 was a cause in which many thousands of women, from Conservatives to Communists, became involved. Pressuring their government to support Spain against Franco and organizing all forms of aid for the Republic offered women activists a range of political and vocational choices. Wilson joined the Birmingham Council for Peace and Liberty (BCPL), an antifascist group founded by the city's Communist Party that included a wide political spectrum of members. It is through this council that Wilson made her first trip to Republican Spain in 1937 and returned there in 1938, arranging facilities for children in Murcia in southeastern Spain. She arrived along with a crowd of refugees from Malaga and saw the need for a children's hospital that she soon helped to open; later she organized a farm colony and a summer camp for orphaned and lost children. She afterward wrote, "Only once or twice in my life have I felt such a bond between myself and a community, sometimes of children and sometimes of grown-ups, as I did in Spain." Indeed, she said, "my mind was full of Spain til the end."[12]

World War II meant new calls for her services. She was fifty-one in 1939, and her professional life would span three decades of war, dictatorships, murder, and starvation. In 1939 and 1940, the Friends sent Wilson to Czechoslovakia, where she was, under the auspices of the Polish Relief Fund, supposed to help Poles who had escaped the Nazi invasion. She ended up, however, helping Czechs reach France or Syria. When she and a coworker were arrested at the Rumanian border, she was not only terrified but feared she would anger the Friends, whose discipline she was under and who did not approve of illegal work. Once she returned to Britain, she worked with the International Commission for War Refugees and then joined the United Nations Relief and Rehabilitation Administration (UNRRA) as a welfare officer in 1944, stationed mainly in U.S.–occupied Germany. Because of her knowledge of Serbo-Croatian, UNRRA also asked her to tour its programs in Yugoslavia in 1946 and 1947. In the 1950s and thereafter, from her house in London, she was a sought-after speaker and author on refugees and the reform of British immigration policies.

Mainly known as a novelist and as the friend of Vera Brittain, **Winifred Holtby** had her own career as an internationalist and anticolonialist that is just beginning to receive scholarly attention. She had not been a suffragist or a wartime peace activist (she was only sixteen in 1914) but became closely associated with WILPF and involved with the disarmament movement in the 1920s. Brittain and Holtby were adopted in the 1980s by feminist scholars such as Lillian Faderman and Sheila Jeffreys, who saw them as a pioneering lesbian-like couple; their unorthodox living arrangement – in which Holtby resided with Brittain's husband George Catlin and their children after 1927 – has also attracted much interest. Later researchers have accepted their friendship as a nonerotic one; Brittain biographer Deborah Gorham understands their friendship as a partnership organized around their mutual calling as writers, a powerful but unequal relationship. Holtby was the far more generous friend – something of which Brittain became guiltily aware after her friend's death in 1935.

From well-off families, neither had to struggle to earn a living, and they devoted their lives to work and politics. Both were equal-rights feminists. Holtby became a pacifist, she said, through witnessing Vera Brittain's unending grieving for her lost brother and fiancé. In the early 1920s, they both became speakers for the League of Nations Union and both joined the Labour Party in the mid-1920s. Together they attended the League's Conference on Reduction and Limitation of Arms in 1932. Two years after Holtby's death, Brittain became a member of the Sheppard's Peace Pledge Union that opposed war for any reason. Holtby, a knowledgeable and alarmed student of Fascism and anti-Semitism as evidenced in her unpublished play, *Hope of Thousands*, might well, like such other feminist pacifists as novelists Storm Jameson and Phyllis Bottome, have come to renounce her earlier pacifism.

Holtby, however, had distinct international commitments and connections not shared with Brittain and rather neglected by scholars. As a director of the weekly review *Time and Tide* from 1926, she often contributed to the journal's "Notes on the Way" section, where she displayed a very wide knowledge of current national and international affairs. She had a vivid interest in film and could be a devastatingly satirical movie reviewer, a skill she put to use in presenting the hilarious legacy of a group of visiting Hollywood filmmakers in the hidden African city of Mandoa in her eponymous novel. She formed a strong connection to the black South African union movement and made public through print and the affiliative groups to which she belonged the growing harshness of race politics in South Africa and in British colonial Africa more generally.

Holtby focused her attention on race and empire after the mid-1920s. She admitted to a childhood fascination with Africa based on an ancestor who had been an early governor of Uganda, and she was probably not a cutting-edge anti-imperialist thinker. Her actual contacts in South Africa began in 1926 when she spent five months giving a series of lectures for the League of Nations Union, travelling to ten different cities. Her letters to Vera Brittain during those months register her shock at the "stupidity and selfishness of the average South African in the face of the colour danger" as well as the "patience of the Bantu." The whites were, she was sure, courting a massive uprising against their cruelty.[13] Holtby found a South African collaborator in the civically involved liberal writer Ethelfreda Lewis, who was interested in supporting a growing black union, the Industrial and Commercial Workers' Union (ICU), formed in 1919. These white liberals' motives certainly included fear of communist influence in the union, whose membership in 1927 numbered 80,000. The union's charismatic head was Clements Kadalie, whose weaknesses as an administrator and poor support from white unions Lewis thought she and other sympathetic whites could help to remedy. Holtby would help as a liaison with sympathetic socialists in Britain.

By the late 1920s, Holtby had become a sort of hostess for South Africans visiting London; "Winifred's Africans" were a frequent presence at the home in Chelsea she shared with Brittain. When Kadalie visited London in 1927, Holtby looked after him while Independent Labour Party contacts arranged for Kadalie to lecture to publicize the new apartheid measures in South Africa and encourage support for his union. With the same colleagues, Holtby arranged to fund a British assistant for Kadalie, though this did not prevent the latter from resigning in disgrace or prevent the union's split into two factions. Although the union project had failed by 1930, in the next few years, Holtby formed new cross-race friendships and joined a number of organizations promoting racial equality, some of them part of the global agitation on behalf of the Scottsboro prisoners: the London Group on African Affairs and the Quaker-led Joint Council to Promote Understanding Between White and Coloured People in Great Britain. She lobbied Members of Parliament, government officials, and others willing to support the cause of the African workers.

Meanwhile, Holtby wrote extensively about South Africa and Africa in general in *Time and Tide*, *The Nation*, *Foreign Affairs*, and *The New Leader*.

Her relative political independence and vivid identification, as a woman, with the disenfranchised, denigrated, and propertyless inform a prose that is fearless and often bitingly humorous. Holtby and her peers were witnessing the step-by-step creation in the mid-1920s of what would become the apartheid system in the newly minted dominion of South Africa. The new policies, she said, evoke the "old African tradition of slavery as well as the Afrikaners' self-definition as a chosen people with a divine mandate to possess the 'Promised Land.'" She mentions the huge disparity in land ownership between the country's 1,500,000 whites and 4,700,000 blacks. New legislation kept blacks out of skilled trades and even industrial jobs in general and heavily taxed those who did not work for Europeans.[14]

Holtby's keen use of print in her anticolonial cause is evident in her report of an October 1934 address by former South African Prime Minister General Smuts at St. Andrews University. Holtby excerpted a section of his speech that deplored the decline of parliamentary government in Europe, which had been "the vision of freedom, of the liberation of the human spirit" and predicted a future "cataclysm."[15] "Smuts should know," Holtby responded, "what a tragedy this is because he has presided over the decline of nearly all rights to non-Europeans" in South Africa. She wondered how Smuts could seem so sincere about the importance of representative government to the human spirit. "Because, for General Smuts and his contemporaries, the human horizon does not yet extend to coloured races, as, for Fox and his eighteenth-century contemporaries, it did not extend to English women." Smuts "does not see them as human beings at all, but rather as "good dogs, merry, obedient, rather stupid servants, gay singers and players..." Holtby insisted on connections between contemporaneous South African, European, and American racist movements. Such "failures of imagination" as Smuts's can be found in many places in history and elsewhere in the world, she noted: the Jews in Nazi Germany, blacks in the American south, Catholics victimized by the Ku Klux Klan, women disparaged by eighteenth-century liberals. Holtby ends her article with the hope that some of South Africa's enlightened whites – people of conscience and of the left – would be willing to work to hasten "the coming of the great day of freedom" in South Africa.[16]

The growing power of such militarists as Mussolini, Hitler, Franco, and Tojo reconfigured both pacifism and militarism in Britain. On the right, Mosley's now hopeful Fascists opposed rearmament and instead launched a peace drive in 1938, cynically featuring a "Women's Peace Campaign." Supporters of peace and collective security underwent more painful changes. The ineffectual League of Nations evaporated as a rallying point; many of the staunchest pacifists hung up their banners, sadly acknowledging that Nazism was even worse than war. Energized by the Popular Front movement – the Kremlin-backed international alliance of left-wing parties – support both for military preparedness and anti-Fascist action expanded. Holtby had died, but Allen and Wilson, both modern women like her, were on starkly opposite sides in the war that was soon to come.

Notes

1 Virginia Woolf, "Thoughts on Peace in an Air Raid," in *Thoughts on Peace in an Air Raid* (London: Penguin Books, 2009), 10.

2 Angela Ingram, "'In Christ's Name – Peace!' Theodora Wilson and Radical Pacifism," in Angela Ingram and Daphne Patai, eds., *Rediscovering Forgotten Radicals: British Women Writers: 1889–1939* (Durham: University of North Carolina Press, 1993), 176.

3 Quoted in Angela V. John, *Evelyn Sharp: Rebel Woman, 1869–1955* (Manchester: Manchester University Press, 2009), 90.

4 Gertrude Bussey and Margaret Tims, *Pioneers for Peace: Women's International League for Peace and Freedom 1915–1965*, reprint ed. (London: WILF, 1980), 14–15.

5 Angela Jackson, *British Women and the Spanish Civil War* (London: Routledge, 2002), 10.

6 Martin Pugh, *"Hurrah for the Blackshirts!" Fascists and Fascism in Britain between the Wars* (London: Jonathan Cape, 2005), 65.

7 Martin Durham, *Women and Fascism* (London: Routledge, 1998), 57, 53.

8 June Horder, *Francesca Wilson: A Life of Service and Adventure* (London: privately printed, 1993), 121; based on Wilson's manuscript autobiography and edited and published by her niece June Horder. My thanks to Mrs. Horder for sharing documents with me and for conversation about Wilson, whom Horder (born in 1920) knew very well.

9 Francesca Wilson, *In the Margins of Chaos: Recollections of Relief Work in and between Three Wars* (New York: Macmillan, 1945), 1–2.

10 Horder, *Francesca Wilson*, 105.

11 Ibid., 107–09, 111.

12 Ibid., 108, 127.

13 Lisa Regan's *Winifred Holtby's Social Vision: "Members One of Another"* (London; Pickering & Chatto, 2012) is one of just a few studies of this kind. See pp. 105, 118.

14 Ibid., 201, 48.

15 "Jan Christian Smuts," from *Time and Tide*, Oct. 27, 1934, excerpted in Paul Berry and Alan Bishop, eds., *Testament of a Generation: The Journalism of Vera Brittain and Winifred Holtby* (London: Virago, 1985), 195.

16 Ibid., 197–99.

Part II

Visual Culture

5
_____

Consumer Culture

Consumer culture transformed in the early twentieth century – and in turn transformed the twentieth century. In Britain and the United States, shopping shifted from a discrete activity to a climate, one that offered a heady mix of entertainment, pleasure, luxury, and the promise of new identities. The reach of marketing expanded through innovative forms of advertising in newspapers and periodicals, on the streets and in subway stations, and in new, brightly lit window displays that turned the night into an additional opportunity to imagine future transformations. More and more spaces – the home, the workplace, the city, the landscape – and more and more times – the weekend, the evening, the day – were infused with reminders that shopping could remake these very places and times. Identity itself, the marketers hinted, might be shaped by selecting new styles or products. Consumers, for example, were invited as never before to experiment with different class and gender associations. The middle-class customer might be promised an enticing view of upper-class luxury or an authentic product made by artisans working in the old techniques; women might be assured that in the carefully appointed new department stores, they were in an exclusive world much like their husbands might enjoy in their all-male clubs. As consumer culture became just that – a culture – stores began to market and sell not just individual products (though they certainly did) but ways of life.

This essay offers a brief tour of some key shifts in consumer culture around the turn of the century. I consider the dramatic rise of the department store in both America and Europe, and the concomitant changes in advertising in newspapers, catalogues, public posters, and window displays. Alongside large-scale ventures, I also explore the rise of niche markets, considering efforts such as the Omega Workshops, which sought to employ artists within a collective yet commercial venture. Not surprisingly, these dramatic changes in consumer culture did not go unnoticed by artists. Writers, filmmakers, painters, and photographers recorded and commented on these transformations, incorporating representations of consumerism into artistic expressions both as critique and as celebration. Inevitably, tensions emerged, with some artists seeking a clear division between what was art and what was suspiciously commercial and others seeing a blurrier picture, an ambiguity that they could translate into the art itself. Marketers in turn were eager to make such divisions into opportunities, evoking ideas of authenticity and the genuine artwork, and promising that products were not tainted by commerce – and yet were the latest thing and might be easily purchased. These same tensions between art and commercialism have kept contemporary modernist critics busy; in the last thirty years, critics have posited various relationships between modernism and consumer culture, a critical history I survey at the end of the essay.

I organize this essay around an experiential shopping trip that moves from the home to the streets to various stores, noting how advertising, store design, and window displays might have been experienced. My default shopper will be a middle-class white woman, as she was the target of so many of the changes, but as we travel, I will consider other types of shoppers and note differences among various locations and times. We begin within the home, the heart of the private sphere in the nineteenth century and the focus of a great deal of the advertising. Over breakfast or a cup of tea, our shopper might have looked through a newspaper or perused an illustrated periodical; in both Britain and America, mass-market newspapers, magazines, and journals multiplied at the turn of the century, so our shopper would have many options, perhaps glancing through the *Daily Mail* (launched in Britain in 1896) or the *Saturday Evening Post* (an American option, redesigned in 1897) or *Cosmopolitan* (launched in America in 1886), as well as venerable choices such as the *New York Times* or London's *The Times*. Her preferences might depend in part on her class and in part on her interests. In most of these publications before the turn of the century, she would have found advertisements that offered a particular product for sale at a particular price, with perhaps a brief description of the item and promises about its quality or special features. Especially in newspapers, the advertisements – if included at all – had often been squeezed close together in cluttered, undistinguished groups. Such groupings relegated shopping to a marginal utilitarian activity, something done after the day's news had been properly digested.[1]

By the early twentieth century, however, a profound shift was occurring in print marketing. As our shopper opened a newspaper or magazine in 1910 in Britain, and somewhat earlier in America, she might have seen advertisements that did not feature products but instead evoked an atmosphere of luxury or enchantment or the refinement of the classical world. Professional artists, some of them postimpressionists, had been hired to paint or draw enticing scenes to catch the eye of our shopper.[2] For instance, opening the *Daily Mail* in March of 1909, she might have seen one of the many artistic ads announcing the grand opening of Selfridges department store in London. One example featured an original drawing of a regal woman in full court dress and a courtier who has flung down his cape in front of her feet – clearly a reference to Queen Elizabeth I and Sir Walter Raleigh (Figure 4). Our shopper was assured that this image represented the quality of service promised by the store; come to Selfridges, the argument ran, and you will be treated like a queen.[3] The American reader might have seen a similar advertisement had she opened *Collier's Magazine* in 1923. One of the biggest advertising designers of the era, Maxfield Parrish, had created a color painting of a generically Renaissance king and queen, sitting on elaborate gold thrones and dressed in resplendent purple robes; here, the courtier who stood between them held up a plate of Jell-O while making a low bow.[4] Such appeals typified new advertising strategies that sought to present a lifestyle or an atmosphere rather than focusing only on a particular product for sale at a particular price. These new advertisements presented a variety of appeals and could also posit many identities: low prices for the careful, discerning shopper who wanted quality on a budget; artistic, one-of-a-kind products allegedly made in cottage industries for those who might fear shopping was vulgar or infected by crass commercialism; a life of ease and service for those who spent much of their time serving others, and so on.[5] What united many of these messages, especially in Britain where commerce had long been viewed with suspicion, was the sense that there was an underlying connection between the store or the product and our shopper's home (though the store might be much more alluring). The reader would be enhancing the home by shopping (or so the promise went), not moving from a sacred private space to a contaminated public one. And if our shopper wanted to stay within the

FIGURE 4 Selfridges' advertisement, "Courtesy" (1909). Reproduced with kind permission from Selfridges & Co. and the History of Advertising Trust (www.hatads.org.uk)

home, in both Britain and America, she could pick up the telephone, order something, and have it delivered.[6]

Marketers usually aimed, though, to draw shoppers out of the home and into the store. Our shopper, whether driving or walking or taking public transportation, would have been inundated with ads from the moment she left her house. In America, from the late nineteenth century on, our shopper might well have been greeted at the threshold of her home by small "advertising cards" delivered to her door that depicted small scenes of activities or places to visit or, somewhat later, stores and goods.[7] She might have tucked the card into her purse so she could paste it in a book displaying her collection of cards, as many Americans did at the time.[8] As she travelled, especially within urban settings, the streets themselves would have been saturated with advertisements on buildings, billboards, trams, and subways, with artists often commissioned to create sophisticated artistic posters designed to capture the eye of the shopper.[9] In both America and Britain, she might have seen brightly lit electric signs highlighting various products,[10] though this advertising often lacked the sophisticated lifestyle aims of the posters or the printed ads consumed within the home. Sandwich men – men with advertisements hanging from their bodies – wandered the streets, as James Joyce describes in *Ulysses* (1922), and marketers were always looking for new ways to catch the attention of commuters (as, indeed, adman Leopold Bloom considers all day). Virginia Woolf reminds us in *Mrs. Dalloway* (1925) that marketers could even take to the air, represented in the airplane that writes a (ambiguous) message across the London sky. In the major cities in America and Britain, advertising on the streets would have been a familiar presence throughout the nineteenth century; what was shifting was the artistry and sophistication of many of the advertising campaigns – and the dazzling new stores they often advertised.

The rise of the department store marked a decisive turn in consumer culture, so one of these new emporiums will be the first stop for our imaginary shopper.[11] By the early twentieth century, she would have had numerous options. As historian Jan Whitaker notes, the end of the nineteenth century saw a huge rise in department store construction;[12] America and Britain scrambled to catch up to Paris, where department stores were already considered the "'eighth wonder of the world.'"[13] In America, smaller department stores began to appear in the mid-nineteenth century, but by 1878, huge ventures such as Wanamaker's in Philadelphia, Macy's in New York, and Jordan Marsh in Boston would have been open to our shopper, as would, by 1907, Marshall Field's hugely expanded store in Chicago.[14] Britain was somewhat slower to develop the large stores, but in 1909, Gordon Selfridge opened his vast new emporium on Oxford Street and transformed both the marketing and the design of British stores; by the 1910s, Harrods and Whiteleys were continuing their expansion from what were essentially collections of small shops into large, consolidated, full-service stores.[15] As our shopper approached such venues, she would first have been invited to admire the building's often palatial exterior. Major department stores at the time were designed to mimic the exteriors of large museums, government buildings, or even palaces. Stores might include classical detailing or draw on more contemporary fashions, such as a Beaux-Arts architectural style (Marshall Field's, Wanamaker's), or Art Nouveau (Schlesinger & Mayer).[16] The exteriors were often elaborately decorated, incorporating clocks and towers and detailed stone carvings. The building's very design would have been a draw for our shopper and thousands of others who were attracted to and even awed by these impressive new spaces.

The key feature of the exteriors would have been the elaborate window displays that encircled most department stores by the early twentieth century. Our shopper would have been invited to pause and admire the carefully designed displays behind the large, clear, plate-glass windows that advances in glass technology made possible. The displays themselves would have been distinctly different from those in the second half of the nineteenth century. Formerly, window displays had been crowded with goods, what the trade magazine *Display World* called "torturing the merchandise," with as many products crammed in as possible.[17] By the 1910s and 1920s, however, displays had started to morph into beautifully crafted settings or scenes or tableaux, often with a minimal emphasis on prices. In America, L. Frank Baum, the popular writer of *The Wizard of Oz* books, was a leading voice in the new displays, promoting window dressing as a profession and launching, among other ventures, the trade journal *The Show Window* in 1900. Baum argued for displays with fewer goods and more artistic atmosphere, and he launched a revolution in display design.[18] If our shopper had been in Chicago and headed to Marshall Field's, she would have seen examples of such new displays created by one of the leading window dressers of the early twentieth century, Arthur Fraser. Fraser's highly stylized windows combined special lighting, full-body mannequins (rather than the headless dummies used previously), and careful selections of color to create alluring scenes of refinement and elegance, not unlike the famous *tableaux vivants* depicted in Edith Wharton's *The House of Mirth* (1905). Fraser's innovative methods quickly influenced the whole profession; he trained, for example, Edward Goldsman, who travelled to London to create dazzling new displays that revolutionized British retail. In both countries, then, our shopper would likely have seen windows that evoked atmospheres and lifestyles rather than the buying and selling of goods more directly.[19] In addition to admiring the windows in the daytime, our shopper could even view the windows at night.[20] Rather than shutter the windows when the sun went down, by the 1910s, store owners kept the windows lit well into the evening, even after the store had closed, enticing viewers to become Baudelaire-like *flâneurs* or *flâneuses*, wandering the streets to gaze and admire.[21] The glass of these displays might offer our shopper an interesting paradox of desire; on the one hand, the glass invited the viewer into a scene or mood or identity (or all three), promising that the desired vision was extremely close (indeed, just in the store and available). On the other hand, however, the glass served as barrier, granting the scene an enticing unavailability, making it seem close but out of reach or exclusive. The implied promise, of course, was that with careful selection, this vision, complete with its elusive quality, could be attained by the discerning (and often well-heeled) consumer.[22]

After all this stimulus from the outside commercial environment, it might well have been a (somewhat ironic) relief for our shopper to step into the luxurious world of the modern department store.[23] While the interior of the stores and the amenities they featured would have been different at various times and locations, certain characteristics gradually began to dominate in the first part of the twentieth century. With the advent of steel frameworks, the interior spaces became palatial, incorporating high ceilings and atriums.[24] Interior adornments were often lavish, profusely decorated with bronze, mahogany, and other materials. Our shopper might walk on soft carpets or cool marble, and live music by string quartets might play in the background. Escalators and elevators could whisk shoppers to different floors, saving on fatigue, and the store's aisles were wide to foster a sense of expansive space in which to wander. By the 1920s, lighting was used to various effects, often diffused to create an aura of mystery or enchantment; at Marshall Field's in Chicago, for example, the designers at Tiffany had created a glass dome of multiple colors, designed to cast a magical light over the interior it covered.[25] Along with light, our shopper would have been surrounded by color schemes often carefully coordinated with the extravagant and changing spectacles within the store. Visiting Wanamaker's in 1895, our shopper would have seen angel figures sailing through the air in the store's rotunda, or in 1908, vast displays centered around a "Bride's Jubilee" theme, infusing the store with pink and white colors and scenes of brides in various stages of wedding preparation.[26] Our shopper could select from among a world of goods within separate departments, each selling various types of commodities focused around different themes. Price tags were often discreet, the goods on display gently purged of associations with trade or commerce.

In addition to the various departments, our shopper could also wander through changing exhibitions held at the store that worked to blur the divisions between shopping and activities or products that might seem noncommercial; such exhibits might feature crafters brought in to show that the old ways of manufacturing were still (supposedly) alive and well, setting up looms or lace stations or wood carving to demonstrate techniques to customers. At the more spectacle-oriented end of marketing, visitors might be encouraged to come view the first plane to cross the Channel, for example, or a famous explorer or celebrity paying a visit to the store. And lest our shopper feel that commerce and art were not compatible, she could visit art shows within the store that displayed original paintings much as a gallery might.[27] What united most of these efforts was a shift similar to what our shopper might have seen in the building's exterior: the message was that this was not simply a store to purchase specific goods but an experience in and of itself that might transport the shopper to any number of places and through any number of atmospheres. At the same time that the goods were associated with various lifestyles and effects, the stores also gave shoppers extensive access to the goods themselves, which were elaborately displayed and available for inspection, or, in echoes of the outdoor window displays, tantalizingly enclosed in clear glass cases.

Our shopper would have experienced an unprecedented level of service and amenities within the store. The sense that these stores were not simply emporiums of buying and selling carried over to the vast array of services offered. Knowledgeable sales staff assisted the customer in any way possible. Our shopper could book theater tickets or have her hair done or arrange to meet friends through the concierge desks. Relaxing lounges and libraries could be found at many stores, with assistants available to cater to particular needs.[28] Lavatories were beautifully decorated and often provided a range of free toiletries. Should our shopper be hungry, she might stop for tea or a full meal at one of the store's restaurants. Roof gardens could provide an open-air experience at the top of the building. Despite all the attentive service, however, stores were careful to give shoppers a sense of complete freedom within the store, as if they were in charge of a vast home with countless servants.[29] The level of service, combined with the sumptuous interiors, could evoke an almost

Gatsby-esque atmosphere, one that suggested an abundant material luxury cleansed of actual commercial transactions.[30]

From the advertisements to the window displays to the carefully orchestrated interiors, our early twentieth-century shopper was invited to radically reimagine identity itself. Rather than thinking of identity as something fixed, consumers were encouraged to think of identity as fluid and capable of being remade (however illusory that promise might turn out to be). In particular, marketers played in various ways with class. Most obviously, perhaps, the middle class was tempted by various iterations of upper-class lifestyles, whether in style or in associations. But the class fluidity promised was actually far more complicated and emphasized movement rather than simply aspirational advancement. Marketers, especially in Britain, where class structure tended to be more rigid, promised links to upper-class lives but also to the authenticity and integrity romantically linked to the peasant or laborer. And commodities could have mixed class associations as well: the products marketed as original, one-of-a-kind objects, created by craftsmen schooled in traditional techniques, might nevertheless evoke associations with a landed gentry class that had possessed such objects for generations. The very spatial layout of the stores extended these different class associations: many stores had bargain basements where prices were low and goods less carefully arranged; as the shopper moved up through the store, class associations often moved up as well, with higher floors and departments catering to higher-priced goods.[31] Various class appeals could also mingle within departments, with the more expensive goods often under glass. Stores were appealing not just to multiple classes but to the promise of transgressing those classes; well-heeled customers could enjoy looking for bargains in the basement, and less-affluent customers were invited to walk through showrooms that resembled upper-class houses. Marketers, in other words, sold blends of class associations, promising consumers products and areas that referenced different classes, (allegedly) shorn of problems or complications. A key innovation in these approaches was often to evoke and sell the tensions between a low commercial culture and a high commercial-free culture, all within commercial ventures.[32]

Our shopper would have experienced a somewhat different marketing ethos depending on whether she was in America or Britain. While both countries saw a revolution in commercial culture in the early twentieth century, they drew on histories that had different associations with commerce and different ideas about the past and the importance of traditions. In America, shoppers would generally have been transported into an atmosphere that emphasized spectacle and novelty. While old and new money distinctions were certainly present in America (see Edith Wharton), there was a less entrenched disdain for trade and commerce – it was how fortunes had almost always been made. America was a young country seeking to define itself on its own terms, and its consumer culture produced, as critic William Leach points out, an attitude often "hostile to the past and to tradition" with a clear focus on "a future-oriented culture of desire."[33] In Britain, however, our shopper would have experienced a different emphasis. When Gordon Selfridge revolutionized advertising and store design in 1909, he knew many people in Britain viewed trade as suspect and even vulgar, a spoiler of traditions and the honored past. He thus worked to show how his store's architecture, design, and goods were perfectly in line with established British institutions and traditions, a marketing strategy that stores like Harrods were quick to adopt (indeed, Harrods tried to paint Selfridges as the novel upstart, run by an American only newly arrived in Britain). These appeals to the past and to tradition were mingled, however, with claims about the novelty and up-to-dateness of their many goods.

Department stores were not the only shopping options, even if they were often the most popular (and here I will leave our generalized shopper behind). Niche markets also developed, and they appealed more narrowly to particular classes of consumers. In London, for example, there was a long-established divide between stores on and around Bond Street – consisting mainly of smaller, exclusive, higher-priced stores – and the larger emporiums that lined Oxford and Regent Streets.[34] Most cities had areas with similar distinctions, though their location could shift as neighborhoods fell in and out of fashion. And there were also particular groups and movements that represented other markets. In London, for example, the Bloomsbury-heavy Omega Workshops, started by art critic Roger Fry, employed artists and craftspeople (and deliberately blurred the line between the two) to produce unique furnishings and décor designed to appeal to the reasonably well-heeled hipster of the 1920s.[35] High-class ventures such as Tiffany & Company in America sought to create luxury items with impeccable craftsmanship and a deliberate blend of new techniques and old traditions, launching, for example, innovative designs in stained glass for the home and drawing on both the Arts and Crafts movement and Art Nouveau.[36] The Arts and Crafts movement itself could been seen as appealing to a niche market and also serves as an example of how such markets could spill over into larger ventures; while the movement was started by William Morris as an alternative to mass-based industrial production, Arts and Crafts design features were exploited by the marketers, who were happy to sell to the mass market an ethos of disdain for the mass market.

These new commercial ventures – and in particular the advent of the department store – often made elaborate claims about the key role they might play in the lives of consumers. While obviously much of this rhetoric was hype, stores did, in fact, function in often surprisingly influential ways. Stores provided entertainment, but ironically, they also could serve as enclaves of structure, order, and normalcy, in particular during the two world wars that so profoundly disrupted everyday life in the twentieth century. Despite the chaos of war, some people found stores were places where civilization might continue; one department store owner in fact coined the phrase "business as usual" during World War I as a way to emphasize this very continuity.[37] A literary magazine, the *Academy*, noted that during this war, enchanting window displays at department stores could function as consolation against

> the death and desolation that reign in the cities on which battle has set its terrible seal. Each beautiful fabric displayed, or product of the lands across the ocean, has a new value of its own. It means that looms are working and factory chimneys smoking; women and children warmed and fed and housed amid the tribulations of war.... Without the streets swarmed with placards shouting war sensationalism; stress and the hint of danger were in the air. Within were beauty and order and steady business, nothing feverish in its atmosphere, but a pervading sense of well-being.[38]

The new advertisements could work in similar ways in the newspapers, pulling the reader's eyes from the devastation described in the articles to the promises of beauty and ease and bargains in the ads themselves. This sense of the store as a bastion of civilization endured throughout the century; as one Chicago consumer remarked during World War II, after the bombing of Pearl Harbor, "Nothing is left any more – except, thank God, Marshall Field's."[39] It is easy to trace the continuity of this sensation to the present moment, as advertising continues to offer alternative worlds and to evoke tantalizing atmospheres in the margins of news screens and in the commercial breaks that give viewers a respite from the often grim breaking news.

The commercial revolution of the early twentieth century – and the very way such ventures could distract people from things like wars and corruption – produced a flood of criticism that continues (for good reason) to the present. Protests ranged from objections to the new lifestyle advertising (as one irate consumer complained to a department store in 1909, "What do you sell? What do you sell? Why don't you say what you sell in your advertisement?"[40]); to scathing commentary on the false promises of marketing, such as H.G. Wells's novel *Tono-Bungay* (1909), which brutally satirized the advertising of patent medicines; to viewing the effects of commerce as contaminating everything from politics to daily life. Modernist literature in part became an important voice within this protest, both representing and at times decrying the effects of commercialism. Modernism's precise relationship to the market has actually been the focus of extended commentary in the last thirty years. In a now familiar narrative, critic Andreas Huyssen posited the "Great Divide" between modernism and mass culture, exploring how modernism pushed against and indeed defined itself against mass cultural production; Fredric Jameson likewise proposed that modernists relied on a "distinction between high and so-called mass culture" in their works.[41] In the last two decades, critics have complicated this story, exploring how modernists from T.S. Eliot to H.D. to Virginia Woolf incorporated aspects of consumer and popular culture into their poems and novels, and not always as a way to protest the deleterious effects of those cultures; other critics have pointed out the often savvy marketing of modernist writers themselves.[42] This critical narrative – moving from "modernism and mass culture are divided!" to "no, they're inexplicably mingled!" – can at times oversimplify how the very divide and its dismantling functioned within early twentieth-century culture. Certainly many modernists criticized consumer culture and decried the pervasive influence of that culture in modern life; at the same time, they deftly wove that same culture into their own works and marketed their own writing. Marketers in turn shrewdly played with a similar divide, assuring their customers that their goods were untainted by commerce and mass production – and promising authentic, brand new, and easily available products. Consumer culture – and modernist culture – became defined in part by how artists, consumers, *and* marketers negotiated these very divides.

Notes

1 See William Leach, *Land of Desire: Merchants, Power, and the Rise of the New American Culture* (New York: Vintage, 1993), 42 for more on earlier advertising in America, and Elizabeth Outka, *Consuming Traditions: Modernism, Modernity, and the Commodified Authentic* (Oxford: Oxford University Press, 2009), 116–18 for earlier advertising in Britain.

2 For more on the new advertising in America, see Leach, 41–55. For a discussion of the dramatic changes in British retail initiated by Selfridges, see Outka, 99–123, 139–42, and 146–47.

3 "Courtesy" appeared in the *Daily Mail*, as well as in the *Leader* and the *Evening Standard*, on March 18, 1909.

4 Leach, 52.

5 Ilya Parkins's essay in this volume explores the way fashion in particular could unsettle dualisms between art and industry and offer amalgamations of both times and identities.

6 Catalog shopping was also becoming increasingly popular in both Britain and America, with catalogs going, as department store historian Jan Whitaker notes, "beyond simply describing and illustrating items for sale" to become "fashion and literary magazines as well" (155). Wanamaker's and Marshall Field's even had their own fashion magazines by 1914 (158); Jan Whitaker, *The World of Department Stores* (New York: Vendome Press, 2011).

7 T.R. Nevett observes that in Britain, while circulars delivered to the door were popular in the nineteenth century, marketers were choosing the postal service for delivery by the century's end (93). Handbills and flyers had been a constant presence on London streets throughout the nineteenth century (95–96); T.R. Nevett, *Advertising in Britain* (London: William Heinemann Ltd., 1982).

8 Leach, 44.

9 See Leach, 46, on the artistic quality of posters in America, and Nevett, 86–92, on the poster in Britain; Nevett notes that by 1894, the poster was "widely regarded as an art form in its own right" (88).

10 Leach, 46; Nevett, 88.

11 A few terms that may be helpful for readers interested in consumer culture at the turn of the century: A "dry goods" store usually meant a store that sold textiles, but it could also refer to stores that sold clothing or sundries more generally. "Millinery" referred to hats or to a store that designed and sold hats. A "draper" was a store or person who sold cloth, and also sometimes ready-to-wear clothing and dry goods. Part of the innovation of the department store was to consolidate all these specializations under one roof.

12 Whitaker, 101.

13 Mary Very, "Au Bon Marche," *The Independent*, July 29, 1875, 6; quoted in Whitaker, 6.

14 Whitaker, 25.

15 Ibid., 31.

16 Ibid., 112, 114.

17 Quoted in Barry James Wood, *Show Windows: 75 Years of the Art of Display* (New York: Congdon and Weed, 1982), 27.

18 See Leach, 55–61, and Whitaker, 177.

19 The history of window displays is told in many places; see Wood's book as well as Whitaker, 174–99, who also includes full-color photographs; and Leach, 39–70.

20 As Len Platt details in this volume, window displays, often like mini stage sets, could remind the shopper of the sense of spectacle within popular theater, with both plays and stores often celebrating the new glamour of consumer culture.

21 Anne Friedberg explores how Baudelaire's vision of the wandering, dreamy male shopper (the *flâneur*) gives way to the female gazer (the *flâneuse*) with the rise of the department store; see both "Les Flâneurs du Mal(l): Cinema and the Postmodern Condition," *PMLA* 3.106 (1991): 419–31, and *Window Shopping: Cinema and the Postmodern* (Berkeley: University of California Press, 1988). Rachel Bowlby explores how the shop window becomes a place of identity formation for women in *Just Looking: Consumer Culture in Dreiser, Gissing, and Zola* (New York: Methuen, 1985); see also Bowlby's analysis of modern shopping and consumerism in *Carried Away: The Invention of Modern Shopping* (New York: Columbia University Press, 2001).

22 See Outka, 147–48.

23 In both America and Britain, our shopper might have been reminded of grand exhibitions, such as the famous Crystal Palace in London in 1851, which featured goods from all over the world (though not, quite, for sale) or any of the World's Fairs, two common experiences retailers had in mind as they designed the new department stores. See Whitaker, 12.

24 Whitaker, 108.

25 Leach, 77.

26 Ibid., 83–84.

27 Numerous sources offer detailed descriptions of the interiors of stores at the start of the twentieth century. For American interiors, see Leach, 71–84; for a look at interiors across a range of countries, as well as photographs, see Whitaker, 98–141.

28 Outka, 113.

29 For more on service at the new department stores, see Whitaker, 222–53, as well as Whitaker's other book, *Service and Style: How the American Department Store Fashioned the Middle Class* (New York: St. Martin's Press, 2006), 219–44. In London, service shifted when retailers abandoned the British tradition of shop walkers, employees who would greet, often aggressively, the customers and escort them to a specific area. Instead, shoppers were encouraged to browse, to arrive perhaps with one purchase in mind, but to be tempted to circulate (and buy) more widely (Whitaker, *World*, 63–64).

30 The atmosphere of enticing (if problematic) material plenty that F. Scott Fitzgerald evokes in *The Great Gatsby* (consider the abundant display of Gatsby's beautiful shirts) both anticipates and echoes changes in retail and advertising in the early twentieth century. *The Great Gatsby*, 1925 (New York: Scribner, 2004).

31 Leach, 72; Outka 121–22. Ilya Parkins's essay investigates how fashion could also blur gender norms, sexual identities, and even different selves – and different ideas about the self.

32 Whitaker offers a longer discussion of class and the department store in *Service and Style*, 31–51.

33 Leach, xiii.

34 Virginia Woolf famously compared the "sublime rites" of Bond Street (where Clarissa Dalloway does her shopping) to the "too blatant and raucous" shopping found on Oxford Street. "Oxford Street Tide," 1932, in *The London Scene: Five Essays by Virginia Woolf* (New York: Random House, 1975), 16–22, 16.

35 For more on the history of the Omega Workshops, see Judith Collins, *The Omega Workshops* (Chicago: University of Chicago Press, 1984).

36 John Loring offers a history of Tiffany's designs in *Tiffany Style: 170 Years of Design* (New York: Abrams, 2008).

37 Pound, 125.

38 Ibid., 130.

39 Whitaker, 6.

40 "Criticising Mr. Selfridge," *Evening News,* March 16, 1909.

41 Andreas Huyssen, *After the Great Divide: Modernism, Mass Culture, Postmodernism* (Bloomington: Indiana University Press, 1986). Huyssen also argues that the avant-garde did take mass culture as a critical part of its aesthetics. Fredric Jameson, "The Politics of Theory: Ideological Positions in the Postmodernism Debate," *New German Critique* 33 (Autumn 1984): 53–65; 64. While these two quotations are frequently cited by critics, Huyssen's and Jameson's arguments are more complicated than these passages suggest.

42 See, for example, Kevin J.H. Dettmar and Stephen Watt, eds. *Marketing Modernisms: Self-Promotion, Canonization and Rereading* (Ann Arbor: Michigan University Press, 1996); Ian Willison, Warwick Gould, and Warren Chernaik, eds., *Modernist Writers and the Marketplace* (London: Macmillan, 1996); Lawrence Rainey, *Institutions of Modernism: Literary Elites and Public Culture* (New Haven: Yale University Press, 1998); John Xiros Cooper, *Modernism and the Culture of Market Society* (Cambridge: Cambridge University Press, 2004); Marsha Bryant, *Women's Poetry and Popular Culture* (New York: Palgrave Macmillan, 2011); and Alissa G. Karl, *Modernism and the Marketplace: Literary Culture and Consumer Capitalism in Rhys, Woolf, Stein, and Nella Larsen* (New York: Routledge, 2009). Jennifer Wicke's work on modernism's ties to advertising and marketing is excellent; see, for example, *Advertising Fictions: Literature, Advertisement, and Social Reading* (New York: Columbia University Press, 1988). Consumer culture and advertising have long been the subject of more general criticism, in particular from the Frankfurt School, including Max Horkheimer and Theodor Adorno's *The Dialectic of Enlightenment*, translated by John Cumming (New York: Continuum, 1994). Pierre Bourdieu, in his well-known *Distinction: A Social Critique of the Judgment of Taste*, analyzes the consumption and marketing of cultural commodities in French society. See also Rachel Bowlby's works, already cited.

6
———————

Fashion

For many critics and theorists of modernity, in the last decades of the nineteenth and first decades of the twentieth century, fashion *was* the modern. Those who, like Charles Baudelaire, Georg Simmel, and Walter Benjamin, sought to understand the unique character of modern life frequently turned to fashionable dress as a material embodiment of the spirit of modernity. But what was it that these critics saw as so uniquely useful about fashion as shorthand for the spirit of the age? Why did they so often turn to this medium to illuminate the lived and ideological dimensions of life in a rapidly changing, industrial, and consumer capitalist society? Some keys are found in the very elements of the preceding sentence: fashion itself changed rapidly, and so its tempo was understood to reflect the accelerated pace of modern life. As well, in straddling the poles of industrial and consumer capitalism, it had a long reach – and it called attention to the importance of *both* aesthetics and commerce as mediating factors in modernity rather than privileging one or the other. The latter point encapsulates perhaps the most important characteristic of fashion in this period: fashion made visually and materially apparent the instability of many of the ideological boundaries that were central to modern culture. Mythical modernity was structured by a series of dualisms: "man" and nature, subject and other, art and industry, east and west, black and white, masculinity and femininity, among many others. Yet this chapter aims to show that the structure and abundance of fashion called into question binary oppositions that had a strong hold in modernity's picture of itself. In this sense, fashion dramatized the underside of modern life, the alternative narratives that structured everyday, lived experiences of modernity, highlighting the gap between ideals and representations.

As potentially both an aesthetic object and a mass-produced one, fashion uncomfortably straddled the divides among art, industry, and commerce. Whereas most clothing had been handmade at the beginning of the nineteenth century, rapid technological change – including the advent of sewing and other machines, such as cloth spreading and cutting machines and buttonhole makers – was followed by a refinement of the division of labor and the ultimate deskilling of the needleworker, who became a "garment worker." Developments like these, which followed the general pattern of standardization in industrial production, led to the capacity to produce clothing more efficiently and inexpensively and to the widespread diffusion of new styles by the early twentieth century – which has been called, controversially, the "democratization" of fashion. On the other hand, the nineteenth century saw the rise of the couturier, a figure whose cachet derived from his or her status as artist-craftsman and who worked in an idiom opposed to mass production. Charles Frederick Worth, who worked in Paris from the 1860s, is generally considered to be the first modern couturier. Cultivating links with cultural elites and selling fashion as a precious and singular commodity, Worth – like those who followed him – encouraged the viewing of fashion as an art form. By the twentieth century, couturiers like Jacques Doucet and Elsa Schiaparelli had firmly established links to the art world and clung tenaciously to their own status as artists – so tenaciously, in fact, as to reveal some anxiety about that status. They were right to be anxious, for fashion sat on the edge of the deeply held divide between art and industry, with its simultaneous positioning as an art, designed by a "creator," and a mass-produced object produced by anonymous factory workers. To use the terms of Walter Benjamin – himself deeply interested in fashion's modernity – mass reproduction sat uneasily with claims that a form like fashion was invested with the singular "aura" of a work of art.[1] The form threatened to reveal the instability of this foundational dichotomy of modernity, which held that art and industry were opposed and insisted on the "purity" of the aesthetic against the "taint" of commerce.[2] As Nancy J. Troy writes, "the couture dress … despite couturiers' claims to the contrary, was never a unique original but rather a copy."[3] Fashion offered a vision of the ways that commerce impinged on the supposedly rarified sphere of art, and aesthetics came to shape consumer capitalism. In this sense, it was exemplary of "the experience of modernity" as, in Marshall Berman's formulation, a dialectic of artistic modernism and industrial modernization.[4]

The tense but mutually dependent relationship between art and industry was not the only dialectic that fashion underscored. With its complex relationship to time, fashionable dress also called into question the boundaries between past, present, and future. Modernity seemed, at a rhetorical level at least, to be defined by its fetishization of the new. Cultural modernists and activists revealed their sense that they were living through the birth of a new society, defined by a new aesthetics, new orders, new ways of relating, of living. As a Russian futurist manifesto declared, encapsulating the widespread sentiment, "We are the new people of a new life."[5] And, too, consumerism was propelled by the promise of the ever-new, selling products on the basis of their innovation. Fashion, in one sense, had a strong kinship with the fetishization of the new, for fashion is "dress in which the key feature is rapid and continual changing of clothes."[6] Though the principle of change had been embodied in fashionable dress since the medieval period, the capacity and will to innovate had expanded with the development of a modern fashion system, as both mass-produced and couture fashion began to introduce seasonal collections. In the words of the major couturier Paul Poiret, in 1914, "the very word, fashions, means something new. Fashions should always develop in an unexpected direction and proceed toward the unknown."[7] The fashion press reinforced the allegiance to novelty, structuring its coverage around the introduction of "new modes" and changing trends.

Yet as much as fashion was imagined, produced, desired, bought, and sold according to its perceived innovation – its undeniable emergence from the present moment – one of the things that made it so compelling to theorists of the modern was its relationship to the past. Here was another paradox. In his essay on the painter Constantin Guys as an exemplar of modernity, Baudelaire argued that Guys's achievement was "to extract from fashion the poetry that resides in its historical envelope, to distil the eternal from the transitory."[8] Seventy years later, he was followed in this vein by Benjamin, who conceived of fashion as both having "an eye for the topical" and representing "a tiger's leap into the past."[9] Fashion, that is, brought together different orders of time – the past, the eternal, the present, and the future – and thus issued an implicit challenge to narratives of progress that became ideologically dominant in the nineteenth century, which viewed the past as securely bounded and isolated from the mobile present and largely dispensed with the concept of eternity as a static construct. Whereas such narratives were preeminently modern, rooted in Enlightenment liberalism's faith in the developmental advancement of the human capacity for freedom, fashion's ubiquity ensured that a temporal counternarrative was visually and materially available. The vogue for Empire-inspired fashions in the first decade of the twentieth century serves as an excellent example. The trend was launched by Poiret, whose 1906 collection of dresses featuring the simple, columnar shape of the French Empire period (1800–1815) – and seeming to dispense with the corset – remains one of the most memorable departures in twentieth-century fashion. Poiret – who I cited above, extolling the importance of the *new* in fashion – explicitly framed this silhouette as inspired by the period of the French Revolution, proclaiming, "I waged war on the corset in the name of Liberty!"[10] Thus, what was framed as innovation called on history for its symbolic force. Making the constellation of new and old even more complex in this case, of course, was the fact that Revolutionary dress itself reached into a distant past – Ancient Greece – with the aim of materially embodying democracy through self-fashioning. Poiret's radical break with dress conventions of his day, though it was framed in the rhetoric of novelty by him and others, actually constellated the present with multiple pasts and provided an alternative model of the present, of time, and of modernity itself as a temporal palimpsest. Nor was this a singular occurrence: cycling back between present and various pasts was already and continues to be central to fashion's structure. Fashion provided a strong counter to the dominant story of progress that sustained the modern era. Because it was so visually prominent, it ensured that other narratives were discernible to modern subjects, providing texture and diversity to the modern imaginary.

The turn to "the East" in late nineteenth- and early twentieth-century fashions also complicated temporal narratives, since the "Orient" was also considered to be caught variously outside of time or in some distant past. Yet in turning time and again to various "Eastern" sources for inspiration, fashion brought the modern body into intimate proximity with an aesthetic that conjured associations of timelessness and stasis. As Richard Martin and Harold Koda note, "[t]he Orientalist objective in dress was to cull from various Easts their spellbinding foreignness for the purposes of rendering Western dress richer and more exotic."[11] One might add that because of the close association of bodies with dress, in rendering dress more "exotic," wearers also took on some of this association. In the nineteenth century, for example, the Persian and Indian design element known as "paisley" became very popular in Britain, especially as a print on cashmere scarves. As the ability to produce these textiles increased and they became more widely available, this design brought a certain cachet – the association with the "exotic" – to its wearers while also becoming naturalized and losing some of its orientalist connotations. In the twentieth century, major couturiers including Poiret and Mariano Fortuny were among those who borrowed liberally from design elements, fabric, and draping central to non-"Western" cultures. For his part, Venice-based designer Fortuny ventured to regions across the world, borrowing and mixing design elements from various cultures. Fortuny had extensive exposure to Italian Renaissance painting masters, and his works often seemed to integrate global design elements with an aesthetic derived from these Renaissance influences. He and other couturiers who took up orientalist themes exemplified a kind of hybrid approach to design; and in doing so, their garments troubled the boundary between the West and the mythical "East."

It was not only haute couture, though, that appropriated design concepts from non-Western cultures. The tendency moved beyond cultural elites as it was taken up by producers and purveyors of affordable clothing for the masses. The curator of the Brooklyn Museum, Stewart Culin, for example – a recognized expert on global dress who amassed, during his tenure, a formidable costume collection at the institution – was involved in numerous industry collaborations that showcased global costume. The majority of these involved the loan of items from his collection to department stores, which used the originals in window and in-store display and offered affordable replicas for sale. Such a promotion took place at Brooklyn department store Abraham & Straus in their 1919 Blouse Week, when the store designed Abraham & Straus–branded blouses that were displayed alongside the original costumes but were distinguished by their distinctly modern silhouettes; the lines of the garments followed precisely those dominant in the fashion of the moment. Not only do these collaborations offer another fine example of the constellation of past and present in fashion, but they were also significant because they subtly opposed a dominant tendency in modern orientalist representations, whereby the paradigmatic Western subject was constituted through his distance from the imagined "Orient." In Timothy Mitchell's words, "what is outside is paradoxically what makes the West what it is, the excluded yet integral part of its identity and power."[12] Since clothing has such a close relationship to the wearer's body – and is a primary technology of identity projection – putting on an orientalist garment involved some degree not only of cultural appropriation but of *incorp-oration* of the other as part of the self. This is not to suggest that hybrid clothing countered racism or orientalism or eroded the dominance of the white, Western subject in colonial relations and the orientalist imaginary – "putting on" different identities through dress was not equally available to colonized people, whose adoption of fashionable clothing was most often ridiculed.[13] It does, though, make visible a different means by which the white subject could exercise her or his power in relation to orientalized people in modernity: by literally "putting them on" and projecting a spectacular fantasy of incorporation. Fashionable clothing provided the material for a complex negotiation of self and other across the charged boundaries of "race," ethnicity, and nation.

Such incorporation, of course, threatened modernity's dominant model of selfhood, subjectivity, and embodiment. Post-Enlightenment modernity was built on the idea of the self as discrete, atomized, and inherently possessed of the capacity for development. The human at the center of liberal humanism was meant to have no need for other subjects in order to actualize the self. Humanity was also, as a generation of feminist scholars has pointed out, premised on the idea of a consciousness divorced from the body. Here, then, was fashion, suggesting something quite different, "an embodied practice" that brought self together with the others, with otherness, with the world. In Joanne Entwistle's terms, "[t]he body forms the envelope of our being in the world, and our selfhood comes from this location in our body and our experience of this. In terms of dress, [this] means acknowledging the way that dress works on our body which in turn works on and mediates the experience of self."[14] That is, dress acted as a hinge between body and world. Certainly, the subject could "express the self" with fashion, with putting something material on the body and letting the body signal identity to the world. But that subject was also, in part, *produced* by the clothing it wore, by something external to the self. Fashionable clothing, then, also drew attention to the complex relationship between the modern body and the modern self and provided a medium through which to dramatize the relationship between self and the world beyond the self. In this sense, it troubled the dominant narrative about identity as discrete and entirely self-constituted, providing glimpses of another way of conceiving of the individual and the social.

This is, indeed, one of the major reasons contemporary theorists of modernity found fashion so representative of their age: it illuminated the interplay between individual and the social world, or, in Georg Simmel's terms, distinction and conformity. He wrote, in a 1904 essay, that fashion simultaneously represented "the tendency to social equalization [and] the desire for individual differentiation and change."[15] Simmel's reference to the "desire" for change is notable here, for it connects fashion's relentlessly present-oriented tempo, its changeability, to the personal sphere of the subject. Change was not simply an abstract principle made visible by fashion. As Simmel told it, fashion showed that change was an intimately experienced phenomenon, one with personal stakes for the individual. Not only did fashion bring together subject and world, but it also could do so without sacrificing the affective or personal dimension of individual life. Fashion is as much an intimate form as a collective one. Subjects have viscerally experienced, emotional investments in their dress. Touching it, trying it on, imagining themselves in it, wearing it to project an identity: all of these were and are activities that can provoke intense responses. Clothing is, after all, linked to memory. Rebecca Arnold writes that "[f]ashion has a great resonance, acting as a collective memory; nostalgic styles are traces of the past, mapping individual and group experiences, recalling both reassuringly familiar and yet ... upsettingly clear invocations of earlier histories."[16] References in the fashion press and modernist literature, too, frequently offered a glimpse of fashion as linked to memories of days past, linking personal histories to the sweeps of epochal histories. The form was often nostalgic, not merely for a particular social world or era but for remembered personal connections and even a past self. A 1922 article from the *Gazette du Bon Ton*, for example, opined that the modes of 1875 or 1900 would return quite soon, perhaps not precisely, "but through details from that era, which was, for some of us, childhood, for some, our youth: memories full of happiness or ... of melancholy."[17]

Further, the act of visually projecting an identity to the world is no trivial matter – in a world defined by its visual culture, mediated through the eye, and attentive to fashion, how one presented oneself was increasingly important. It could lead to a new sort of anxiety. Virginia Woolf's diaries beautifully capture the ambivalence that was often provoked by fashion. Woolf vacillated between extreme emotional responses to clothing and how it was perceived in the world. On one hand, she evidenced a certain fascination with clothing – "My love of clothes interests me profoundly,"[18] she wrote – but this was tempered by constant references to anxiety about not dressing well: "Everything to do with dress

still frightens me … or at least makes me shy, self-conscious, uncomfortable,"[19] and, tellingly, "This is what humiliates me. To walk in Regent St,
Bond Str &c: & be notably less well dressed than other people."[20] These
anxious confessions speak to the very real way in which the increasing
importance of fashion and its intimate relevance to the self brought with
it an attendant host of concerns about how one might be positioned and
read within a variety of cultural settings.

A further anxiety arose from the way that fashion seemed to complicate and even undermine class and other social distinctions. A 1935 article in American fashion and beauty magazine *Harper's Bazaar* sketched a
picture of "the female of the species." The cosmopolitan young woman,
the author asserted in this somewhat negative appraisal, self-fashioned
without tethering herself to any single class or milieu: "the ideal is to be
beyond positive identity as this or that."[21] Clothing enabled the woman to
remake herself, potentially giving her some control over how she would
be read and interpreted in relation to various social markers. Further,
with the deterioration of strict sartorial codes in the modern era, as many
pointed out, the dominant anxiety was not about women merely dressing "to be beyond positive identity"; it was about how easily one could
dress as "someone else." Fashion thus bore yet another contradiction: it
was seen to represent the depth or interiority of the person – a trope constantly reinforced in the fashion press, which exhorted women to express
themselves through dress – and yet it simultaneously offered the distinct
possibility of self-invention or reinvention, imitation, masquerade – in
short, "deceit." In claiming allegiance with some concept of a "true self"
all the while enabling masquerade, fashion discourses subtly undermined the very concept of a core or essential self. In this, fashion was
aligned with currents in the broader modernist culture. Nietzsche's
philosophy, for instance, invoked femininity as the sign of a modern
deconstruction of the style-versus-substance paradigm; he pointed to
the fallacy of the very concept of deep interiority "hidden" behind an
ornamental surface.[22] Fashion was in this instance a fine manifestation of
influential intellectual tendencies.

Fashion's affinity for masquerade and identity play seemed to open up
the potential for wearers to transgress cultural boundaries in a wide range
of settings, a fact that was regarded variously as liberating and threaten-
ing. As Mary Louise Roberts traces in the case of France, for example, the
panic that accompanied changing clothing and hairstyles for women
in the 1920s was tied to the perceived erosion of visually identifiable

markers to differentiate them from men. She quotes a French student in 1925, brimming with anxiety about the difficulty of interpreting women wearing the new fashions: "Can one define *la jeune fille moderne*? No, no more than the waist on the dresses she wears. Young women of today are difficult to locate precisely ... it would be a barbarism, in my opinion, to call our pretty *parisiennes* young women. These beings – without breasts, without hips, without 'underwear,' who smoke, work, argue and fight exactly like boys ... – these aren't young women."[23] Here the commentator suggests that women's fashion (among other visual and behavioral markers) contributed not only to the impossibility of defining women but to the possibility of their *mis*identification as boys or men. As a 1922 *Gazette du Bon Ton* article on women dressing in masculine-inspired styles suggested, the fashions were leading feminist women, in particular, to "disguise" themselves as men.[24] The word "disguise" is telling, of course, because it suggests that women were seen to have an ulterior motive for their adoption of changing fashions: they would benefit in some way from their apparent masculine masquerade, perhaps by claiming some of the power associated with men, surely an anxiety-producing proposition for many. And so here is another area in which fashion trafficked in the instability of deeply entrenched cultural oppositions, this time highlighting the shifting relationship between masculinity and femininity in modernity.

Stylistic change was only, of course, one of many ways that modern fashion called attention to or even subtly eroded boundaries between appropriately "masculine" and "feminine" ways of being in the world. The very *public* culture of fashion provided another very important challenge. Alongside the development of the technological capacity to produce fashion came the public spaces in which to sell it: the department stores that are explored at length in Elizabeth Outka's chapter in this volume first arose across the Western world in the 1840s. The title of Émile Zola's 1883 department store novel *The Ladies' Paradise* (*Au Bonheur des Dames*), inspired by pioneering Parisian store Bon Marché, hints at the implications of the development of these massive and lavish temples of consumption: they were imagined as spaces for women. Often these stores were explicitly designed with the female consumer in mind; they contained tea rooms, lounges, and bathrooms explicitly designed for the comfort of women shoppers. Though they may be so naturalized as to appear unremarkable today, these developments contributed to the gendered revitalization of public space. Class-bound ideologies of public and private prevailed in the nineteenth century, relegating the ideal woman to the domestic sphere and reserving the public sphere for men (of course, women of color and working-class white women already negotiated the public sphere daily in their real lives). Yet here were department stores, inviting respectable women into public life and public spaces. As Erika Rappaport argues with respect to London – and her argument is generalizable across many modern metropolises – discourses of shopping as leisure, of the city as a site of consumption "altered the way many Victorians viewed their city, produced new notions of desire, and rewrote gender ideals, producing a bourgeois femininity that was born within the public realm."[25] Rappaport shows how particular districts of a city, when they were oriented around fashion and consumption, effectively became feminized. The Ladies' Mile in New York City is a particularly good example; this was an area of department and luxury fashion stores centered on approximately one mile of Broadway. The presence of an entire shopping district organized around fashion signaled the uncontroversial entry into public space of a certain class of white women. It shows how perceptions of fashion and its consumption as fundamentally feminine did not merely reproduce a set of gendered stereotypes but also can be said to have enabled a new set of possibilities for bourgeois women.

It was not only the spatial organization of cities and their shopping districts in the nineteenth century that revolutionized women's relation to public life; so too did the means of displaying and visualizing fashion in such spaces. Advances in technologies for merchandising – cheaper plate glass for display windows, electric lights, new display conventions that merged commercial principles with aesthetic ones, such as the use of surrealism in display windows – led to the proliferation of particular kinds of visual interactions with fashion, especially in larger metropolitan centers; Outka's chapter on consumerism in this volume traces these at some length. William Leach situates these technological developments in the context of related changes in public spaces ranging from opera houses to hotels to museums, all of which required and indeed generated a new sort of visual literacy for the consumer, whether they were consuming an art form or merchandise.[26] One of the most significant characteristics of this new visual regime as it related to fashion and consumption was its feminization. Window displays, for instance, were not neutral tableaux; they almost invariably featured women's clothing and female mannequins. So did the displays inside of stores. Displays were matched by developments in the print culture that marked the increasing inclusion of photographs of living women in the pages of women's and fashion magazines in the 1920s – where they replaced illustrations – and developments in street culture that saw more and more women pictured in advertisements. Altogether, a spectacular culture of images of fashionably clad women, most often using their bodies to sell things, came to pervade public life. Christopher Breward quotes J. B. Priestley's 1937 novel, *Angel Pavement*, to capture the significance of fashion's feminization of everyday life in the metropolis of London:

> Everything he saw spoke to him of women and love. The shops he passed were brilliant with hats and clothes that Lena might wear; they showed him her stockings and underclothes; they were piled high with her entrancing little shoes; they invited him to look at her powder bowls, her lipstick, her scent bottles; there was nothing she wore, nothing she touched, they did not thrust under their blazing electric lights ... The very newspapers, under cover of a pretended interest in Palm Beach or feminine athletics, gave him day by day photographs of nearly naked girls with figures like Lena's.[27]

This feminization of the cityscape through the presence of women was an intensification of a nineteenth-century phenomenon that was often captured in paintings, especially those depicting Parisian life: the informal "parade" of fashionable dress on city streets, when people went out to look at others and to be looked at themselves. Fashion was a key ingredient in the intensification of a visually oriented or "ocularcentric" culture in modernity, in which visual spectacles functioned as a major source of knowledge about the world. Thus not only were women actually pervading public space through their shopping and consumption, but femininity also imprinted the visual organization of modern public space in significant and spectacular ways, with fashion and dress mediating this entry into a formerly masculinized terrain.

Though there was anxiety about the supposed erosion of gender roles that this entry into public space effected, it was also recognized as an inevitable part of everyday life in modern cities, and enterprise often capitalized on the association of fashionable women with mobility, speed, and urban street life. Consider the prevalence of women in advertisements for motor vehicles. These were found throughout fashion magazines alongside articles about new styles that would facilitate women motoring, but such images were also featured in other types of publications. Mary Louise Roberts notes, in fact, that in France women were featured in automobile advertisements much more frequently than were men. A survey of auto ads from the United States seems to bear out the same imbalance. Such representations, as Roberts notes, "created the image of a woman who leads a busy, fast-paced, and independent life, and who is empowered by the "mannish" fashions she wears."[28] Advertisers recognized the market created when middle-class women entered the public sphere of consumption through displays of their fashionability; women had come to be imagined as quintessential consumers not just of fashion but of everything. They also, crucially, recognized that a fashionably clad woman had become a selling point in itself – hence sometimes cars were not even featured in ads for automakers, with the ads using fashionable women as objects of desire, thereby making them, in a sense, interchangeable with the goods they were selling. In this way fashion prompted a different kind of entry into the public sphere. In making women coextensive with the clothing they wore – often in order to sell something ostensibly unrelated – advertisements that mobilized fashion positioned femininity and women's bodies as commodities on the very same market in which fashion was bought and sold. Like Walter Benjamin's figure of the prostitute, the use of fashionable women's bodies in advertising made them "seller and sold in one."[29] This connected them to the public sphere of commerce in undeniable ways, and it cemented the feminization of the spectacular visual culture that was so central to modernity.

Another visually mediated development in which dress and fashion positioned people in relation to central binaries of modernity – including those of masculinity and femininity, heterosexual and homosexual, and public and private – took place at the level of sexual subcultures. The growth of a range of sartorial codes and forms of expression took place as communities developed around newly imagined sexual identities (such as "sexual invert" and "homosexual"). For some working-class women in the United States, for instance, the development of "butch-fem(me)" (or, in some African-American communities, "stud-fem") dynamics allowed for a distinct, original way of organizing and signaling sexual desire, one that was largely facilitated by dress. As butch women dressed in masculine-identified clothing, and fem(me)s in conventionally feminine clothing, they forged means of connecting that allowed them both to be visible to each other in the right milieus and to protect themselves in more hostile spaces. Clothing thus played an important role in the development of modern sexual minorities; it was a medium that could both reveal and conceal varieties of sexual desire and gender expression. In this way, dress enabled what was, for queer people in the early part of the twentieth century, a rare ability to communicate with and find each other.

Of course, precisely because dress facilitated such connections, it also fell under the scrutiny of authorities who recognized its capacity to support burgeoning sexual minority communities. Across the United States, for instance, local laws that regulated clothing along the lines of gender were in effect well into the twentieth century. To take one of hundreds of instances, Ordinance 816 was adopted in 1892 in Oakland, California, making it "unlawful for any person to appear in any public place naked or in a dress not belonging to his or her sex, or in an indecent or lewd dress."[30] In some places, laws were even more specific and made it illegal not to wear at least three items of clothing understood as "appropriate" to one's biological sex. These laws were enforced, often brutally, and often in raids of the bars that had become significant gathering spaces for lesbians, gay men, and transgendered people.[31] The enforcement of laws about dress suggests once again that it was a site of significant anxiety about the erosion of social distinctions, in this case both those between masculinity and femininity and between homosexuality and heterosexuality – the latter because both butch and femme dress suggested that lesbians could potentially "pass" as something they "were not" (straight men or women).

Indeed, as modernity accelerated, dress came into its own as a visually ubiquitous consumer item that allowed people an unprecedented degree of control over their self-presentation. Its facilitation of self-fashioning provoked potential "misreadings" of identity and pointed obliquely to the complexity of identifications in a modern context that was dependent on the organization and management of easily recognizable types. Though it occasionally seemed to confirm these types, fashion's propensity for playfulness threw them into question, just as it threw into question a whole host of other seeming certainties about the changing social order of modernity. The interest of the form for theorists of the modern becomes clear: they turned to it over and over again because it provided a powerful key to the complexity that undergirded the homogenizing ideological tendencies of the age. Contemporary historians of modernist culture might take a cue from them: using fashion as a lens through which to excavate the early twentieth century unearths the inconsistencies, contradictions, and overall richness of the relationship between ideology and everyday life, ensuring that we bring needed texture to our accounts of the modern.

Notes

1 Walter Benjamin, "The Work of Art in the Age of Mechanical Reproduction," in *Illuminations*, translated by Hannah Arendt (London: Fontana, 1973), 223.

2 Elizabeth Outka's chapter on modern landscapes of consumption, in this volume, exposes this binary at some length.

3 Nancy J. Troy, "Paul Poiret's Minaret Style: Originality, Reproduction and Art in Fashion," *Fashion Theory* 6, no. 2 (2002): 118.

4 Marshall Berman, *All That Is Solid Melts into Air: The Experience of Modernity* (New York: Simon and Schuster, 1983).

5 Hylaea Group, "Untitled," from *A Trap for Judges* (Sadok sud'ei), *2* (St. Petersberg: Zhuravl', 1913). In Anna Lawton, ed., *Russian Futurism through Its Manifestos* (Ithaca: Cornell, 1988), p. 54.

6 Elizabeth Wilson, *Adorned in Dreams: Fashion and Modernity*, 2nd edition. (New Brunswick: Rutgers University Press, 2003), 3.

7 Paul Poiret, "Crinolines," *Harper's Bazaar*, August 1914, 12.

8 Charles Baudelaire, "The Painter of Modern Life," in *Baudelaire: Selected Writings on Art and Literature*, ed. P.E. Charvet (London: Viking, 2006), 402.

9 Walter Benjamin, "Theses on the Philosophy of History," in *Illuminations*, translated by Hannah Arendt (London: Fontana, 1973), 263.

10 Paul Poiret, *King of Fashion: The Autobiography of Paul Poiret*, translated by Stephen Haden Guest [1931] (London: V&A Publications, 2007), 36.

11 Richard Martin and Harold Koda, *Orientalism: Visions of the East in Western Dress* (New York: Metropolitan Museum of Art, 1994), 12.

12 Timothy Mitchell, *Colonizing Egypt* (Cambridge: Cambridge University Press, 1988), 166, quoted in Meyda Yeğenoğlu, *Colonial Fantasies: Toward a Feminist Reading of Orientalism* (Cambridge: Cambridge University Press, 1998), 49.

13 See Liz Conor, "The 'Primitive' Woman in the Late Colonial Scene," in *The Spectacular Modern Woman: Feminine Visibility in the 1920s* (Bloomington: Indiana University Press, 2005): 175–208.

14 Joanne Entwistle, "Fashion and the Fleshy Body: Dress as Embodied Practice," *Fashion Theory* 4, no. 3 (2000): 336.

15 Georg Simmel, "Fashion," *International Quarterly* 10 (October 1904): 133.

16 Rebecca Arnold, *Fashion, Desire and Anxiety: Image and Morality in the Twentieth Century* (London and New York: I.B. Tauris, 2001), 7.

17 Jeanne Ramon Fernandez, "De Mil Huit Cent Soixante Quinze à Mil Neuf Cent," *Gazette du Bon Ton*, June 1922: 148. ("Il me semble voir venir à nous, d'ici une ou deux saisons, peut-être, non pas l'exact mode de 1875 ou de 1900, mais des détails se rattachant aux atours de ce temps, qui fut pour quelques-unes d'entre nous l'enfance et pour d'autres la jeunesse: souvenirs plein de gaîté ou...de mélancolie.")

18 Virginia Woolf, "A Sketch of the Past," in *Moments of Being*, ed. Jeanne Schulkind (San Diego: Harcourt Brace, 1985), 68.

19 Virginia Woolf, *The Diary of Virginia Woolf*, ed. Anne Olivier Bell (New York: Harcourt Brace Jovanovich, 1977–84), Vol. 3, 21.

20 *Ibid.*, vol. 3, p. 75.

21 Louis Bromfield, "The Female of the Species," *Harper's Bazaar*, October 1935, 79.

22 See, for example, *The Gay Science*, ed. Bernard Williams, trans. Josefine Nauckhoff (Cambridge: Cambridge University Press, 2001). In fact, in *The Gay Science*, Nietzsche famously used an item of women's clothing – the veil – to explore this question.

23 M. Numa Sadoul, excerpted from "Une controverse: L'émancipation de la jeune fille moderne est-elle un progrès réel?" *Progrès civique*, June 13, 1925, Dossier Féminisme, XXième Siecle, Bibliothèque Marguerite Durand. Cited in Mary Louise Roberts, "Samson and Delilah Revisited: The Politics of Women's Fashion in 1920s France," *American Historical Review* 98, no. 3 (1993): 671.

24 Roger Boutet de Monvel, "Les Masculines," *Gazette du Bon Ton*, May 1922, 101.

25 Erika Rappaport, *Shopping for Pleasure: Women in the Making of London's West End* (Princeton: Princeton University Press, 2001), 5.

26 See William Leach, *Land of Desire: Merchants, Power, and the Rise of a New American Culture* (New York: Vintage, 1993), chapter 2.

27 J.B. Priestley, *Angel Pavement* (London: Heinemann, 1937), 501–02, quoted in Christopher Breward, *Fashioning London: Clothing and the Modern Metropolis* (London: Berg, 2004), 111–12.

28 Roberts, "Samson and Delilah Revisited," 675.

29 Walter Benjamin, "Paris, the Capital of the Nineteenth Century <Exposé of 1935>," in *The Arcades Project*, translated by Howard Eiland and Kevin McLaughlin (Cambridge: Belknap Press, 1999), 10.

30 This law is examined in Joan W. Howarth, "First and Last Chance: Looking for Lesbians in Fifties Bar Cases," *Southern California Review of Law and Women's Studies* 5 (1995): 160.

31 For documentation of such enforcement, see Elizabeth Lapovsky Kennedy and Madeline D. Davis, *Boots of Leather, Slippers of Gold: The History of a Lesbian Community* (New York and London: Routledge, 1993).

7

Modernist Film and Cinema Culture

Many excellent histories of film, taking up its various strands and development, double as histories of the twentieth century itself.[1] Most accounts of cinema's emergence trace it back to the magic lantern, already known by the ancients and passed on to Leonardo da Vinci as the camera obscura, the small darkened box that used a mirror to project an image of what lay outside. Yet cinema at the turn of the century revolutionized former technologies of perception and embodiment. Miriam B. Hansen has called cinema "the single most expansive discursive horizon in which the effects of modernity were reflected, rejected or denied, transmuted or negotiated."[2] There has been, according to Hansen, a "critical fixation on hegemonic modernism" that has unnecessarily separated artistic practices from "the political, economic, and social processes of modernity and modernization, including the development of mass and media culture."[3] This chapter will not trace the incremental development of film but rather will underscore major cultural tensions and paradoxes peculiar to modernity through citing a range of films.

Modernity was riddled by many paradoxes, not least of which was its time problems, anchored in an overarching claim to newness, semisynonymous with the materiality of trains, autos, skyscrapers, and cinema itself. G.A. Caillavet aptly declared in 1912: "The cinema is the diary of modern life."[4] Film held a mirror up to the modernity that created it. It also became a medium that itself criticized modernity and technology. Later, this will be evident in a sequence of representative films: King Vidor's *The Crowd* (1928), Fritz Lang's *Metropolis* (1929), and Charlie Chaplin's *Modern Times* (1936). The aesthetics of modernity boasted newness yet continuously cited tradition, especially in fragmented forms. Film, the most modern of modern mediums, epitomized this duality, and even the naming of theaters, such as The Egyptian in Hollywood, harkened back to the past.

This chapter covers the silent period through the "talking films" of the 1940s, to designate the onset of the "classical period" of Hollywood dominance in perfecting a "mechanism for producing an illusion of Renaissance space, flowing movements compatible with the human eye."[5] Film production took numerous directions, flowering into nearly unlimited experiment in both popular and avant-garde films. While low budget avant-garde films showed in Europe, D.W. Griffith perfected the two-reeler melodrama of the silent era, using for instance Tennyson's poem "Enoch Arden" for a narrative film, using the poem for intertitles, of the same title in 1911. Griffith introduced and later perfected intercutting in his full-length films: here the woman longs for her husband lost at sea, awaiting his return with telescope; many years pass (her infants become adults within ten screen minutes) between shots of Enoch's island solitude and his wife's struggling to remain a Penelope. Charlie Chaplin, between 1914 and 1921, made dozens of Mack Sennett shorts, popularizing his resonant comic gags. These brief films, constrained by the projector's capacities, dazzled with succinct speed, counterpoint to Griffith's slower, dreamier pitch. In other words, silent films were not merely stepping stones on the road to the talkies, ushered in by *The Jazz Singer* (1927), the first film employing dialogue as integral.

In some sense, modern film began with Eadweard Muybridge's motion studies in Palo Alto, California, in 1878 when he set up twenty-four cameras across a racetrack, engineered so that the galloping horse would trigger each shot and frame, and, in essence, capture the lifting and falling of horse hooves. The French physician Etienne Jules Marey went further in 1882 when he invented a photographic gun that had lenses in its chambers and could capture consecutive movement, for instance his fragmented sequence of a flight of birds. Yet a further ancestor was Louis Daguerre in partnership with Nicéphore Niépece (who managed the first photograph c. 1816); together they fine-tuned photographic method, with its own specific fate. For the cultural film historian Kracauer, "[i]n a photograph, a person's history is buried as if under a layer of snow."[6] With film, a person could be brought back to temporality, if only as a haunting specter. This might be one reason so many Expressionist films portray doubles, notably Robert Weine's *Cabinet of Dr. Caligari* (1919) up through Fritz Lang's *Testament for Dr. Mabuse* (1932); the patient in both undermines the doctor's authority so that the line between madness and sanity turns frighteningly thin.

Photography belonged to an emergent film sensibility. It energized the poet Baudelaire, who saw the self as a "kaleidoscope endowed with consciousness," a prototypic camera that could plunge into the metropolis as "into an enormous reservoir of electricity."[7] Baudelaire detected the growing symptoms of the "the transient, the fleeting, the contingent" that he subordinated to "the eternally subsisting portion as the soul of art." He concluded that art must have contact with the timely in order to attain the Timeless. As modernity unfolded, ephemerality increasingly trumped the eternal. From Daguerre's first positive daguerreotypes as early as 1839, to almost a half century later, the Lumière brothers' premiere films in 1895 (*Workers Leaving the Lumière Factory* or *The Train Coming Into the Station*) provide a kind of sequence, from photography to cinema, that acts as a metaphor for modernity, with its mixed desire for fixity as promised by the photo and for motion; for a static past alongside a relentless strip of movement into the future, a "continuous present," in Gertrude Stein's phrasing, as she called it, "in the period of the cinema."[8]

With the codifying of cinematic conventions, such as the shot/reverse shot where bodies operated in the same space, a starker division between mainstream and avant-garde productions emerged. However, in the silent film period, works geared for scientific document, entertainment, or avant-garde experiment unintentionally and intentionally depicted fractured spaces and bodies. Griffith deliberately dislocated narratives, manipulating parallel action, particularly in *Intolerance* (1916), a three-and-a-half-hour film that intercut four periods, the Babylonian, the early Christian, the French Renaissance, and the modern day, each era marked by a different color tint and punctuated by the image of a mother (Lillian Gish) rocking a baby. Griffith's controversial *Birth of a Nation* (1915) relied upon the iconoclastic methods of montage, parallelism, and rapid intercutting. Sergei Eisenstein formalized these techniques, stitching narrative through the shocking juxtaposition of images.

In spite of ideological differences, the avant-garde Soviet Eisenstein and the more popular Griffith were both attracted to layered, complex narratives. Eisenstein wrote: "Let Dickens and the whole ancestral array, going back as far as the Greeks and Shakespeare, be superfluous reminders that both Griffith and our cinema prove our origins to be not solely as of Edison and his fellow inventors, but as based on an enormous cultured past; each part of this past in its own moment of world history has moved forward the great art of cinematography."[9] Eisenstein privileged cinema as the capstone of cultural and literary development; it could cultivate a maximum of discomfort with the political status quo.

As an example of novel-turned-film, we might think of Erich von Stroheim's *Greed* (1924), inspired by Frank Norris's 1899 *McTeague*: if screened as Stroheim wanted, it would have been eight hours long, a Greek tragedy in which human beings confront their basest motives.[10] *Greed* also reminds us that films honed attention in a way that the digital era almost takes for granted in what Garrett Stewart calls its "attention surfeit disorder."[11] In the modern era, spectators could not rewind or fast forward, even if they endured several showings. The "whole" was the "flow." The process of seeing invited a nostalgia that made the very act of viewing related to the affective senses of loss and temporality.

Disregarding notions of what constituted the "high" culture of film, many found cinema's difference from literature its most exciting exponent. For example, Franz Kafka, who attended many programs at Prague's Kinematograph theatre, watched the ultimate "trash film," a Danish one-reeler titled *The White Slave Girl* (1911), presenting a woman lured from home to a strange land, forced into prostitution, and finally rescued.[12] The film reinforced the anxious distinction between whiteness and otherness keenly present in modernity; yet like many early popular films, what audiences, including Kafka, responded to, perhaps more than the story, were the mechanics presenting it: for the first time in human history, bodies and objects in motion, projected upon the screen in flickers, emphasized the ephemeral. Mass audiences could communally experience the cinema as sarcophagus foregrounding their shared mortality. Laura Marcus observes that silent film was itself "a form of hieroglyphics, a thinking in pictures rather than words," a process "fuelled by the discoveries and translations of Egyptologists and the opening of Tutankhamen's tomb in 1922."[13]

In counterpart to the modern impulse toward grand narratives of cultural representation, there existed a modern investment in the hieroglyphic object, fragment, and the part that threatened to override the whole. Tom Gunning has argued that early cinema was "not dominated by narrative" but rather partook of the "sensual and psychological impact" of the fairground.[14] Throughout Man Ray's *Emak Bakia* (1927), for example, the revolving movement of a brightly lit merry-go-round at night destabilizes and hypnotizes the viewer to the point of vertigo.

In contrast to painting's reliance upon a meditative state, film's physical piecing together of strips of flammable celluloid (literally cellulose nitrate), as with *Emak Bakia*, likely induced vertigo or other heightened sensations provoked by movement. Like other avant-garde films, *Emak Bakia* further used superimposition, out-of-focus shots, animation, and double exposures to emphasize cinematic materiality, but whether experimental or popular, film recorded kinesthetic processes, "lived experiences of time."[15]

In its rudimentary forms, cinema both represented and provoked sensory experience, crossing the very surface of the viewer's body. This might explain why Eisenstein compared some montage effects to the dizzying ride of a roller coaster.[16] Similarly, according to Kracauer, film offered "redemption" of physical reality because "representations of movement do cause a stir in deep bodily layers."[17] Bodies projected on the screen were both present and mutable, whole and piecemeal, an embodiment dependent upon both mechanical representation and an imagined viewer's body.

Christian Metz describes the way the screen itself often presented a unified bodily gestalt, "a veritable psychical substitute, a prosthesis for our primarily dislocated limbs."[18] Film technology revealed that the individual's embodied vision was limited and partial, whereas the cinematic apparatus could record both wider and stricter perspectives. Walter Benjamin aptly described a parallel between film and psychoanalysis: "The camera introduces us to unconscious optics as does psychoanalysis to unconscious impulses."[19] These optical possibilities were repeatedly self-consciously referenced in avant-garde and entertainment films alike: for instance, Buster Keaton's silent *Cameraman* (1928) shows the comic's desire to get "the perfect shot" with his ungainly tripod in order to impress the film's ingénue. In his confusion, he misses the Tong War in Chinatown, the baseball game at Yankee Stadium, and, dislocated by urban chaos, he tries to shoot a fire engine, fragmented through multiple shots.

Popular slapstick artists, like Chaplin and Lloyd, reverberated with experimental filmmakers, who in fact took these artists as their ego ideals. Perhaps the most blatant example of the incorporation of gags in an avant-garde film occurs in Luis Buñuel's surrealist *Un Chien Andalou* (1928): insects pour out of a hand, a mouth is wiped off a face to superimpose upon an underarm. In another example, Fernand Léger's short nonnarrative *Ballet Mécanique* (1924), a literal ballet of pistons and sensual body parts, begins with an animated cubist version of Chaplin, seen in fragmented motion. The Soviet director Dziga Vertov made the ultimate self-referential film with *The Man with the Movie Camera* (1929), in which the main character is the camera eye ("kino-eye"), the "high-speed eye" in an "assault on the visible world," as Vertov framed it.[20] With its omnipotent yet mechanical ability to penetrate visibility, this camera, attached to the cameraman, navigates under the train, between trolley cars, on a high tower, in an air balloon, and secreted in a boudoir, where the camera records a woman's sleeping body. Less comically, Vertov's "conquest" of reality through the camera highlighted how the cameraman, as in Keaton's rendition, was often subordinated to or misled by the apparatus.

Modernity and cinema arrived more or less simultaneously. The one-shot 1895 *Train Arriving at the Station* induced immediate shock; the film was purportedly a documentary that used strangers for actors. Audiences quickly understood the representation's artificiality when they remained unscathed by the locomotive barreling at them. Fear, anxiety, and excitement bundled together in this incipient moment. The short film's main protagonist, the train, was key, given that the train illustrated modernity's paradoxical excitement about new technology and fear of its oppressive presence. The train, with its framing consecutive windows, the blurring and separation of images, its speed and movement, resonated as the epitome of nostalgic departures; the railway was also a significant site in physics. Einstein's landmark "Special Theory of Relativity" (1905) demonstrated that space and time were malleable and mobile; in a later "thought experiment," he showed subjective positions on various "still" platforms that undermined a fixed spatio-temporal model.[21] Perspective could be multiple, as the modernist poem, novel, or painting recorded; the self, figured as part of a tissue of objects and landscapes, was no longer the central locus of the visible.

Arrival of the Train was coincident with studies in physics that incited more expanded literary investigations (think of Proust's long meditation upon the circularity of temporality in his six-volume *In Search of Lost Time*, 1913 to 1927). Early film, partaking of shock and the fairground, helped open up self-conscious questions of epistemology that would plague and intrigue modernity's myriad thinkers, dancers, musicians – and filmmakers. On a material level, the train functioned in tandem with modern crowds (which I return to), urban life, and economic exchange, providing essential ingredients for film: movement and multifold perspective.

Einstein believed "every reference body has its own particular time," and he proved through his groundbreaking theories that we could "have as many clocks as we like," given no absolute time and space exists. Cinema pushed home time's relativity in making divergent temporal and spatial zones open to radical manipulation, as when comic Harold Lloyd hangs precariously above distant city bustle from a second hand on a skyscraper clock in *Safety Last* (1923). Slapstick stars brought home both the emblematic workaday clock and the sensational going out on a limb, often breaking from linear time to create uniquely filmic sensations. Clocks become pawns of "reality": think of *The Pawnshop* (1916), where Chaplin, surrounded by clocks, broken or ticking at different paces, makes the visual pun of attaching a stethoscope to one of many presumably ill clocks.

The idea of relativity, embedded in the modern worldview, fed various experiments within film representation. Film demonstrated that both space and time were infinitely alterable through acts of montage, editing, lighting, and composition. While the medium offered enormous possibilities for verisimilitude, it questioned the very premises upon which a supposedly stable realism rested. The camera could break down the barrier between interior and exterior worlds, calling directly upon the spectator's subjectivity in making the film, just as new filmmakers, with their cameras and lenses, projectors and screens, revolutionized how the imagination recreated three-dimensional conditions to elicit emotional and mental responses. An avant-garde filmmaker could create new connections through metaphoric and literal cuts: reflect only upon the opening scene in *Un Chien* with its shot of a bisected moon followed with that of a razor crossing a woman's eye.

Einstein was not the only "great man" to contribute to film culture. Two years before *Arrival of the Train*, Sigmund Freud with Joseph Breuer published "On the Psychical Mechanism of Hysterical Phenomenon," linking somatic disease with traumatic memory.[22] *The Interpretation of Dreams* (1900), perhaps Freud's writing most influential upon film, exposed a vast realm of unconscious dream life. Directors played upon the kinship between dream analysis and film: G.W. Pabst in *Secrets of a Soul* (1926) revealed the dramatic shifts in psychic life by intercutting imagined or dreamed experience with the so-called waking state, and later, Hitchcock's *Spellbound* (1945) cemented the bond between film and dreams. An extended dream sequence, created by Salvador Dali, transcribes the protagonist's (Gregory Peck) dream and helps his analyst (primarily Ingrid Bergman) unlock the solution to solve the film's ostensible or "manifest" mystery.

Freud further provided a psychic structure of the unconscious that most resembled the process of going into a cinema, entering the darkness as if the viewer were in a trance, tapping into his or her own primal identifications, enhanced by the spiraling of memory and flashback afforded by film techniques. Freud's writings permeated, refined, and reflected upon cinematic technique, including his central ideas of identification and projection, for after all, "the bodily ego" was for him a "projection of a surface."[23] *The Uncanny* (1919), which scrutinized how the familiar turned unfamiliar, would provide the template for many modern films. *Beyond the Pleasure Principle* begins with mention of traumatic injury from a train accident to explore the more recent injuries of war shock and trauma to the "bodily ego."[24] The "war neurotic" was implicitly compared to the hysterical female, a pair that would populate the silver screen after World War I. Antiwar films like King Vidor's *The Big Parade* (1925) drew upon every filmic method possible, from the tracking shot of foot tapping to a snaking convoy to the front, until the spectator discovers the hallucinatory close-up in the trenches. The film cuts back home, where the hero, effeminized by war trauma, returns with an amputated leg. Debilitations and disabilities found expression in a filmic medium that did not resist the unidealistic; rather, cinema, generally speaking, presented the novel, whether sublime, attractive, ordinary, or grotesque.

Psychic time, in modernity and cinema, was recursive: it moved forward and backward, depending on subjective perception. Mention of Einstein and Freud leads to mention of at least three other major male genii of modernity: Darwin, whose theory of evolution traced the present back to a past that had evolved in intermittent difficult steps, purporting a kind of deterministic thought that led to novels and films like *Greed*; Nietzsche, who preached the "eternal return" and the death of god, would find fulfillment in the dark cave of cinema where time was both in a "continuous present" and attached to mythical figurations of the past; and, finally, Marx, whose theories of class structure and economic exchange infiltrated all aspects of film representation, particularly in the Soviet films of Eisenstein and Pudovkin, of which the cultural critic Bryher (born Annie Winifred Ellerman) writes: "Cutting … is considered far more important than the story."[25] In *Battleship Potemkin* (1925), Eisenstein uses shock effect through "dialectical montage," a Marxian-inspired aesthetic that provokes emotional responses from the viewer:

the famous "Odessa Steps" sequence, filmed with rhythmic repetition (conveying a sense of endlessness), shows a massacre of civilians, among them a woman shot in the eye (her pince-nez shatters) and a mother gunned down, her baby carriage rolling without control down the steps towards the fleeing crowd.

These five fingers on the hand of modernism (Einstein, Freud, Darwin, Nietzsche, and Marx), while well recognized, cannot be forgotten if we are to understand film's centrality to the phenomenological and cultural realities of the time period. Many other influential thinkers come to mind, but this hand or grip illuminates the seeming absence of female thought, as if women were to be assigned the role of spectacle, the "to-be-looked-at-ness" Laura Mulvey outlines in her groundbreaking essay on visual pleasure.[26] Mulvey and other feminists have since understood that women spectators were not limited to identification with the female characters who serve merely as the hero's objects: women spectators could identify across genders. And yet making films for female viewers was a two-edged problem: matinee sex idols like Rudolph Valentino who appealed to heterosexual women also reinforced sexual binaries in exotic films like *The Sheik* (1921), even as many female viewers were disjointed through their postwar loss or gain of greater mobility – one effect being the ability for women to literally see films on their own, without chaperones. Women also exercised agency through the venue of film criticism: Bryher and her second husband of convenience, along with the poet H.D., engineered the first film journal in English, *Close Up* (1927–1933), which highlighted experimental practices, publishing for instance a first translation of Eisenstein's film essay, "Fourth Dimension in the Kino." The conflict between shots results in a montage effect as "one of shock" that will, according to Eisenstein, have "reflex-physiological essence."[27] Eisenstein mastered this tactic in *Potemkin*: in his studied opening sequence "Men and Maggots," the sailors are drowsing in their hammocks until confronted by the captain with the contaminated meat they are expected to ingest; the ship's doctor, using his spectacles, lectures the crew and cinema audience; the doctor's intertitle, "These are not worms," makes the image more shocking, especially when the meat with its microscopic maggots takes up the whole screen. The spectacles act as prosthetic camera.

Through the lattices of film aesthetics and cinema culture, one observes the emergence of women linked to moribund fatality, like Louise Brooks as femme fatale in Pabst's *Pandora's Box* (1928) as well as modernity's "New Woman," as she was dubbed. When the men came home from war and reclaimed their jobs, women became even more motivated to break the barrier between private interiors and public spaces. One of the spaces that became sacrosanct for some women was the film theatre itself. Popular women filmmakers were scarce besides the lesbian Hollywood director Dorothy Arzner, who had a successful career in the twenties and thirties; her films include *The Wild Party* (1928) and had no overt tones of lesbian desire but featured women together in sensuous contact. In spite of the lack of women as directors, a large majority of the early screenwriters were women, including Lang's wife, Thea von Harbou, and Hitchcock's spouse, Alma Reville, who collaborated on screen adaptations of films like *The Secret Agent* (1936) and *The Lady Vanishes* (1938). These women, and many others, were close collaborators, quietly unrecognized or dimly acknowledged.

The journal *Close Up* epitomizes intensive writing about film by modernists and reflected film theory in its early stages. It often highlighted the sexual and gender element in viewing film.[28] In her first "Continuous Performance" column for *Close Up*, titled "The Film Gone Male," Dorothy Richardson describes attending a Monday-afternoon matinee with an audience of "almost entirely mothers," "figures of weariness at rest," and observes that film allowed a necessary "forgetfulness," even escape.[29] She further warned of the bluntness of "talkies," their capacity for propaganda, while silent film could be as "intimate as thought," engendering a space for a fluid, freely circulating set of emotions and ideas. This vision of filmgoing and filmmaking seems at loggerheads with Eisenstein's ideas of dialectal montage that called for a "collision" of shots, but if we think more of the dream settings and atmospheric moods offered by silent film, it is easier to reconcile films like Pabst's *Joyless Street* with its long shots and close-ups, rendered in eerie light and shadow, with those that Richardson alludes to without naming.

Richardson objected to the break into the subjective processes of incorporating a film, the compulsion, almost unawares, to absorb stylized propaganda supported through dialogue. As the Nazis gained more power, they turned to media such as radio and film to make their programs heard, and words, as Richardson suggests, locked down interpretation rather than opened it up. This was a facet of Benjamin's anxiety in "The Work of Art in the Age of Mechanical Reproduction"; the philosopher was excited by the possibilities of dialectical montage yet still worried about cinema's capacity to foster ideological thinking.

Patrice Petro describes the moodiness of Weimar film as an expression of war exhaustion, and for our purposes, it was exemplary of women's developing roles in film. In rethinking Weine's *Caligari* through Tony Kaes, Petro views the somnambulist as a victim of trench warfare linked to female boredom, as opposed to male hysteria, an ennui embodied by the sexual icon and "sexually decadent star" Marlene Dietrich. In Stroheim's *The Blue Angel* (1930), Dietrich enacts "Lola's blasé sexuality – her seeming lack of affect," which "suggests that sex, as much as modernity, promises nothing to the woman; or, if it does, that this promise is always already broken."[30] By 1930, many silent directors entered sound, as did Stroheim, but they used it sparingly. Stroheim, for instance, continues to concentrate on silent montages, such as a whimsical one in which the smitten professor blows on a postcard of the music hall Lola and we see the strings of her skirt rise up with his gentle puff of air. The same year as *Blue Angel*, Stroheim produced another Dietrich vehicle, *Morocco*, which titillated audiences with the cabaret performer's cross-dressing costume in top hat and tails: Dietrich struts about as the object of the gaze, until she finally kisses a woman – purposefully confusing her own and the audience's identification and desire, though she quickly pivots from the shocking kiss to toss a flower to Gary Cooper.

It was the very experience of the cinema that gave some women relief not just from everyday life but also from sexual and aesthetic norms. When H.D. first saw Pabst's *Joyless Street* (1925), she was riveted: "Greta Garbo as I first saw her, gave me a clue, a new angle, and a new sense of elation. This is beauty, and this is a beautiful and young woman not exaggerated in any particular, stepping, frail yet secure across a wasted city."[31] In her poetry, H.D. transformed Garbo into a mythic Helen and the postwar landscape of Vienna into Troy, thus linking the past to the present. The theatre for H.D. and many of her cohorts was "a sort of temple" awaiting "our Aeschylus, our Sophocles, our Euripides," a place where a fragmentary "bit of chiffon" could evoke erotic possibility. Along similar lines to Richardson, H.D. described a "sinking" into the cinema as into an underground where identification and metamorphosis might happen:

> Then we sank into light, into darkness, the cinema palace (we each have our favorite) became a sort of temple. We depended on light, on some sub-strata of warmth, some pulse or vibration, music on

another plane too, also far enough removed from our real or intellectual stimulus. We moved like moths in darkness, we were hypnotized by cross currents and interacting shades of light and darkness and maybe cigarette smoke. Our censors, intellectually off guard, permitted our minds to rest. We sank into this pulse and warmth and were recreated.[32]

Film was born in part from a vision of the crowd, from the sweat of a growing urban population, where E.A. Poe's "Man in the Crowd" (1840) anxiously watched the passerby fade into anonymity and Baudelaire's *flaneur* strutted, stunned, before the phantasmagoria of crowds. No wonder the philosopher Georg Simmel called for "strategies of delimination" so that the individual would not feel swallowed by the crowd.[33] Films could mirror mass culture and help to preserve a sense of a singled-out subjectivity embodied in the spectator. Many films in the modernist period specifically addressed the anxieties over anonymity in urban settings such as in the atmospheric *Sunrise* in 1927; F.A. Murnau won an Oscar for it, although the film was a commercial failure. The film relies upon a drastic division between the city and the country: both end up as dangerous places where gender and class coalesce to show the male hero tempted by the "metro girl" to murder his "pastoral girl."

This chapter has already alluded to modernity's critique of itself through film. King Vidor's *The Crowd* is paradigmatically modernist, blending slapstick, melodrama, and montage, with intricate flashbacks and superimpositions. Yet the story is a popular one: the country boy follows the American Dream that poignantly sours amid crowds and amusement parks such as Coney Island and through the very technologies that make film possible. *The Crowd* is famous for its clever use of a mobile, continuous camera action, including "the famous shot ... what Mitry called 'one of the most beautiful tracking shots in the whole silent cinema': the camera advances into the crowd, against the flow, makes its way toward a skyscraper, climbs up to the twentieth floor, frames one of the windows, discovers a hall full of desks, goes in to arrive at a desk where the hero is sitting."[34] The camera pulls out again to reveal the mass of desks from an aerial view. The film linked the automated reproduction of human life, paralleling the office with the maternity ward, each worker and mother in their identical cubicles. Driven by the large clock above their desks, the workers punch in and punch out. The fantasy of standing out from the crowd as well as being part of a larger force turns out to be doubly crushing for our hero, who ends up losing his child to an auto accident and working, dressed as a clown, wearing a sandwich board for advertisement on a busy New York street.

The factory setting in *Modern Times* of the next decade provides Chaplin with many opportunities to mock mind-numbing automation and immersion in crowds. The assembly line mechanizes the body so that Chaplin, whose job it is to fasten screw after screw, ends up chasing a woman during his break, automatically fastening the buttons on her dress, daringly close to her breasts. Chaplin, as factory worker, also gets caught up in a socialist workers' march and is hauled off to jail. One of his fellow prisoners hides cocaine in the saltshaker, and after Chaplin generously salts his food, he becomes even more jerky and sped up than usual. Chaplin makes a powerful equation between addiction and the demands of work. *Modern Times* acts as a comic counterpoint to both *The Crowd* and *Metropolis*, Fritz Lang's vision of a dystopic city. *Metropolis* was a great segue for Lang's film noirs, which were produced in America after he left Germany in 1933. The modernist aesthetics of Expressionism induced a feeling of menace, rendered through chiaroscuro and exaggerated facial and bodily expression, tactics that continued to ensue in Hollywood film.

An after-image of the modernist silent era persisted. The "modernist" filmmakers, mostly German Jews fleeing the Nazis – Fritz Lang, Billy Wilder, Otto Preminger, to name several – carried the experimental styles they had practiced in Europe into Hollywood. Thus Lang's *Metropolis*, a classic of modernist filmmaking, is linked to a keen class critique that films like *The Crowd* and *Modern Times* unfolded at the onset of and during the American Depression. In *Metropolis*, slaves in the pit of an insular world with imposing clock and baroque levers grind away in mechanical labor to supply the energy for those very few living at the top, the leisure class who play lawn tennis or, like the main character's father, practice surveillance of workers on a massive scale in a spacious techno-ready office. The workers look like inmates, closely resembling the refugees that were starting to populate Europe when the film was made in 1927. Kracauer identified *Metropolis* as predictive of the passivity of Germans before Nazi control. Yet the film, modern to the core, criticized both technology and rigid social control.

It is the self-same individual, threatened by the mob or crowd, that struggles for life in totalitarian societies as well as supposed democracies; Lang's *Big Heat* (1953), a Hollywood noir, tracks a cop's (Glen Ford) necessary vigilantism to revenge his wife's death by institutionalized gangland crime. Similarly, *The Fury* (1936), Lang's first Hollywood film, shows Spencer Tracy, falsely accused of a crime, hounded into becoming a cynic and criminal because of mob arson attacks. Billy Wilder's *Witness for the Prosecution* (1957) was among other Hollywood "contraband" incorporating the still immediate European past with Dietrich playing a double role, a refugee and betrayed wife. Such self-conscious performances (Dietrich ventriloquizes a Cockney "lowlife" with a scar) entered the veins of mainstream Hollywood, suggesting the enduring marks of modernist sensibility upon popular films. Similarly, Hitchcock, who had studied with Munrau in Berlin in the twenties, began making political "comedy/thrillers" like *The 39 Steps* (1935) with its vaudeville "memory man" (an automaton of facts who holds a spy ring's secret code) and its double agent, a woman without a country, whose murder initiates the political detective plot. Hitchcock had learned well the Expressionist methods of distortions and perverse or tilted camera angles to convey the camera's subjectivity.

Hitchcock flourished in part through his continued use of intensive camera work, precise and loaded compositions in which every image counted. Starting in the silent period, in *Blackmail* (1929), Hitchcock's camera dissected the process of police work, which starts to resemble crime work – shadowing, fingerprinting, booking, parade lines, and persecutory pursuits that in this story culminate with the blackmailer falling through the high glass dome of the British Museum. Thus began Hitchcock's obsession with vertiginous heights.

Entertainment films were not as far off from avant-garde films as they progressively became from the 1940s onward. Maya Deren's silent *Meshes of the Afternoon* (1943) gave the uncanny power of objects their due, the camera filming almost with a power of its own, tracking the repetition of a woman returning home and seeing herself fractured into multiple selves. Deren's film opposes Leni Riefenstahl's propagandistic glorification of mass assembly, specifically in *Triumph of the Will*, which filmed the 1934 Nazi Congress in Nuremberg, through mesmeric cohesion and long sweeps of the militants in organized salute. Yet films like Deren's sort took a different path of humility rather than the triumphal Riefenstahl or even the large-scale Eisenstein.

In the early period, Chaplin (and many others like Lang, Vidor, Pabst, and Griffith) combined entertainment with technical play and composition, doting upon small details as well as larger frames. Silent-era film aggregated many of its sister arts so that it is arguably the most inventive, hybrid, and enduring of the cinema periods. It borrowed from music and collage. Think of Walter Ruttmann's *Berlin: Symphony of a Great City* (1927) with its impressionist movement across the rainy city and its diverse inhabitants from beggars to prostitutes, Germaine Dulac's *L'invitation au Voyage* (1927), a film based on a Baudelaire poem, that makes tiny worlds within worlds in its dreamscape, or Man Ray's *L'Etoile de Mer* (1928), a "cinematographic poem" with its cryptic image constellations of shells, fish, and humans diving into dream-like states. These lyric films, like Deren's emphatically opposed to narrative cohesion, created an aesthetic cinema, without subtitles, that could offer the aficionado a peak experience in viewing the unexpected. In spite of resistance to the avant-garde, many of its techniques were absorbed by longer films and eventually by popular films.

Modernist cinema looks extremely inventive and collaborative, especially when considering the auteur theory that came to dominate film studies in the 1950s. We might consider Dali and Disney's attempt to collaborate on an animated short *Destino* (1945), recently reconstructed from archival drafts of drawings and paintings. Following a screening of the newly constructed *Destino* in 2003, one of Disney's *Silly Symphonies* appeared. These cartoons, shorts made between 1929 and 1939, echoed familiar motifs in avant-garde cinema, with its dislocated bodies, impossible traversals of space, myriad music from lyric to cacophonous, to orchestrate modernism's multiple possibilities for knowing and seeing.

Notes

1   Most recently, a five-DVD set, *The Story of Film: An Odyssey* (2012), created by Mark Cousins, surveys the history of film with an epic scope and lyric tone; the Belfast-born Cousins calls it his "love letter" to film.
2   Miriam B. Hansen, "America, Paris, the Alps: Kracauer and Benjamin on Cinema and Modernity," in *Cinema and the Invention of Modern Life*, eds. Leo Charney and Vanessa R. Schwartz (Berkeley: University of California, 1995), 365.
3   Ibid.
4   Quoted in Hanns Zischler, *Kafka Goes to the Movies* (Chicago: University of Chicago Press, 2003), 33.
5   Laura Mulvey, "Visual Pleasure and Narrative Cinema" (1975), in *The Sexual Subject: A Screen Reader in Sexuality* (London: Routledge, 1992), 33.
6   Siegfried Kracauer, "Photography," in *The Mass Ornament: Weimar Essays*, ed. Thomas Y. Levin (Cambridge, MA: Harvard University Press, 1995), 51. Originally published in German in 1927.

7   Charles Baudelaire, "The Painter of Modern Life," in *Modernism: An Anthology of Documents*, eds. Vassiliki Kolocotroni, Jane Goldman, and Olga Taxidou (Chicago: University of Chicago Press, 1998), 105–06.

8   Gertrude Stein, *Portraits and Prayers* (New York: Random House, 1934), 177.

9   Sergei Eisenstein, "Dickens, Griffiths and the Film Today," in *Film Form: Essays in Film Theory*, ed. Jay Leyda (New York: Harcourt Brace & Jovanovich, 1949), 232–23.

10 The film's original eight hours was, against Stroheim's wishes, cut to two and a half hours.

11 Garrett Stewart, *Between Film and Screen: Modernism's Photo Synthesis* (Chicago: University of Chicago Press, 1999), 138.

12 Hanns Zischler, *Kafka Goes to the Movies*, 33.

13 Laura Marcus, "The Contribution of H.D.," in *Close Up 1927–1933: Cinema and Modernism*, eds. James Donald, Anne Friedberg, and Laura Marcus (Princeton: Princeton University Press, 1998), 102.

14 Tom Gunning, "The Cinema of Attractions: Early Film, Its Spectator, and the Avant-Garde" (1986), in *Early Cinema: Space Frame Narrative*, ed. Thomas Elsaesser (London: BFI Publishing, 1990), 59.

15 Edmund Husserl, *The Phenomenology of Internal Time Consciousness* (1905), translated by James S. Churchill (Bloomington: Indiana University Press, 1966), 28.

16 Quoted in Gunning, "The Cinema of Attractions," 59.

17 Siegfried Kracauer, *Theory of Film: The Redemption of Physical Reality* (Princeton: Princeton University Press), 158.

18 Christian Metz, *The Imaginary Signifier: Psychoanalysis and Cinema*, translated by Celia Britton (Bloomington: Indiana University Press, 1975), 4.

19 Walter Benjamin, "Work of Art in the Age of Mechanical Reproduction" (1936), in *Illuminations*, ed. Hannah Arendt and translated by Harry Zohn (New York: Shocken Books, 1968), 3.

20 Dziga Vertov, "The Birth of Kino-Eye" (1924), in *Kino-Eye: The Writings of Dziga Vertov*, translated by Kevin O'Brien (Berkeley: University of California Press, 1984), 41.

21 Einstein's thought experiment employed two light rays starting at both ends of the platform. See Albert Einstein, *Relativity: The Special and General Theory* (1916), ed. Nigel Calder (New York: Penguin Editions, 2007).

22 Joseph Breuer and Sigmund Freud (1893), *The Standard Edition of the Complete Psychological Works of Sigmund Freud*, translated by and ed. James Strachey (London: Hogarth Press, 1953–1974), Vol. 2, 6. Other references to the *Standard Edition* will be referred to as *SE*.

23 Freud, *The Ego and the Id* (1923), *SE* 19, 26.

24 Freud, *Beyond the Pleasure Principle* (1923), *SE* 19.

25 Bryher, *Film Problems of Soviet Russia* (Riant Chateaux: Pool, 1928),14.

26 Mulvey, "Visual Pleasure and Narrative Cinema," (1975).

27 Eisenstein, "Kino in the Fourth Dimension," in *Close Up* 6, no. 3 (March 1930): 185.

28 See Laura Marcus, *The Tenth Muse: Writing about Cinema in the Modernist Period* (Oxford: Oxford University Press, 2007), for multiple forums of early critical writing about films. I offer *Close Up* as exemplum of this film culture and writing.

29 Richardson, *Close Up* 1, no. 1 (July 1927): 35–36.

30 Patrice Petro, *Aftershocks of the New: Feminism and Film History* (New Brunswick: Rutgers University Press, 2002), 122.

31 Richardson, H.D., "Beauty," *Close Up* July (1927): 28.

32 Richardson, H.D., "The Cinema and the Classics III: The Movietone," 1, no. 5 (November 1927): 23.

33 Simmel, "The Metropolis and Mental Life" (1903), in *Modernism: An Anthology of Sources and Documents*, ed. Vassiliki Kolocotroni, Jane Goldman, and Olga Taxidou (Chicago: University of Chicago Press, 1998), 54.

34 Gilles Deleuze, *Cinema I: The Movement-Image* (Minneapolis: University of Minnesota Press, 1986), 22.

8
———————

Dance

Dance's ambivalent duet with modernity, its contradictory tendency to celebrate innovation and the primitive past, was a crucial aspect of modernist cultures. Dance featured new bodily techniques, stage designs, and lighting effects while representing non-Western cultures and ancient societies. This was true of dance's many forms in the period, from popular vaudeville performance to the experimental ballet most commonly associated with Sergei Diaghilev's Ballets Russes to the new modern aesthetic dancing. Partially because of its apparent antimodernism, dance has not, until recently, been sufficiently incorporated into conceptions of modernism. And yet, dance brings into more revealing focus some of modernism's most interesting provocations, including its well-known fascinations with a primitive past, movement, and bodies. As the art of bodily motion, dance inspired artists working in many fields, yet modernist studies tends to privilege that other art form centrally concerned with movement: film. This chapter will use the relationship between dance and film to demonstrate dance's function as an aesthetic register of modernity and its challenge to our more static conceptions of modernism.

It has long been recognized that experiments with protocinematic technologies in the late 1870s through 1890s were conducted in the midst of aesthetic movements that heralded modernism: symbolism, aestheticism, and impressionism, among others. Critics frequently identify film as a privileged form for recording experiences of modernity, even "the most modern of modern mediums," as Susan McCabe suggests in her excellent chapter in this volume. The form we call modern dance also took to stages around the world at the end of the nineteenth century, often playing the same venues where early films were screened. Today, dance is rarely touted as a medium well suited for registering the shock of modernity or shaping the sensibilities of modernism. Yet, as early as 1912, art enthusiasts proclaimed a "modern revival of dancing" and celebrated the ability of the Ballets Russes to present "a series of pictures for the painter, statues for the sculptor, stories for the romancer, psychology for the scientist and a Thing of Beauty for every eye."[1] Film is not named among the forms that benefit from the revival of dance, but its concern with movement and prominent position in modernist studies makes it a useful counterpoint to dance. The challenge of documenting the dancing body led to new cinematic technologies and performance techniques, from the tracking shot to montage – and now 3D.[2] Film technologies were even modeled on the moving body as they attempted to replicate, for example, the mobile eye that can focus on an object, turn away to look at something else, or close. This chapter examines three sites where innovations in dance influenced the cinema and modernism more generally: Paris, Hollywood, and Berlin.

In claiming that dance is a crucial register of modernity, I have already broached a series of definitional problems surrounding the terms "modernity," "modernization," "the modern," and "modernism."[3] Dance offers additional terminological challenges that can help identify (although not resolve) these problems. A robust culture of dance existed in the modernist period, with many different forms of dance competing for stages and audiences. There was no single "modernist dance" that constituted a riotous break from the past similar to the iconoclasm we presume in the other modernist arts. Some critics suggest that modernity was most visible in popular dance forms like the skirt dancing craze initiated by Loïe Fuller after 1891.[4] Others point to the renovations of classical ballet in, for example, Vaslav Nijinsky and Igor Stravinsky's *Le Sacre du Printemps*, which famously provoked a riot at Paris's Théâtre des Champs-Élysées on opening night, May 29, 1913. Accounts of this now-celebrated Ballets Russes production reveal the historical neglect of dance; critics tend to accept Stravinsky's claim that the audience was inflamed by the music's innovations in polyrhythm and dissonance rather than Nijinsky's choreography of primitive ritual in asymmetrical poses, stomps, and pigeon-toed jumps.[5] The story of a musically inspired riot is suspect given that the crowd was too noisy to hear anything for most of the performance, yet the score is still cited as the first clamor of modernist music. Stravinsky's *Sacre* appears in the 1913 list for the chronology of *The Cambridge Companion to Modernism* and the chapter on "Modernism in Drama," but Nijinsky is not mentioned.[6]

Those we now call "modern dancers," beginning with Isadora Duncan, rejected rather than sought to renovate ballet in the first decades of the twentieth century.[7] Duncan never referred to herself as modern; in fact, "modern dance" was first used in the 1880s as a term of derision by, for example, the American minister Rev. G.F. Pentecost, who compared "modern social dance" to the old-fashioned square dance, concluding that it was a foreign form and "[e]very posture, every motion was the invention of licentiousness."[8] Even eminent scholars in the new discipline of psychology, such as Harvard Professor Hugo Münsterberg, condemned dance, claiming, "The modern dance is erotic and sex-inciting."[9] Münsterberg was far more enthusiastic about film in his *The Photoplay: A Psychological Study*, one of the first books of film theory (1916).[10] In order to avoid such accusations, Duncan and other dancers invoked the elite aesthetics of ancient Greece, appealing to the popular interest in viewing art that offered the uplift of classical distinction or the shiver of ancient barbarism.[11] As the poet Shaemas O'Sheel points out, "It was customary to refer to Isadora's dancing as 'Greek.' But she herself wrote that she went to nature as primitive man had done. She wrote that the dance was the earliest of the arts."[12] Greek, primitive, and natural dancing seem like antonyms for "the modern," yet they reflect a dominant antimodern impulse that runs through canonical modernist art, evident in Stravinsky's use of pre-Christian Slavic culture as the inspiration for *Le Sacre*, Cubism's roots in Picasso's encounter with African masks, and Ezra Pound's advocacy of classical Chinese and Japanese poetry as models for Imagism. Music, painting, and poetry, like dance, are all ancient arts, and it might seem that the past would be poor material for film, modernism's newest medium. That isn't the case. As my Hollywood example demonstrates, dance popularized representations of ancient cultures and made them available for cinematic "remediation," or transfer between media.[13]

All forms of dance in the modernist period challenged the ability of other arts to represent moving bodies. Because of its pride of place in modernist studies, cinema serves as a useful example of that challenge. Early cameras flattened the body into two dimensions, presented movement from one angle, and added a jerky quality to human motion because early projection techniques were not fast enough to hide the gaps between frames. While later technologies resolved this problem, it reemerged with 3D, as I discuss in the final section of this chapter. Dance is composed of three movement vectors that establish a three-dimensional choreographic space, which film (and other modernist arts) sought to represent: 1. Dance is motion and stillness in space that creates a *formal pattern* or, translated into film language, *shot composition*. 2. Dance choreography alters the body's *proximity* to the audience, which film achieves through *camera distance* and *angle*. 3. Dance movement takes a certain amount of time to create a *rhythm* or tempo, which in film is established by the camera's *frames per second* and the *frequency of cuts*. Efforts to accommodate these dance dimensions on film led to innovations that not only changed cinema but also altered the way modernism represented the human body and its movement.

Projecting Attractions in Paris

The origins and intersections of popular dance, modern aesthetic dance, and cinema are evident in Loïe Fuller's performances in Paris in the 1890s (Figure 5). Her protocinematic choreography experimented with each of the dance dimensions I have isolated: pattern, proximity, and rhythm.

FIGURE 5   Portrait of Loïe Fuller by Falk (1901), Library of Congress, Prints & Photographs Division, LC-USZ62-63147

She completely surrounded and concealed her body with flowing fabric and attached long wands to these skirts so that she could lift them and create swirling patterns that also brought her movement closer to her audience. With this prosthetic device extending her arms, she transformed her skirts into a 3D screen. A century before 3D technology became the hallmark of contemporary film, Fuller realized multidimensional projection by casting colored lights onto her skirts from different angles, even from underneath her, to produce the illusion of a ghostly partial body. She developed moving pedestals for her lights and used a protocinematic stereopticon to project moons, stars, flowers, faces, and other images onto her 3D skirts.

Fuller generally performed a series of dances with titles such as *The Serpentine*, *The Butterfly*, and *The Violet*. She represented bucolic natural images but also technological themes as in *Radium Dance*, inspired by Madame Curie. Fuller offered what might be called a *dance of attractions*, a term I borrow from Tom Gunning's "cinema of attractions," his famous designation for early cinema's investment in spectacle, tricks, and theatrics.[14] Fuller refused the plots commonly presented in nineteenth-century ballet, and her followers in modern aesthetic dance, from Isadora Duncan to Pina Bausch, continued to suppress narrative and emphasize dance form, emotional expression, and abstraction. Fuller's fame led to a bevy of less notable followers who performed popular "skirt dances" in variety shows alongside acrobatics, magic tricks, and short films with many "attractions."

Given Fuller's projection of light and images onto her moving 3D skirt-screens, it's not surprising that she interested the Lumière brothers, who filmed her skirt dance imitators in 1896.[15] Fuller herself turned to filmmaking with *Le Lys de la Vie* (1921), a journey film that features a series of dances she had previously performed live onstage. A princess searches for the magical lily of life that will save the ill prince who had abandoned her for another lover. She secures the lily but dies of unrequited love. After being resurrected by the fairies she encountered during her voyage, the princess joins their mythical world, escaping the heteronormative fairytale plot.[16] The prince was played by a young René Clair, who, after this introduction to dance and cinema, went on to produce the famous Dadaist film *Entr'acte* (1924) featuring an iconic dance scene. Clair collaborated with Jean Borlin's Ballets Suedois, and *Entr'acte* was created as a cinematic intermission act for *Relâche*, a ballet choreographed by Francis Picabia.[17]

While Fuller was transforming herself into a protocinematic 3D moving image and then remediating her dances on film, another artist working in Paris, Georges Méliès, employed music hall dancers and developed new cinematic techniques to represent and manipulate human movement. In *A Trip to the Moon* (1902), he brought the moon closer with an imaginary launch that takes the magician-like Barbenfouillis, played by Méliès, and his Astronomic Club to the surface of the moon.[18] In the famous lunar landing sequence, a dissolve transforms a theatrical backdrop of the sky and moon into a man-moon-face that enlarges, as if the camera were moving closer to the moon from the perspective of the projectile. In reality, the man in the moon is the face of an actor who was rolled toward the camera. Méliès ingeniously portrayed motion by enlarging the moon rather than moving the camera, recognizing motion is perceived when the viewer's proximity to an object changes. A stop-camera substitution splice then makes the projectile appear to implant in the moon's eye. This trick was produced by stopping the camera and manually adjusting one aspect of the set (in this case repositioning the projectile). It was an "attraction" Méliès used to great effect in many films. The shell piercing the eye of the moon could be considered a projection of the technologies of film into the human body.

Scholars have recognized that early films like *A Trip to the Moon* created a "hybrid" and "multidimensional" space drawn from both theater, with its flats, traps, and flies, and cinema, where single shots merge into the "flow of action."[19] An overlooked element in this hybrid is a *choreographic space*, in which film attempts to represent the dimensions of the human body shaping space with patterned movement and exteriorizing emotion or conveying character through gesture. The intersection of choreographic space with cinematic and theatrical space is evident in the lunar scenes in *A Trip to the Moon*. With the early astronauts sleeping out of the way in the lower part of the screen, Méliès uses the upper part of the screen to provide some of the nonnarrative attractions for which he is famous. A comet travels across the lunar sky, followed by the appearance of the Big Dipper, its stars featuring the heads of popular Parisian dancers from the music hall. Phoebe, another showgirl/moon maiden, appears seated in the crescent moon, and a bearded man gestures angrily from a mock-up of Saturn, leading to a very theatrical snow flurry. These visual attractions are not crucial to the film's "action" and are partially derived from the theatrical space of burlesque and variety shows – where *A Trip to the Moon* was screened as one of the acts.[20] The lunar scenes use stage techniques within the cinematic medium, but they also remediate dance movement and dancers themselves. The theatrical flats merge with the cinematic superimposition as a dancer poses serenely on the stage flat of a crescent moon. The gestures of Saturn are the conventional expressions of anger in melodrama, and this gestural language was adapted as a primary mode of expression in silent film and dance.

When Saturn's flurry awakens the bold space explorers, they encounter dancing, mildly ominous Selenites (moon dwellers) who borrow their choreography from *féerie* operettas and popular jungle dances. They crouch on all fours and hop about in movements that adapt the choreographic images of primitive peoples to aliens. Méliès also took themes from adventure novels, especially Jules Verne's *From the Earth to the Moon* (1865) and H.G. Wells's *The First Men in the Moon* (1901) and from museum exhibitions of art and artifacts imported from France's extensive colonial holdings in Africa and the Pacific islands.[21] These imperial exhibits encouraged the late-nineteenth-century primitivism of artists like Paul Gauguin, who became the muse of Pablo Picasso and other modernists.[22] Ragtime music was introduced to Paris at the 1900 *Exposition universelle*, followed shortly thereafter by the Cakewalk and other so-called Negro dances.[23] Méliès's *A Trip to the Moon* makes an early cinematic entrance into this cultural milieu, which would soon be admiring Josephine Baker's dances and bouncing to the rhythms of that "jungle music" jazz.[24] In this context, the Selenite dances can be read as a gentle send-up of French primitivism.

The Selenites disappear when struck by Barbenfouillis's heroic umbrella, a spectacle created by stop-motion substitution splices. Méliès as Barbenfouillis wields his umbrella in a comedic sword dance, producing another gentle satire of the colonialist as magician. This was not Méliès's only dance on screen. His interest in the new hybrid of choreographic and cinematic space is evident in another 1902 film, *The Human Fly*, in which he plays a Russian dancer in a Cossack tunic who opens with an energetic *Kazatsky* dance. He then appears to run up and across the walls, where he performs somersaults, splits, handstands, and other acrobatics while well-attired ladies point and clap.[25] He also joins an extreme version of primitivism, in the figure of a fly crawling on the walls, to the orientalist magician from Europe's far east. The Ballets Russes would later exploit the fascination with the Orient upon their arrival in Paris in 1909 with ballets such as Michel Fokine's *Cléopâtre* (1909).

Posing for Hollywood

Better known today for spectacles and commercialization than for innovation, Hollywood was an important site of experiments in dance and film in the second decade of the twentieth century. As in Paris, many Hollywood films engaged and remediated orientalist and primitivist dance styles. One of the most influential Hollywood directors, D.W. Griffith, not only cast dancers in his films but also used dance schools to train his silent film stars. His famous *Intolerance* (1916) turned back to ancient times to comment on modernist culture, as did many other artworks of the period. The stories of the fall of ancient Babylon to Persia in 539 BCE and the Crucifixion of Jesus are juxtaposed with the 1572 St. Bartholomew's Day Massacre of Protestant Huguenots in France and a modern American conflict between workers and puritanical capitalists. Contemporaneous reviews suggest that audiences were far more interested in the orientalist spectacle of Babylon than in the modern critique of capitalism. "*Intolerance* Impressive," claimed *The New York Times* (September 6, 1916), touting the Babylonian story as the most masterful of the segments:

> It is the Babylonian portion of the film that will commend it to the great public. These pictures of the wals [sic] of Babylon ... of the great gates thronged with picturesque caravans, of the palace of Belshazzar with its myriad slaves and dancing girls, and of the siege and fall of the city are indeed masterpieces of the cine.[26]

The "dancing girls" were primarily cast from Denishawn Dance Company, and much of the company was featured in the repeated scenes of celebration on the Babylonian steps. The sequence opens with a cut to the Babylonian walls followed by a tracking shot that moves toward the dancers on the steps and brings viewers closer to the celebratory dance, finally positioning them within the throng of moving bodies. The camera then draws back slightly, as if to distance the viewer, and focuses on the pas de deux performed by a man and woman at the center of the steps.

The choreography performed on the steps creates exotic images by combining the movements and costumes of popular "Oriental" dances with poses derived from ancient statuary. The adaptation of these elements for film manipulates the three dance dimensions I have identified to enhance the exotic flavor of the choreography. The shot composition emphasizes the dancers' parallel legs and hips (as opposed to the turned-out positions of ballet) as they lunge forward and perform leg extensions with bent knees. The dancers in the chorus frequently turn their heads to a profile view and hold their arms and wrists bent at right angles, all positions that invoke the two-dimensional quality associated with ancient Mesopotamian and Egyptian art. This choreographed flattening of the body is exaggerated by the two-dimensional frame of film and by the camera shots from one angle, positioned directly in front of the dancers.

The cuts away from the steps and to the interior of the palace also slice parts of bodies from the screen. In the first cut, a woman dancing on a table is visible from her chest down while men gaze at her; other bodies are strewn about the ornate room in profligate postures. A second cut from the dance on the steps reveals only the knees of a seated woman before the light rises on her legs and the camera lifts to show her torso – but never her head – while other women bend as if in supplication. The segmented female bodies invoke damaged ancient sculptures with missing heads and other delicate body parts. They also call attention to film's ability to frame a body and literally cut it apart at a time when Griffith and other filmmakers were discovering the power of montage as a particularly cinematic organizational device. In the Babylonian subplot of *Intolerance*, the repeated dance scenes suggest that the eroticization of the female body, decadent sexual practices, and the court's excess contributed to the fall of Babylon. The juxtaposition of these exotic, partial bodies with shots of bodies clothed and moving in the styles of different times in the film's other subplots reinforces the message about the differences between cultures and the continuity of human intolerance.

Griffith's "masterpiece" depended on his collaboration with many dancers and choreographers, but particularly with the Denishawn Company founded by Ruth St. Denis and Ted Shawn in Hollywood in 1915. They specialized in choreography representing "exotic" cultures, a style St. Denis had been performing since her career-making *Radha* (1906) depicted the Hindu goddess celebrating and spiritualizing the five senses. This and other early dances were inspired, St. Denis claimed, by a poster featuring the goddess Isis in an advertisement for Egyptian Deities brand cigarettes. She saw the poster in 1904 while touring with the David Belasco theatrical *Du Barry* and first performed *Radha* at Proctor's Vaudeville in New York alongside a pugilist and a pack of trick monkeys.[27] The choreography she developed for *Radha* and other "exotic numbers" influenced the dancing in *Intolerance*. The Egyptian Deities anecdote moves from the

FIGURE 6 Ted Shawn in *Gnossienne*, by Witzel (1919). Denishawn Collection. Courtesy of the Jerome Robbins Dance Division, The New York Public Library for the Performing Arts, Astor, Lenox and Tilden Foundations

cigarette ad as an example of early twentieth-century consumer cultures to the orientalism and exoticism of popular vaudeville performance to modern aesthetic dance and finally film, bringing together many aspects of modernist culture discussed separately in this volume.

St. Denis's partner, Ted Shawn, also capitalized on the dance of other cultures and historical periods. *Japanese Spear Dance* (1919) imagines the movements of a samurai, and *Gnossienne* (1919) depicts a priest of ancient Crete worshipping a Snake Goddess. The latter piece, like the choreography for *Intolerance*, features a sequence of poses derived from ancient statues and frescoes, and Shawn whitened his body to make himself look even more like a statue come to life (Figure 6). This choreography reflects his interest in popular Delsartism, particularly in the statue posing the movement advocated as a training method for physical expression. American Delsartism was loosely based on the theories of François Delsarte (1811–1871), a French performer and teacher who developed a system of gestural expression in which poses, often derived from ancient art, were associated with a specific emotion. The practice of posing in

Delsarte classes and semiprivate theatricals was promoted as a regimen that would enable the performer to recover an "authentic" and "expressive" self that was supposedly present in ancient cultures.[28] Dancers like Shawn and St. Denis adapted the poses and the emphasis on classical art from Delsartism in pieces like *Gnossienne*. Ted Shawn's book about Delsarte, *Every Little Movement* (1954), claims he studied extensively with the influential Delsartean Henrietta Hovey and invited her to teach at the Denishawn school.[29] The next generation of modern dancers, including Martha Graham, Doris Humphrey, and Lester Horton, practiced Delsarte's gestural code and statue posing, as did many of Hollywood's silent film stars. Griffith asked actors such as Lillian and Dorothy Gish and Blanche Sweet to take Delsarte classes at Denishawn twice a week. There, they learned a code of gestures linked to specific emotions that they could use as the language for their silent film performances. Delsartism provided a training regimen for performers in dance, theater, and film, as well as for amateurs, primarily upper-class women, who studied Delsarte for self-cultivation. The extensive reach of the movement meant that Delsartism also trained audiences to *read* the meanings of gesture. Delsartism established a language of gesture that was adapted for use in many modernist media.

Influenced by Denishawn, popular Delsartean performance, and his own research in classical and Christian art, Griffith uses posed compositions throughout *Intolerance*, even in the episodes that did not cast dancers. The repeated interlude image of Lillian Gish as the woman who rocks the cradle, dressed in Greek-style robes with a veil, might have been taken from one of the Delsarte manuals featuring such pantomime-recitations as L. Blinn's "Rizpah" with poses by A.M. Morgenroth: the biblical mother of *Samuel 21* protects her sons' bodies from "beasts" and "dies crooning to and rocking an imaginary child."[30] The influence of Delsartism is most evident in the Babylonian and Judean chapters of *Intolerance*, but the modern American sequence also emphasizes emotional gestures and poses, with Mae Marsh featured on publicity posters in a version of the mother-protecting-her-child pose. Delsartism and dance made classical gestures and ancient cultures available for cinematic representation and particularly influenced acting techniques on silent film. The challenge of filming dance, for Griffith and others, also encouraged innovations in camera movement and montage, film's particular way of cutting and making moving bodies mean.

Le Sacre in Three Dimensions

Montage may have been the cinematic innovation that most profoundly transformed film aesthetics in the early twentieth century. Leaping a hundred years forward, 3D is likely to do the same. Just as Fuller's skirt projections achieved a version of 3D before the cinema, dance has been influential in the development of the new technology. The 2011 film *Pina* by German director Wim Wenders was touted as the "world's first 3D art house film" and "the first artistic masterpiece of 3-D cinema."[31] The dance documentary is a tribute to the choreographer Pina Bausch, who died in June 2009, two days before the rehearsal shoot and five days after being diagnosed with cancer. The film features four long works: *Vollmond* (*Full Moon*, originally choreographed in 2006), *Café Müller* (1978), *Kontakthof* (1978), and Bausch's 1975 version of that epitome of modernism, *Le Sacre du Printemps*. Bausch's work joins more than two hundred others inspired by the famous Ballets Russes production in the century after its riotous debut. Her *Le Sacre* is danced on a stage covered with black earth and crowded with thirty-two dancers, generally separated into groups of men and women. As they stomp, convulse, and fall, their bodies and flesh-colored costumes become smeared with dirt. A sacrificial maiden is chosen by one of the men, who forces her to wear a red dress and leads her to her death dance. The choreography comments on the misogyny submerged in our fascination with primitivism.

Bausch's work is often designated "modern dance" even as she is called a postmodern choreographer, a contradiction that reflects the ways dance troubles common periodizations of twentieth-century art. Bausch is also touted as a cinematic choreographer who translates techniques like montage and cross-fades into dance stage space.[32] She and Wenders had been discussing making a film together ever since they met in 1985. Only in 2007, when Wenders saw a 3D film of a U2 concert, did he believe there was a cinematic medium capable of capturing Bausch's choreography.[33] Even then, he had to delay for two years until 3D technology could document more than what he called "an attraction or a carnival ride."[34] "It was good enough for animation and blockbuster movies," Wenders said, "but to render movements naturally we had to wait."[35] Wenders suggests all new cinematic technologies initially promote what Gunning calls "attractions." Digital technology was first used in advertising and for special effects on expensive Hollywood films. Wenders points out, "At that time no one would have thought that digital cinema would ultimately save and re-invent documentary filmmaking. I think it will be similar for 3D technology."[36] *Pina* is a reinvention of the documentary, the dance film, *and* the cinematic tribute.

Wenders and his team used 3D technologies to cinematically represent each dance dimension: *formal pattern* or *shot composition*; *proximity, camera distance*, and *angle*; and *rhythm* or *tempo*. Two-dimensional film has struggled to accurately record the depth of motion through space and communicate, for example, *Le Sacre's* configurations of dancers in the foreground and background of the stage. To alter the viewer's proximity to the dancing bodies on film, Wenders and his 3D team developed "a long telescopic crane," which the 3D producer Erwin M. Schmidt described as a "giant dancing eye" that could track the dancers and position the viewer right on stage.[37] Alain Derobe, the creator of the crane prototype, pointed out, "The camera literally dances with them … Everyone had to know exactly where the dancers would move."[38] Wenders shot the film at two focal lengths, both quite wide so that they would "have the angle of our natural vision. Overall, we tried to follow as much as possible the physiology of human eyes," he claimed.[39] Imagining a shot composition that mimicked natural vision, Wenders disrupted the classical rules for filming dance, which were established in Hollywood in the 1930s: film from head to toe; no close-ups; hold takes for as long as possible. Wenders intercut the four ensemble pieces filmed on stage with solos and duets set outside in Wuppertal, Bausch's hometown, and close-ups on the immobile faces of dancers as they commented on Bausch's work in voiceover. His dancing camera could put the audience close enough to be engaged in a duet with a dancer, even inside her head, or take viewers outdoors.

As for the dimension of time, it might seem that the infamously difficult rhythms of Stravinsky's *Le Sacre* would govern the tempo of Bausch's choreography. Yet she adapted cinematic techniques to manipulate the experience of time; she used movement to produce an intense close-up–like focus on the red dress of the Chosen Maiden and included long periods of stillness, as when the man lies on his stomach before choosing the maiden. At other moments, quick entrances and exits give the choreography a feeling of montage. As Wenders worked to document this cinematic choreography, he was also concerned with tempo and fought with the American Film Institute to allow him to play *Pina* at 50 frames per second rather than the standard 24. At the faster speed, the jerkiness of the pan shots disappeared, as did the occasional multiplied limbs of the dancers, which 3D could aggravate. The Institute would not alter the standard, just one example of the confrontation between aesthetics and the standardization of the cinema.[40]

On April 3, 2013, as celebrations of the centennial of *Le Sacre* were taking place all over the world, yet another version was staged at the Palace of Arts in Budapest. Klaus Obermaier's *Le Sacre* was billed as "an interactive real-time generated stereoscopic dance and music project."[41] First performed in 2006, years before James Cameron's *Avatar* initiated the 3D craze, Obermaier immerses his Chosen Maiden in a computer-generated virtual world, where she dances with her own computerized avatars in curiosity, delight, and terror. If Nijinsky and Stravinsky's *Le Sacre* staged modernism's fascination with primitive rituals and the deadly tributes paid for the return of spring and survival of the community, Bausch's version suggests that the violent ritual had more to do with gender than nature, and Obermaier takes up the danger of sacrifice to the new rituals of technology. Today, the virtualization of our communities, relationships, and even bodies prevents us from celebrating spring's return. In adapting *Le Sacre* one more time, Obermaier highlights the cyclical nature of modernity's crises. We worship new technologies for the same reasons we worship old religions: the promise of a return to utopia, the garden of Eden, or a perfect spring.

Dance in the modernist period has correctly been associated with that utopian desire for a return to a primitive paradise. Dance also enabled the remediation of this story and its exotic images on film and in other art forms, even as dance challenged film technology's ability to document choreography's formal structure, manipulation of the body's proximity to viewers, and rhythms. This challenge has spurred the development of new cinematic techniques, from stop-motion substitution splices to tracking shots, montage, and now 3D. Rather than refusing the technologies of modernity, dance has been their ambivalent but consistent partner.

Notes

1 Caroline and Charles H. Caffin, *Dancing and Dancers of Today: The Modern Revival of Dancing as an Art* (New York: Dodd, Mead, 1912), 155.
2 For a similar argument, see Erin Brannigan's *Dancefilm: Choreography and the Moving Image* (New York: Oxford University Press, 2011).
3 See Susan Stanford Friedman, "Definitional Excursions: The Meanings of Modern/ Modernity/Modernism" *Modernism/Modernity*. 8.3 (2001): 493–513.

4 See Rhonda K. Garelick, *Electric Salome: Loïe Fuller's Performance of Modernity* (Princeton: Princeton University Press, 2009).

5 See Richard Taruskin, "A Myth of the Twentieth Century: *The Rite of Spring*, the Tradition of the New, and 'The Music Itself,'" *Modernism/Modernity* 2.1 (1995): 1–26. Peter Hill details Stravinsky's initial admiration for Nijinsky and subsequent disparagement in *Stravinsky: The Rite of Spring* (Cambridge: Cambridge University Press, 2000), 115–16.

6 Christopher Innes, "Modernism in Drama," in *The Cambridge Companion to Modernism*, ed. Michael Levenson (Cambridge: Cambridge University Press, 1999), xiv, 141.

7 Ballet, modern aesthetic dance, and other forms all influenced each other in the period. Ballets Russes star Nijinsky cited Duncan among the dancers he admired, claiming, "Isadora Duncan is a very great artist … Before her time dancing was under the restraint of an exacting technique. Isadora has danced to give freedom to movement, and has broadened the dancer's horizon." Millicent Hodson, "Ritual Design in the New Dance: Nijinsky's Choreographic Method," *Dance Research* 4.1 (Spring 1986): 68.

8 Rev. G.F. Pentecost's *The Christian and the Modern Dance* was published by the Mennonite Publishing Company in 1884, selected and reprinted as "The Christian and the Modern Dance," *Vision: A Magazine for Youth* II.12 (December 1889): 545–46.

9 Quoted in Thomas A. Faulkner, *The Lure of the Dance* (Los Angeles: Kessinger, 1916), 89.

10 Hugo Münsterberg, *The Photoplay: A Psychological Study* (New York and London: Appleton, 1916).

11 For clarity, I will call the tradition following Duncan "modern aesthetic dance."

12 Shaemas O'Sheel, "Isadora Duncan, Artist," in *Art of the Dance*, ed. Sheldon Cheney (New York: Theatre Arts, 1969): 31–36, 34. See also Isadora Duncan, "The Dance of the Greeks," in Cheney, 92–96.

13 *Remediation* describes the transfer of performance material between media but with substantial alteration based in the representational capabilities and structural properties of each medium. See Jon McKenzie, "Smart Media at the University of Wisconsin–Madison," *Enculturation: A Journal of Rhetoric, Writing and Culture* 15 (2013), http://www.enculturation.net/smart-media; "Towards a Sociopoetics of Interface Design: etoy, eToys, and TOYWAR," *Strategies: A Journal of Theory, Culture and Politics* 14.1 (2001): 121–38.

14 Tom Gunning, "The Cinema of Attractions: Early Film, Its Spectator and the Avant-Garde" in *Early Cinema: Space, Frame, Narrative*, ed. Thomas Elsaesser (London: BFI, 1990), 56–62.

15 The clip of the Lumière film called *Danse Serpentine* is available, along with a useful timeline of dance on film, at: http://www.dancefilms.org/resources/dance-and-media-timeline/.

16 Julie Townsend, *The Choreography of Modernism in France: La Danseuse 1830–1930* (Oxford: Legenda, 2011), 88–89.

17 The seventeen-minute film is held in the Museum of Modern Art, New York: http://www.moma.org/collection/object.php?object—id=91485.

18 *A Trip to the Moon* is available in a restored, original, hand-colored copy released by Flicker Alley (2012) and on YouTube.

19 Tom Gunning, "Shooting into Outer Space: Reframing Modern Vision," in Matthew Solomon's *Fantastic Voyages of the Cinematic Imagination: Georges Méliès's* TRIP TO THE MOON (Albany: State University of New York Press, 2011), 103.

20 Ibid.

21 Ian Christie, "First-Footing on the Moon: *Méliès*'s Debt to Verne and Wells and His Influence in Great Britain," in Matthew Solomon's *Fantastic Voyages of the Cinematic Imagination: Georges Méliès's* Trip to the Moon (Albany: State University of New York Press, 2011), 65–80.

22 For a discussion of Gauguin and colonial artifacts, see Jean-François Staszak's "Primitivism and the Other: History of Art and Cultural Geography" *GeoJournal* 60.4 (2004): 353–64.

23 For the Parisian response to African art and African American music, see Jody Blake's *Le Tumulte noir: Modernist Art and Popular Entertainment in Jazz Age Paris, 1900–1930* (University Park: Pennsylvania State University Press, 1999).

24 The term appears in Walter Kingsley and William Morrison Patterson's "Why 'Jazz' Sends Us Back to the Jungle. A Broadway Ethnologist Tells the Savage Origin of this 'Delirium Tremens of Syncopation,'" published in *Current Opinion* (1918). Quoted in Sieglinde Lemke's *Primitivist Modernism: Black Culture and the Origins of Transatlantic Modernism* (New York: Oxford University Press, 1998), 62.

25 Natasha Elena Staller discusses Méliès's performance and innovative camera tricks in *A Sum of Destructions: Picasso's Cultures and the Creation of Cubism* (New Haven: Yale University Press, 2001): 151–54.

26 "'Intolerance' Impressive: D.W. Griffith's New Picture is a Stupendous Spectacle," *The New York Times* (September 6, 1916), online archive, http://query.nytimes.com/mem/archive-free/pdf?res=9501E1DF143BE633A25755C0A96F9C946796D6CF.

27 Jane Desmond, "Dancing out the Difference: Cultural Imperialism and Ruth St. Denis's 'Radha' of 1906," *Signs* 17.1 (1991): 38.

28 This section is adapted from my book, Carrie J. Preston, *Modernism's Mythic Pose: Gender, Genre, Solo Performance* (New York: Oxford University Press, 2011). See also Nancy Lee Chalfa Ruyter, *The Cultivation of Body and Mind in Nineteenth-Century American Delsartism* (Westport: Greenwood, 1999).

29 Ted Shawn, *Every Little Movement* (New York: Dance Horizons, 1954).

30 Howell L. Piner, *Werner's Readings and Recitations* No. 23 (New York: Werner, 1899), 180.

31 *Pina: A film for Pina Bausch by Wim Wenders*, http://www.pina-film.de/en/.David Jays, "Dancing into a New Dimension," *Sunday Times*, April 10, 2011, http://www.wim-wenders.com/news—reel/2011/05-May/SundayTimes.pdf.

32 Brannigan, *Dancefilm*, 4–5.

33 Jeffrey Overstreet, "Learning to Read a Dance (in 3D!)," in *Image* (February 10, 2012), http://imagejournal.org/page/blog/learning-to-read-a-dance-in-3d.

34 Steven Pill, "State of Grace: An Interview with Wim Wenders," in *British Journal of Photography* (May 17, 2011), 27–33.

35 Wim Wenders, "New Cinematic Territory 3D: Interview with Wim Wenders," *Pina: A Film for Pina Bausch*, http://www.pina-film.de/en/about-3D.html.

36 Wenders, "New Cinematic Territory 3D," http://www.pina-film.de/en/about-3D.html.

37 Erwin M. Schmidt, "3D Producer Erwin M. Schmidt Talks About the Production Process," *Pina: A Film for Pina Bausch by Wim Wenders*: http://www.pina-film.de/en/about-3D.html.

38 Scott Wilkinson, "Pina 3D Dazzles," *Home Theater* (February, 21, 2012), http://www.hometheater.com/content/pina-3d-dazzles.

39 Wenders, "New Cinematic Territory 3D," http://www.pina-film.de/en/about-3D. html.

40 Ibid.

41 Klaus Obermaier and Ars Electronica Futurelab, featuring Julia Mach, "Le Sacre du Printemps," by Igor Stravinsky" (2006). Most recently performed at the Budapest Spring Festival, Budapest, Hungary (April 3, 2013), http://www.exile.at/sacre/ project.html.

9
_____

Visual Art

*Presented as a list because modernism can be understood as beginning with doubt
so radical as to necessitate the prioritizing of method, what follows is a mimetic
attempt to highlight some key aspects of modernist visual art as fractured,
historical, and vast: multimedia (painting, collage, sculpture, photography),
international, and stretching from the nineteenth century through the
mid-twentieth. This account begins with painting and ends with photography.
It moves between the declarative and the anecdotal as a means of capturing both
ken and idiosyncrasy. Some links are chronological, some thematic.*

Thirteen Ways

1. Just as Wallace Stevens's poem "Thirteen Ways of Looking at a
Blackbird" suggests the uneasy relation between looking and writing, visual art is beset by two distinct, contradictory stories about modernism.

Story one: Modernism is the purification of a medium – the respective
arts will come to terms with their respective limits, and in those limits,
their possibilities; and thus flourish as purified.

Story two: Modernism entails nudging at or even shoving beyond the
hitherto accepted boundaries between the arts.

For the first story of modernism, we have the purification of the
medium. In this tale's most famous version, the critic Clement Greenberg
writes,

> The history of avant-garde painting is that of a progressive surrender
> to the resistance of its medium; which resistance consists chiefly
> in the flat picture plane's denial of efforts to "hole through" it for
> realistic perspective space. In making this surrender, painting not

only got rid of imitation . . . but also of realistic imitation's corollary confusion between painting and sculpture. . . . But most important of all, the picture plane itself grows shallower and shallower, flattening out and pressing together the fictive planes of depth until they meet as one upon the real and material plane which is the actual surface of the canvas.[1]

Painting is about flatness. This is medium specificity (and the first word is a noun, not an adjective). Modernist painting was to come to terms with what made painting *painting*: canvas and paint. Modernism entails a revolutionary and inexorable understanding of the terms of its production (Marx lurks). This is why, in one long history of modernism, Jackson Pollock for Greenberg and others presented such a breakthrough: even as for Greenberg the nineteenth-century Impressionists "[left] the eye under no doubt as to the fact that the colors they used were made of paint that came from pots or tubes,"[2] Pollock's twentieth-century abstraction stopped us from looking through the canvas as one would a window, forcing us to see what was before our eyes. No more windows: behold the canvas!

In the second story of modernism, Horace is right; "as painting, so poetry" *(ut pictora poesis)*. Simonides, via Plutarch, and echoed by the poet and Asian art historian Lawrence Binyon (who "has said that a precisely identical saying is proverbial among the Chinese"): "Painting is mute poetry, and poetry a speaking picture."[3] The arts are mingled. The muses after all were related, with Calliope (epic poetry) from the same bloodline as her sister Terpsichore (dance and song). "[T]he movement belonging to the aesthetic regime, which supported the dream of artistic novelty and fusion between art and life subsumed under the idea of modernity, tends to erase the specificities of the arts and to blur the boundaries that separate them from each other and from ordinary experience."[4]

The "sister arts" theory, buttressed by interarts analogies and the "union of body and soul, picture and word,"[5] underpins one of the most well-known examples of the crossing of the visual and literary arts: the "literary impressionism" that the writer Ford Madox Ford espoused.[6] Ford's literary school sprang from a painterly source (as did Ford) and was demonstrated by Joseph Conrad, who had stated in 1897 that writing's ultimate mission is "before all, to make you *see!*"[7] In crossbreeding verbal and visual, Ford was echoing the mixed origins of his source. Painterly Impressionism began, as the poet Stéphane Mallarmé pointed out, as a "nameless school" that included the literary, with the writer Émile Zola as its exemplar.[8]

2. The avant-garde shocks. "The avant-garde" can designate either an artistic current like Dada or, more generally, art ahead of the cultural curve. The militarism of the term – the avant-garde is the advance guard, the troops out in front – along with its Frenchness suggests the force (and foreignness) of that aesthetic assault. Debate continues as to whether shock is possible as a repeated event. Cubism's multiple perspectives and jumpy geometries of negative space; Futurism's 1909 command to "destroy the museums"[9] in order to make way for canvases that capture time – a dog wags its tail on the canvas in the course of frantic, multipawed perambulation (Giacomo Balla's *Dynamism of A Dog on a Leash* [1912]) – and sound (Umberto Boccioni's *The Street Enters the House* [1911]); "an explosion in a shingle factory," as Marcel Duchamp's 1912 *Nude Descending a Staircase* was termed, drawing crowds to the 1913 New York Armory's Cubist Room, aka "The Chamber of Horrors"[10]: each bears witness to an economy of surprise. In 1917, Duchamp reshocked the Society of Independent Artists, which ostensibly accepted any artwork for exhibition by anyone with $6, by submitting a urinal signed by one "R. Mutt" and titled "Fountain." They declined. This wasn't art; it was "a familiar article of bathroom furniture," as the *New York Herald* delicately phrased things.[11] Twenty thousand people attended the show in which it did not appear.

3. One way modernism shocks is by bringing together the hitherto distinct categories of life and art, as with Duchamp's "readymade." "Hitherto" in the visual life of Western Europe is best captured by the French Salon system, for it embodied institutionalized art.

The Paris Salon was the juried biennial exhibition run by the Academy of Fine Arts, an outgrowth of the Royal Academy of Painting and Sculpture (founded 1648). The Salon constituted national aesthetic standards. It was "the first public space for art in the modern sense";[12] there was no charge for entry, and the public could absorb what was deemed fine art.

United primarily by the problems each artist had with this institutionalized system, the first truly modernist painterly avant-garde was Impressionism – a word taken from a painting named almost flippantly (Claude Monet's 1872 *Impression: Sunrise*)[13] and first used derisively, by a journalist now remembered for being forgotten. In reviewing the 1874 show put on by *La Société anonyme coopérative des Artistes – Peintres, Sculpteurs, Graveurs, etc.* (Cooperative Association of painters, sculptors, engravers, etc.), which included Paul Cézanne, Edgar Degas, Monet, Berthe

Morisot, and Camille Pissarro, Louis Leroy outsources his contempt by inventing a companion driven mad by what he sees. "In vain I sought to revive his expiring reason... but the horrible fascinated him." The review ends with the madman mistaking a guard for a portrait of a guard, critiquing it on the grounds of anatomical exactitude ("From the front, he has two eyes... and a nose... and a mouth!"), breaking into a war dance, and becoming the aesthetic itself, "crying in a strangled voice: 'Hi-ho! I am impression on the march, the avenging palette knife, the *Boulevard des Capucines* of Monet, the *Maison du pendu* and the *Modern Olympia* of Cézanne. Hi-ho! Hi-ho!'"[14] In having his interlocutor mistake a human for a painting (the show's guard "has two eyes") and having the madman dehumanize himself as a principle ("I am impression on the march"), Leroy showed that life had become art, twice. This was the review of what became known as the first Impressionist show.

Thus "The very idea of the avant-garde ... was inseparable from a commercial system of investment and exhibition."[15]

4. Exhibition means display. Stacking paintings floor to ceiling, "salon-style" presentation, was typical in the nineteenth century, as it had been for centuries. (The expectation of a high hanging led to compensation for that angle of view; bring the painting down to eye level and you meet some very long-legged eighteenth-century individuals.) As Oscar Wilde's Lord Henry summarizes the experience of picture viewing at one of the most important sites in late–nineteenth-century London, "Whenever I have gone [to the Royal Academy of Arts, founded 1768], there have been either so many people that I have not been able to see the pictures, which was dreadful, or so many pictures that I have not been able to see the people, which was worse."[16] Worse than Wilde's worse was seeing (barely) one's painting "skied," hung so high as to be virtually unviewable, as happens in Zola's 1886 novel *L'Œuvre* with the Cézanne/Manet character.

For that first Impressionist exhibit, Degas wanted his paintings displayed in two neat horizontal rows, allowing breathing room and a more direct view; the *Société anonyme* hanging committee, headed by Renoir, agreed. This suggests what it can mean to have artists rather than academicians in charge, prioritizing the manner of view rather than the amount of paintings one can cram into a room. It wasn't the only difference. French Salon walls were red, a tradition with which the avant-garde would break. The Impressionists would coordinate wall colors with their paintings, the Neo-Impressionists employed a "neutral gray," and by the 1920s, when the founding director of New York's new Museum of Modern Art (est. 1929) Alfred H. Barr, Jr., travelled with his assistant (the not-yet-famous architect Philip Johnson) to German galleries, the two men would export the wide spacing and eye-level positioning of paintings to MoMA, "hanging works on off-white 'monk's cloth' and later moving to walls painted bright white, in a clean architectural setting with no decorative elements to distract the eye."[17]

The "white-cube" ethos has remained largely in place for modern museums. It bespeaks the changing modes of comportment expected from viewers. The fact that earlier one might be picnicking in a museum room, or that a gallery, like a private home, might allow people "to move the furniture wherever they like,"[18] or find refuge on "the great circular divan which at that period occupied the centre of the Salon Carré, in the Museum of the Louvre," as does a Henry James character – all embody alternative ways of moving in the public spaces of display.[19]

Modes of display differ too based on purpose: Alfred Barnes (1872–1951) was clear that his spectacular Pennsylvania collection of modern art was not a museum; it was an educational institution, closed in his lifetime for the most part to the general public. The paintings were grouped in order to emphasize not a chronological history of art but a primarily formal means of looking that cultivated appreciation – so a curvy Renoir displayed beneath a curvy door hinge pressed directly onto the wall is par for the educatory course. On the other hand, Isabelle Stewart Gardner (1840–1924) would prohibit any sketching, note taking, or instructional material in her collection, which became Boston's Fenway Court museum; *Pense Moult, Parle Peu, Ecris Rien* – "Think Much, Speak Little, Write Nothing" – was one of her mottos. The body would absorb even at the subliminal level, so the sound of a fountain splashing was as much a part of the experience as the painting or sculpture or desk on which one's eye falls. Living with art entails a different level of engagement still; in the mid-twentieth century, Manhattan's 151 Central Park West, the home of Ben and Pat Heller, housed one of the most famous private collections of modern abstract art (alongside pre-Columbian, ancient, and African sculpture), including important work by Jackson Pollock, starting with *One: Number 31, 1950*. At the point of selling *Blue Poles* to the Australian National Gallery, Heller would remark of that Pollock painting, "It is very different in a home." Its departure was toasted with a 1928 burgundy, veal, and a chocolate mousse – in another room. "[W]ith the painting no longer being mine, we didn't want to risk any damage to it."[20] The daily brings distraction. "Visitors to his home could not have studied the paintings under what we, today [2013], would consider ideal conditions: they would see them partially obscured, their focus fragmented by the competing claims of the decor as a whole. Assuming it were a social occasion, rather than a study tour, they would likely glance at them in an even more distracted manner."[21]

The juxtaposition of daily life with the artwork reveals not just two aesthetic strata (is this fine art or decoration?) but two phenomenologies of looking. One takes attention and distraction as distinct; another understands them as part of the same economy. The question of how to look revolves around, as Merleau-Ponty said, eye and mind; aesthetics has been for centuries a "science of sensual cognition."[22] Even while "aesthetics is born as a discourse of the body,"[23] the desire to escape its confines may underlie a purified account of attention. Visual modernism can take the body as its point of liberation or as the mind's meat: food for thought.

5. Exhibition is a hair's breadth from spectacle. Édouard Manet's 1882 *Un Bar aux Folies-Bergère* (*A Bar at the Folies-Bergère*) is a quintessentially modernist painting: it demands to be looked at, asks what it means to see, and appears to look back – in both senses of "appears": the painting "seems to" (which suggests it may not look back) and "comes into being in order to" (which suggests it exists as a function of looking). While all paintings entail looking, or fantasies of seeing, not all of them force the process to its surface. The painting resolves looking into an enterprise – both in the sense of undertaking and commerce – that makes the process of seeing literally a tricky business (Figure 7).[24]

The painting is of the famous café-concert hall in Paris. The Folies-Bergère charged admission and was therefore on a slightly higher plane (we are on its second floor, as it happens) than other café-concerts, with its décor and stage acts accordingly ritzier (or gaudier). A young woman leans on a marble countertop, her gaze direct. Before her range bottles of alcohol: Champagne (the foil tops announce this), beer. With its red triangle, the Bass Ale label became an early triumph in the marriage of marketing and art; it was the first to register under the UK 1875–76 Trademark Registration Act. The label's geometry was an opportunity for abstraction that would continue to appeal to artists; while in the throes of Cubism, Pablo Picasso would repeatedly depict the image.[25] Manet has signed his name and given the date on the corner of the bottle[26] label to

FIGURE 7 Édouard Manet, *Un Bar aux Folies-Bergère* (1881–82). The Samuel Courtauld Trust, the Courtauld Gallery, London

the furthest left; the rhyme between modern art and marketing is clearly a point of remark.

Further, the woman offers her services, which may or may not include her body. Par for the café-concert course. The writer Joris-Karl Huysmans would be less amazed by the "gaggle of whores" at the Folies-Bergère than the skill with which they used the press of the audience to titillate potential customers.[27] The bottle that Manet signed, if an *apéritif*, would have rhymed with the slang *"apéritive,"* defined by an 1889 slang dictionary as "a woman of easy virtue who was to the high-class hooker what the chrysalis is to the butterfly";[28] the joke rode on metonymy, with female prostitutes in bars asking men to buy them an *apéritif*, an overture to an overture. Whether enticing for a price or blasé and depersonalized – the exemplary metropolitan subject[29] – she continues to evade us precisely by looking straight on.

Her name was Suzon. She tended bar and worked as a model. Manet saw her on site, where he made preliminary sketches, and hired her to pose at the bar he assembled in his studio.[30] Even as she remains "invisible"[31] (was she or was she not a prostitute?), her archetype's historical contours have been sketched.[32] Most importantly, as Richard Shiff points out, "In the literature on modernity, the concept of prostitution – etymologically, a setting-before, a (visible) displaying or offering of oneself – has traditionally been linked to commodification; hence to 'spectacle' and the production of desire through representation."[33]

The spectacle of the female and/as commodity is mirrored by the spectacle for which the Folies-Bergère was officially known: its stage acts. The Hanlon-Lees, an English troupe with a breathtaking repertoire of acrobatic daredevilry, aerial juggling, and madcap skits, performed there, as would Loïe Fuller, Mistinguett, and Josephine Baker. The "café-spectacle" could feature acrobatics, animal acts, ballet. On the upper left of Manet's canvas, tiny green-slippered legs balance on a trapeze. They are easy to overlook (or underlook): the official spectacle, however spectacular, is denied full view. A woman with high-powered spectacles – opera glasses – observes the stage (or something else) that exceeds the painting's frame. We have all that, and the world (through windows, the street is visible), through the mirror behind the bartender.

This mirror captures the attention of viewers most of all. Its reflection has a male customer standing more or less where we are; the female's reflection is askew; the bottles on the counter do not align with the bottles reflected. When the painting was shown in the 1882 Salon, critics complained. "[A]s to the lack of correspondence between the reflected objects and their images, we shall not insist on these things: they are lacunae which are common to these Impressionist gentlemen, who have excellent reasons for treating drawing, modelling, and perspective with disdain."[34] Critics still argue over how the scene might be staged so as to resolve things optically: putting us at an oblique angle to the counter, having the customer to the left of the female, angling the female's body in terms of the counter so as to face us, not him.[35] Problems remain.

One historian, however, has quietly noted that the same "discarding [of] conventional perspective" was "common" "in fashion illustrations from the 1830s onward"; "an 'illogical' mirror view" could show the back of an outfit. He refers to (but does not reproduce) the following image from an April 1835 fashion magazine in an article instructing one on the latest outfits when you go off to the races at fashionable Longchamp (Figure 8).[36]

FIGURE 8 "Modes de Long-champs," in *Petit Courrier des Dames, Journal des Modes,* April 20, 1835, between pages 170 and 171

(Manet repeatedly painted those races from 1864 to 1872, showing its speeding horses and the elegant crowd of observers.[37] One *dressed* for it.)

The Folies-Bergère had first been a department store.[38]

In displaying spectacle from every angle, Manet got it exactly right.

6. Exhibitionism is a hair's breadth from the psychoanalytic body (the collective drawing game the Surrealists played was called the Exquisite Corpse), and modernist visual art can embody the world of the mind. See, for example, the Surrealist fetishizing of the unconscious discovered by

FIGURE 9 Méret Oppenheim, *Object* (Paris, 1936) Fur-covered cup, saucer, and spoon, Cup 4 3/8" (10.9 cm) in diameter; saucer 9 3/8" (23.7 cm) in diameter; spoon 8" (20.2 cm) long, overall height 2 7/8" (7.3 cm). Purchase. © 2014 Artists Rights Society (ARS), New York / ProLitteris, Zurich. Photo Credit: Digital Image © The Museum of Modern Art/Licensed by SCALA / Art Resource, NY

Freud. "Dream and reality ... seemingly so contradictory" will resolve, according to Surrealism's founder André Breton.[39] As its etymology makes plain, sur-realism is the world above the real; the everyday is made strange by Méret Oppenheim's furry teacup (Figure 9).

On the other end of the spectrum of the mind's body is abstraction. In the 1940s, the Abstract Expressionist Ad Reinhardt, later famous for his black paintings (they're not), drew a wickedly smart series of "Art Comics" under the aegis of "How to Look"; two were "How to View High (Abstract) Art" and "How to Look at Low (Surrealist) Art." "The only committed modernist to tease out-of-school"[40] opposed the two currents, with abstraction on top, of course: "The surrealist claims his dream world is more interesting than your dull, nasty, everyday one."[41] Abstraction, on the other hand, is pitched as the alternative to being reminded of New Jersey.

The roots are rhizomatic. Wilhelm Worringer's best-selling German art-historical treatise *Abstraction and Empathy* (1907) was picked up by the critic T.E. Hulme and conveyed to artists including Jacob Epstein, Ezra Pound, and Wyndham Lewis in London in 1914, connecting Egyptian art to Cubism via Cézanne and vaunting "a new geometrical art": "You will find artists expressing admiration for engineer's drawings, where the lines are clean, the curves all geometrical, and the colour … gradated absolutely mechanically. You will find a sculptor … expressing admiration for the hard clean surface of a piston rod." Abstraction had a heritage in "Byzantine art" and "Indian sculpture."[42]

In the course of purifying the medium, Reinhardt would invoke another one: "Because music is the most abstract of the arts, abstract painting is often compared to chamber music and jazz."[43]

7. There are two stories about modernism. They are contradictory.

Story one: While its birthplace differs – the frontal and shameless ("the French for 'shameless,' *effrontée,* suggests a play on the notion of facing"[44]) stare of Manet's *Olympia* from an increasingly thinning picture plane, the corpse-planted trenches of the Somme, "the first heave" of breaking the pentameter,[45] the audience's uproar spurred by the 1913 premiere of *The Rite of Spring* – modernism emerges from rupture. The new is its watchword.

Story two: Because modernism depends on the new, it is in fact indebted to the old: Pound's ideogram is drawn from classical Chinese sources; Manet "did not do anything without thinking of Velázquez and Hals [1599–1660, 1582–1666]. When he painted a fingernail, he would remember that Hals never let the nails extend beyond the fingers themselves, and proceeded likewise."[46] The word "modern" is from Latin, deriving from an adverb meaning a new way of doing things, and the Quarrel of the Ancient and the Moderns happened in the seventeenth century.

Just so, primitivism cuts both ways. Witness, as many did not wish to do, Picasso's 1907 *Les Demoiselles d'Avignon,* with its African-mask visages as women's faces. Whether it was the British Vorticists' reckoning themselves "modern primitives" – with the artist Sophia Brzeska referring to her lover Henri Gaudier-Brzeska as a "savage messiah," and his direct-carving the phallic *Hieratic Head of Ezra Pound* – Man Ray repeatedly photographing the bohemian It girl of the Left Bank Kiki de Montparnasse alongside an African Baule Mblo mask; Nancy Cunard's stacking of tribal bracelets; Worringer's attribution of abstraction to the ancient Egyptian; or the American collector and educator Alfred Barnes collecting Native American textiles, pueblo water jars, and African sculpture alongside the "wild beasts" known as the Fauves, primitivism is a key aspect of the modernist visual arts. Eurocentric and racialist as the term is, it is imperative to recognize that as much as modernism has been and will be associated with industrialism, the machine is in a garden.

See Brancusi. His sculpture *Golden Bird*, stripped of plumage, echoes an earlier mode of making, "bare as the brow of Osiris."[47] Its futuristic hyperpolished metal rests, literally and metaphorically, on a stacked series of pedestals, which must be made of wood or stone – crude but not rude. All humans are base at base: look down. Janus-faced, modernist visual art looks backward to look forward.

8. The fate of realism in the age of modernism unveils the slippery relation between subjectivity and objectivity. By the time modernism gets done with them, it is difficult to unthread the two. This blurring had been going on for some time. Even while "there is no atlas in any field that does not pique itself on its accuracy, on its fidelity to fact," by the eighteenth century, the artifice of objectivity caused no anxiety. The scientific illustration of an eighteenth-century flower is of no actual flower: it is a composite, a "morphological prototype,"[48] assembled according to the maker's eye. Subjectivity is also composite. Martin Jay remarks on "the permeability of the boundary between the 'natural' and the 'cultural' component in what we call vision."[49]

This "permeability" helps account for multiple forms of modernist realism. The major movement in late–nineteenth-century American painting was termed realist; Weimar avant-gardists invoked a New Objectivity. The trompe l'oeil of John F. Peto and William Harnett and the grotesque exactitudes of Otto Dix and George Grosz are worlds apart, yet both reference a world it is possible to identify.

And disavow. For all its dazzling feats of verisimilitude, American realism's prestige steadily waned. By midcentury, Abstract Expressionism *was* modernism; realism was middlebrow. Andrew Wyeth, after Edward Hopper the most distinguished realist painter of his day, "came to represent middle-class values and ideals that modernism claimed to reject, so that arguments about his work extended beyond painting to societal splits along class, geographical and educational lines."[50] But modernism, we see now, includes the marketplace and the popular (Norman Rockwell). What we have understood as modernism continues to change. We see facts differently; the subjectivity of objectivity is what modernism shows us again and again.

9. Decoration and utility seem similarly opposed but can be as tightly interlaced as the threading of a corset. The Austrian journalist and architect Adolf Loos protested the florid heavings of Art Nouveau, crying out in 1908 that ornament was crime – aesthetic, economic,

moral. The German Bauhaus ("house of construction") would follow suit, with Walter Gropius founding a workshop system in 1919 that emphasized the aesthetic of use. "Today, something is beautiful if its form serves its function," writes the painter and photographer László Moholy-Nagy in 1923.[51] The point was to seek the total artwork – hence the unification of art and craft, or art and industrialism: "The artist is an exalted craftsman."[52] Art and life are again joined.

The Omega Workshops in England – Roger Fry, taken by William Morris's nineteenth-century ideal of art "by the people and for the people" – tried the same thing in 1912, putting painters to work on making chairs. The chairs broke. On the other hand, it was the last time that the Bloomsbury Group would be in the same room with what became the Vorticists. Vanessa Bell's book covers for Hogarth Press, founded by her sister and brother-in-law Virginia and Leonard Woolf, are visual events, putting an artwork in your hands.

"Stop color patching on moth-eaten canvasses. Stop decorating the easy life of the bourgeoisie," shouted the Left Front of the Arts (*LEF*) in 1923, Soviet Constructivists who helpfully gave the address to which reader-converts could report.[53] No one dare drink from Oppenheim's teacup, but the Soviet State Porcelain Factory (formerly the Imperial Porcelain Factory) served its propaganda on a plate; the Bolshevik government was short on paper, but long on porcelain. "Science Must Serve People," reads Sergei Chekhonin's 1918 plate, edging sickle and hammer alongside flowers.[54]

10. The word can be a visual event. Manifestos took typography as a means of grabbing the eye, with sans-serif facilitating speedy reading. Under the aegis of Italian Futurism, the word was set free (*parole in libertà*); "Words-in-Freedom (Premier Récord)" (1914) has its *"moi"*'s dotting a page featuring jumping horses, automobiles, and spiraling airplanes whose speeds are recorded. "The poem-painting" is "a kind of advertising poster."[55] Sonia Delaunay's and Blaise Cendrars's accordion-pleated art book *La Prose du Transsibérien et de la petite Jehanne de France* (*Prose of the Trans-Siberian and of little Jehanne of France*, 1913) is simultaneous repeatedly: telling the story of a railroad journey and time, displaying it as "poems, simultaneous colors,"[56] and interpenetrating color and word. Delaunay and her painter husband's theory of simultaneity came from Michel Eugène Chevreul's 1839 color treatise. Delaunay (1885–1979) painted, opened her Boutique Simultané in the 1920s, and designed textiles for

the fashion-forward Metz & Co. department store in Amsterdam from the 1930s through the 1960s. Among her clients was Elaine Lustig Cohen (b. 1927), who, along with her husband, brought modernist design to the dust jacket.

11. Godless critics notwithstanding, modernist visual art is not adamantly secular. See Frieda Kahlo, Kazimir Malevich, Barnett Newman's *Stations of the Cross*, Marc Chagall, Agnes Martin.

12. The entire story of modern visual art could be told in terms of Paul Cézanne. He was represented at the first Impressionist show and the 1910 Post-Impressionist show at London's Grafton Gallery, which some critics have supposed as the occasion for Virginia Woolf's clever proposal that "on or about December 1910 human character changed";[57] he was called upon by Cubists, Fauves, and the twenty-first–century artist Banksy: "All pictures painted inside, in the studio, will never be as good as those done outside."[58] Particularly in light of the relocation of the world's largest Cézanne collection to a space that makes the work appear newly washed (the Barnes Foundation, now in Philadelphia), he will be reevaluated. There are blues you have never seen before.

It is rumored Cézanne took twenty minutes between brushstrokes. Or an hour. Or hours. "He could also paint *fast.*"[59]

13. Fast and slow, having shimmered into existence with modernism itself, photography is arguably the quintessentially modernist visual art. Born in the 1830s (along with Manet), it was a contested medium: is this art or evidence? "Originality in photography as distinct from originality in painting lies in the essentially objective character of photography." And as Bazin's translator points out, "the lens ... is in French called the 'objectif.'"[60]

Is this image made by human or by machine? The uneasy relation of artificial to fleshly forms of production is reflected in Umbo's *The Racing Reporter* (discussed in Chapter 2) with its gargantuan cyborg journalist, assembled from modern technologies, bestriding the earth and making news by making news. He is literally typing his heart out, with the most significant marker of humanity, the human face, obscured by the camera. The trope of merging with the camera to become something other than mere flesh could be read as hiding behind the lens. It is not (Figure 10). Ilse Bing's 1931 self-portrait reflects, literally, on the multiple ways of accessing both selfhood and the prosthetic means by which art allows access

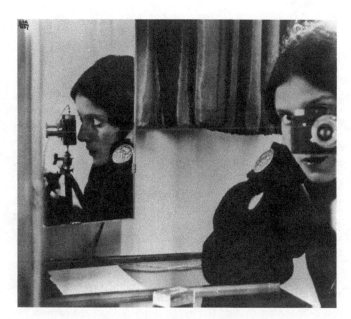

FIGURE 10   Ilse Bing, *Self Portrait with Leica* (1931) © Estate of Ilse Bing

to or constitutes it. Vision is prosthetic. It extends the body's reach, and photography literalizes the fact that this means we have of knowing ourselves and the world is inherently alien. Photography records the drive to capture the world as seen by something other than the human eye. Self and world are both made strange. They always were, but photography shows it.

Eugène Atget (1857–1927) took more than ten thousand photographs, recording Paris from 1897 through the 1920s. The ex-actor stayed offstage; his park benches and city streets were deserted. Walter Benjamin observed, "It has quite justly been said of him that he photographed them like the scenes of crime"[61] (Figure 11). He photographed the quotidian and the overlooked. And never once the Eiffel Tower.

Unexpectedly, that eye for the outside would accord with Surrealist taste: the everyday is again made strange. Living on the same street as Atget, Man Ray bought his prints and had four run in the magazine *La Révolution Surréaliste*. Atget's small attentive crowd viewing a 1911 eclipse is on the 1926 cover, captioned – surreally – "Les Dernières Conversions" (Figure 12). As Man Ray reported of the transaction, Atget's stipulation was of anonymity: "Don't put my name on it. These are simply documents that I make."[62]

FIGURE 11 Eugène Atget, *St. Cloud*. Library of Congress, Prints & Photographs Division, LC-USZ62-99199

FIGURE 12 Eugène Atget, *Eclipse, 1911*. Library of Congress, Prints & Photographs Division, LC-USZ62-99200

Alfred Steiglitz's magazine *Camera Work* (1903–1917) brought photographic art to American view, urging as well other artists like Matisse. Matisse dismissed the medium.

The Impressionists' first show, so savaged, was held in the vacated Paris studio of the photographer Nadar. Nadar photographed Baudelaire. Baudelaire dismissed the medium.

That indexical relation to the objective is its key; photography is the only art bearing "an imprint or a transfer off the real."[63] Modernists collaged it; Dada's Hannah Höch *Cut with the Kitchen Knife Dada Through the Last Weimar Beer-Belly Cultural Epoch of Germany* (1919–20), repeatedly assembling images of what women were to look like, according to fashion magazines and ethnographic photographs.

The photograph gives us both sides of Baudelaire's account of modernity: contingent and immune to time. That's what Emmanuel Radnitzky wanted when he became the multimedia artist Man Ray (1890–1976) and what the Marchesa Luisa Casati (1881–1957) meant when she said, "I want to be a living work of art."[64] Casati was painted by Augustus John, Giovanni Boldini, Kees van Dongen; sculpted by Jacob Epstein, Sarah Lipska, Balla, and Renato Bertelli; and photographed by Cecil Beaton, Adolf de Meyer, and Man Ray. And others. Known for her eyes, she enhanced them with kohl and belladonna (the etymology shows why). Man Ray's photograph of Casati in 1922 (Figure 13), the miracle year of modernism, has her triple-eyed: looking, looking, looking.

Coda

14. Modernist visual art is premised on the imposition of order – be it a grid (Mondrian); theory (Mondrian, Delaunay); utopian ideal (Mondrian, Bauhaus, Constructivism, Corbusier); science (Seurat, Henry Tonks); religion (see above); or canny systems that encompass even entropy and anarchy (Duchamp). However, all this – systems, lists – refuses to add up.

(A) First, because it is a list.
(B) Second, because someone is writing it. (Absent here is any account arising from Australia, South Asia, Cuba, Spain, Scandinavia, the Middle East, and the Caribbean, to name a few major elisions.)
(C) Third, because modernist visual art, despite its indebtedness to language, will continue to exceed the words available to describe it. Ekphrasis has no counterpart.

FIGURE 13 Man Ray, *Marquise Casati* (1922). © Man Ray Trust / Artists Rights Society (ARS), NY / ADAGP, Paris 2014. Photo Credit: © CNAC/MNAM/Dist. RMN-Grand Palais / Art Resource, NY

Notes

1 Clement Greenberg, "Towards a Newer Laocoon" (1940), in *The Collected Essays and Criticism*, ed. John O'Brian, vol. 1, 34, 35.

2 Greenberg, "Modernist Painting" (1960), in *Collected Essays,* ed. O'Brian, vol. 4, 86–87.

3 Jean Hagstrum, *The Sister Arts: The Tradition of Literary Pictorialism and English Poetry from Dryden to Gray* (Chicago: University of Chicago Press), 10.

4 Jacques Rancière, *Aisthesis: Scenes from the Aesthetic Regime of Art*, translated by Zakir Paul (New York: Verso Press, 2013), xii.

5 Hagstrum, *Sister Arts*, 97.

6 See Jesse Matz, *Literary Impressionism and Modernist Aesthetics* (New York: Cambridge University Press, 2001), esp. 12–52.

7 Joseph Conrad, "Preface to *The Nigger of the Narcissus*," in Ford, *The Good Soldier*, 2nd edn, ed. Martin Stannard (New York: W. W. Norton & Co., 2012), 268.

8 Stéphane Mallarmé, "The Impressionists and Édouard Manet" (1876), in Charles S. Moffett et al., *The New Painting: Impressionism, 1874–1886* (San Francisco: Fine Arts Museum of San Francisco, 1986), 28.

9 F.T. Marinetti, *Let's Murder the Moonshine: Selected Writings*, edited and translated by R.W. Flint (Los Angeles: Sun and Moon Press, 1991), 50.

10 Milton W. Brown, *The Story of the Armory Show* (New York: Abbeville Press, 1988), 137.

11 "His Art Too Crude for Independents," *New York Herald,* April 14, 1917, 6.

12 Bruce Altshuler, *Salon to Biennial – Exhibitions That Made Art History*, vol. 1: 1863–1959 (New York: Phaidon, 2008), 12.

13 Different versions exist of the title's arrival and of which canvas occasioned it; see John Rewald, *The History of French Impressionism* (New York: Museum of Modern Art, 1973), 318.

14 Quoted in Rewald, 323–24.

15 Altshuler, *Salon to Biennial*, 14.

16 Oscar Wilde, *The Picture of Dorian Gray*, 2nd ed., ed. Michael Patrick Gillespie (New York: W.W. Norton and Company, 2007), 6.

17 Altshuler, *Salon to Biennial*, 17.

18 Diana Fuss and Joel Sanders, "An Aesthetic Headache: Notes from the Museum Bench," in *Interiors*, ed. Johanna Burton et al. (New York: Sternberg Press, 2012), 67.

19 Henry James, *The American* (New York: Penguin Classics, 1981), 33.

20 McCandlish Phillips, "Farewell Party for 'Blue Poles,'" *The New York Times,* October 2, 1973.

21 Lynn Cooke, "Dialogue," in *Interiors*, ed. Burton et al., 179.

22 Alexander Baumgarten, quoted in Timothy Costelloe, *The British Aesthetic Tradition: From Shaftesbury to Wittgenstein* (New York: Cambridge University Press, 2013), 2.

23 Terry Eagleton, *The Ideology of the Aesthetic* (New York: Wiley-Blackwell, 1990), 13.

24 A zoom-able viewing of the painting is at http://www.courtauld.ac.uk/vr—tour/new/index.shtml?pano=room—06.xml, provided by the Courtauld Gallery.

25 Thanks to Julian Barnes for showing this, and the Manet, to me. Nothing of what I say should be conflated with what he saw.

26 Whether this is red vermouth, a liqueur, or another alcohol (it has been called grenadine and reddish wine) remains definitively indeterminate. Thanks to Barnes again, and Bill Lindsey of the SHA/BLM Historic Glass Bottle Identification & Information Website, for patient knowledge decanting.

27 J.K. Huysmans, "The Folies-Bergère in 1879," in *Parisian Sketches*, translated by Brendan King (Gardena, CA: Dedalus, 2004), 34.

28 The term is used by Huysmans in his 1880 sketch of the Parisian prostitute; the definition appears in Alfred Delvau, *Dictionnaire de la Langue Verte*; and the translation is by Brendan King (Huysmans, *Parisian Sketches*, 171–72).

29 See T.J. Clark, *The Painting of Modern Life: Paris in the Art of Manet and His Followers* (Princeton: Princeton University Press, 1984), and Georg Simmel, "The Metropolis and Mental Life," translated by Edward A. Shils, in *On Individuality and Social Forms*, ed. Donald Levine (Chicago: University of Chicago Press, 1971), 324–39.

30 Georges Jeanniot describes Manet working on the painting in the studio ("En souvenir de Manet," *La Grande Revue* 46 [August 10, 1907]: 853).

31 Richard Shiff, "Ascribing to Manet, Declaring the Author," in *12 Views of Manet's* BAR, ed. Bradford R. Collins (Princeton: Princeton University Press, 1996), 16.

32 See Ruth E. Iskin, "Selling, Seduction, and Soliciting the Eye: Manet's *Bar at the Folies-Bergère*," *The Art Bulletin* 77:1 (March 1995): 25–44.

33 Shiff, "Ascribing to Manet," 20 n3.

34 Jules Comte, *L'Illustration,* May 20, 1882, 335; quoted and translated in Clark, *Painting of Modern Life*, 240.

35 See Thierry de Duve, "Intentionality and Art Historical Methodology: A Case Study," *nonsite.org* 6 http://nonsite.org/article/intentionality-and-art-historical-methodology-a-case-study; Malcolm Park, *Ambiguity, and the Engagement of Spatial Illusion within the Surface*

of Manet's Paintings (Ph.D. diss., University of New South Wales, Australia, 2001); Clark arrives at a wonderful preview of the "solution" without touching on optics per se.

36 Robert L. Herbert, *Impressionism: Art, Leisure, and Parisian Society* (New Haven: Yale University Press, 1988), 309 n46.

37 Herbert, *Impressionism*, 152–70.

38 Herbert, *Impressionism*, 79.

39 André Breton, "The First Manifesto of Surrealism 1924," translated by Richard Seaver and Helen Lane, in *Modernism: An Anthology of Sources and Documents*, ed. Vassiliki Kolocotroni, Jane Goldman, and Olga Taxidou (Chicago: University of Chicago, 1998), 308.

40 Robert Storr, "Diogenes of the Funny Pages," in *Ad Reinhardt, How to Look: Art Comics* (New York: David Zwirner, 2013), 7.

41 Reinhardt, "How to Look at Low (Surrealist) Art" (March 24, 1946), in *How to Look*, 27.

42 T.E. Hulme, "Modern Art and its Philosophy" in *Speculations: Essays on Humanism and the Philosophy of Art*, ed. Herbert Read (1924; New York: Routledge and Kegan Paul Inc., 1987), 93, 97.

43 Reinhardt, "How to View High (Abstract) Art" (February 24, 1946), 25.

44 Michael Fried, *Manet's Modernism: or, The Face of Painting in the 1860s* (Chicago: University of Chicago Press, 1998), 284.

45 Canto 81, *The Cantos of Ezra Pound* (New York: New Directions, 1986), 532.

46 Degas, quoted and translated in Rewald, *History*, 86.

47 Mina Loy, "Brancusi's Golden Bird," in *The Lost Lunar Baedeker* (New York: Farrar, Straus and Giroux, 1997), 79.

48 Lorraine Daston and Peter Galison, *Objectivity* (Cambridge: MIT Press, 2010), 66. "Morphological prototype" comes from an earlier version, in *Representations* 40 (Autumn 1992): 88.

49 Martin Jay, *Downcast Eyes: The Denigration of Vision in Twentieth-Century French Thought* (Berkeley: University of California Press, 1994), 7.

50 Michael Kimmelman, "Andrew Wyeth, Painter, Dies at 91," *The New York Times*, January 16, 2009, http://www.nytimes.com/2009/01/17/arts/design/17wyeth.html?pagewanted=all&—r=0.

51 László Moholy-Nagy, "The New Typography" (1923), in *Modernism*, ed. Kolocotroni et al., 303.

52 Walter Gropius, "Manifesto of the Bauhaus, April 1919," translated by Frank Whitford, in *Modernism*, ed. Kolocotroni et al., 302.

53 "*LEF* Manifesto 1923" (English version), in *Modernism*, ed. Kolocotroni et al., 305–06.

54 *The Great Utopia: The Russian and Soviet Avant-Garde, 1915–1932* (New York: Guggenheim Museum, 1992), 625.

55 We are still catching up to Marjorie Perloff, *The Futurist Moment: Avant-Garde, Avant Guerre, and the Language of Rupture* (Chicago: University of Chicago Press, 1986), 9.

56 Cendrars, quoted and translated in Perloff, 3.

57 "Character in Fiction," *The Essays of Virginia Woolf*, ed. Andrew McNeillie, vol. 3 (New York: Harcourt Brace Jovanovich, 1988), 421.

58 Cézanne as quoted on Banksy website, October 2013, "Better Out Than In" month-long tagging New York project, http://www.banksyny.com/, accessed October 19, 2013.

59 Alex Danchev, *Cézanne: A Life* (New York: Pantheon, 2012), 361.

60 André Bazin, "The Ontology of the Photographic Image," translated by Hugh Gray, in *What Is Cinema?* (Berkeley: University of California Press, 1967), 13.

61 Walter Benjamin, "The Work of Art in the Age of Mechanical Reproduction," in *Illuminations*, translated by Harry Zohn, ed. Hannah Arendt (New York: Schocken Books, 1968), 227.

62 "Interview: Man Ray," *Camera* 74 (February 1975): 39–40.

63 Rosalind E. Krauss, *The Originality of the Avant-Garde and Other Modernist Myths* (Cambridge, MA: MIT Press, 1996), 110.

64 Scot D. Ryersson and Michael Orlando Yaccarino, *Infinite Variety: The Life and Legend of the Marchesa Casati* (New York: Viridian Books, 1999), 1.

Part III

Entertainments

10

Urban Pleasures

It was March 8, 1941, a Saturday night in wartime London. Four flights under the Rialto Cinema, dancing and music were going full force in the subterranean spaces of the luxurious Café de Paris. Outside, the sirens were sounding for the first big raid in weeks, and most of London had descended into shelters. But these warnings were unheard or unheeded by the "happy band of youth" sitting at the tables or moving around the dance floor.[1] The nightclub's wartime occupants were a cosmopolitan mix: uniformed airmen and naval officers on leave, British aristocrats in evening dress, Canadian nurses, refugees from Hitler's Europe, Italian waiters, and Danish owner. What was new and remarkable about this smart nightspot was the all-black British swing band, the first of its kind to establish residency in West End nightclubs.

Ken "Snakehips" Johnson's West Indian Dance Orchestra had just struck up the Andrew Sisters' hit, "Oh Johnny." Patrons felt secure because the Café was falsely advertised as London's safest restaurant. But at 9:50 p.m., two bombs fell on the Rialto's glass roof. One of them traveled down an airshaft and exploded on the dance floor just in front of the bandstand. A second did not explode but covered everyone with corrosive yellow dust. When the smoke cleared, thirty-four people were dead and eighty seriously injured. The dead included the owner Martin Poulsen, the bandleader Johnson, and one of his musicians.

The blast was tremendous. Rescuers and wardens arriving on the scene were shocked at the macabre sight of mangled bodies and physical wreckage. The smell and chaos were indescribable. Legs and hands were blown off. Perhaps most disturbing were the eerie waxwork effects of people who had died instantly when the explosion sucked the air out of their lungs, leaving them frozen in dancing position or sitting around a table, while the bubbles of the champagne bottles were still rising under a layer of plaster dirt. When Berkeley Ballard, a West End actor and special constable arrived with the rescuers, he was appalled at the sight of looters cutting off fingers "to get the rings." He later declared the Café de Paris to be the "most horrifying sight" he witnessed during the Blitz.[2]

What made the bomb scene at the Café de Paris so memorable was its combination of horror and glamour. The wrecked nightspot inverted the fantasy of the nightclub as a hedonistic pleasure zone. *Time* summed up the shocking twist of fate: "What had been a nightclub became a nightmare."[3] Yet pleasure and danger had always been entangled features of the interwar nightclub. The nightclub gained popularity as a modernist interzone, where individuals immersed themselves in risky social practices to disrupt the routines of daily life. The nightclub promised an alternative version of modernity, an informal refuge from the regimented, homogenizing processes of modernization. It promoted itself as a dynamic site of international cultural exchange where social boundaries could be tested, surprising occasions materialized, and bodies revitalized through intense sensation.

But on March 8, 1941, instead of providing an environment of controlled risk and social experimentalism, the Café de Paris descended into surreal chaos, the distinctions of inside/outside obliterated, bodies and selves literally disintegrated. Trying to put a positive spin on the grisly incident, news accounts praised the nurses who tended the wounded and the debutantes who tore off their satin gowns to make bandages. They commended the carefree survivors who went on to dance at a nearby club in their bloodstained clothes, determined to show Hitler that he could not destroy West End morale. But they also noted the sinister presence of looters crawling around the dance floor in search of jewels, cigarette cases, and money.

Female hedonism, defiant pleasure seeking, transnationalism, conspicuous consumption, and predatory lawlessness: this chapter charts these pleasures and dangers of the nightclub between the 1920s and World War II. To this list, it adds another theme present in the coverage of the Café de Paris bombing: race. Within a week of the bombing, news media turned to the tragic death of Ken "Snakehips" Johnson, who was fast becoming Britain's first superstar of swing and who declared that he would "make London swing" or "die trying."[4] Journalists praised Johnson for the "unerring rhythm" of his West Indian band and for the "restless grace with which his body swayed to it."[5] *Melody Maker*, the trade journal for dance musicians, anointed him "one of the most progressive disciples of modern swing in this country." It pointed to his blighted ambitions and posed the following question: "Who is there to take Ken Johnson's place?"[6]

Jazz historians continue to treat Johnson's death as a lost opportunity for black British music. They frame the backstory of his brief success around the career paths of black British musicians who joined Johnson's band, having sharpened their musical skills and gained a political education in the black clubs of Soho in the thirties. Yet these studies give scant attention to the consumers of this entertainment, the patrons of the Café de Paris, whose passion for live black music and dancing enabled "Snakehips" to obtain a residency in the first place. Their enthusiasm was shaped by racial thinking as well as by an appetite for transnational forms of pleasure that reordered public intimacy and bodily styles among white urban sophisticates. These shifting practices provoked intense media scrutiny of the female hedonist as an emblem of sexualized femininity and nightclub transgressions. The entwining of black American cultural forms and elite pleasure-seeking dates back over many decades, to the turn of the twentieth century. It gained momentum during the Great War, when American bands replaced German orchestras. Consumer demand for American dancing and music reached a new threshold during the Roaring Twenties, when the Café de Paris first opened and the flapper held sway as the modern girl.

Café de Paris and the Roaring Twenties

In 1924, the new Café de Paris entered a nightclub economy divided into two market niches: the legal, swanky resorts of the West End and the illegal, shady nightclubs of Soho. These two competitive zones had developed during the Great War. The 1915 Defense of the Realm Act (DORA) imposed restrictions on the hours of drinking and dancing that curtailed the prosperity of legal nightclubs and inadvertently drove late-night drinking and dancing underground. Hundreds of unregistered nightclubs mushroomed in the dingy basements of Soho, a proletarian, foreign district just to the east of London's West End commercial center. After the Armistice, wartime restrictions on drinking hours continued while the nightclub scene expanded. Luxurious restaurant cabarets sprouted in fashionable Mayfair or, like the Café de Paris, materialized along the illuminated commercial thoroughfares bordering Soho's dark streets. These smart places tended to stay on the right side of the licensing laws, but they had to close early and compete with a dynamic, raffish scene in Soho.

These were the conditions facing the Café de Paris when it welcomed its first patrons. Seating 400, the new establishment promised a world of traveling pleasures. Its elegant chrome-plated, mirrored interior resembled the saloon of an ocean liner. It featured a symmetrical set of staircases descending from the balcony to the dance floor that provided ladies with a theatrical entrance to show off their gowns. Its site on Coventry Street, in the entertainment center of Piccadilly Circus and Leicester Square, was convenient to the fashionable residential area of Mayfair and the gentlemen's clubs of St. James. But Coventry Street also had a notorious reputation as a resort of pimps and prostitutes. To gain distinction as a society place, the Café de Paris management undertook a savvy publicity campaign. The African American singing duo of Layton and Johnston proved to be an early draw for the Café, but it was the recruitment of the Prince of Wales, a great aficionado of ragtime dancing and syncopated sounds, that consolidated its popularity among the social elite. Once the Prince bestowed his favor, the Café de Paris became a magnet for Café society, an expanded social elite of aristocrats augmented by actresses, writers, artists, deposed foreign royalty, plutocrats, sports celebrities, film stars, and dance hostesses.

Young members of society frequented the Café de Paris to escape the boredom of dinner parties and balls and the controlling supervision of chaperones and mothers. While hardly a democratic space, the main saloon fostered the impression of intimacy, informality and variety. The crowded dance floor forced people to mix, yet the tables allowed them to return to their own group. Apart from the bandstand, there was no further demarcation of space, no proscenium stage separating the performers from the audience. In many ways, the audience was the entertainment.

The cuisine and service of the Café de Paris conformed to the international standards of haute French cuisine, but the rituals of dining were subordinated to the evening's paramount activity – dancing. The food in such places "was always crammed down between dances, drowned with gin-and-tonic, blown over by cigarette-smoke."[7] Cabaret acts were also streamlined and lacked the political punch of their Continental equivalents. During the interwar decades, headliners often included well-known British entertainers, from female impersonator Douglas Byng (a favorite of royalty for being "bawdy but British") to playwright and songster Noël Coward.

Increasingly, however, the cabaret became a showcase for musical and dancing novelties imported from New York. Take the case of the Charleston. In 1925, Londoners witnessed a live version of the Charleston for the first time when Louise Brooks, then a young American dancer, performed it during her engagement at the Café de Paris. Even before its London debut, the Charleston had already migrated across racial, social, and geographic divides in Manhattan, making its way downtown from Harlem nightclubs to the Broadway stage. One enthusiastic *New Republic* reviewer marveled at the capacity of black dancers in the Broadway black musical *Running Wild* (1923) to transform the "most awkward postures" – knock-knees, legs akimbo, toes turned in, squatting – into a graceful pattern which was "gay and orgiastic and wild."[8] Before it was exported to London, the Charleston underwent considerable alteration, as white celebrity dancers, with the assistance of African-American choreographers, popularized it and toned it down: they eliminated the hip and pelvic thrusts while accentuating athletic movements that showed plenty of leg. Even so, the Charleston was regarded as too wild and vulgar for elite Londoners until it was adopted by the Prince of Wales, who took instruction in the afternoon from a Café de Paris hostess.

Brooks had some disparaging things to say about the "Bright Young Things" (so named by novelist Evelyn Waugh) who attended her Charleston performance, finding them glum and moribund. Like Brooks herself, this London coterie of top-drawer blue bloods and down-at-the-heel bohemians served as trendsetters for a new style of femininity intimately linked to social dancing. In the pages of the middle-market press, female BYTs appeared as quintessential flappers, sporting bobbed hair, short tubular dresses, easy smiles, and slender, elongated bodies. While fashion columns advanced the flapper look as a sign of mobility, bodily autonomy, female sexual desire, and urban self-confidence, editorials and correspondents often deplored the careless pleasure seeking of the nightclub habitué and her deviation from women's proper sphere. Besides promoting new styles of female attire and embodiment, the dancing culture of debutante nightbirds and their escorts reordered the intimate rituals of society to approximate a modernized, Americanized variant of elite heterosexuality. One columnist went so far as to insist that dancing undermined the homosocial world of gentlemen's clubs, arguing that men now enjoyed feminine company in the evening because it contained more erotic promise. Dancing in the dark also changed elite mores by fostering adulterous transgression in public. As one former debutante recalled, "the idea of the darkness was that you'd be dancing with someone else's husband and your husband was across the room with the man's wife." "The dancing," the ex-deb emphasized, "was so important."[9]

While performing important cultural work, this elite dancing was neither inspired nor proficient. Foxtrots, where the feet did all the work and the upper body remained rigidly erect, remained the norm. Musicians who worked at elite West End clubs described the dancing guests as "moving wallpaper," walking and talking, hardly moving at all.[10] To assist patrons in their foxtrots around the dance floor, musicians were required to keep to a strict tempo, muted orchestrations, and evenly balanced instrumentalism.

Soho's Shady Nightclubs

Elite couples brought this mundane dancing culture with them when they went on to the shady nightclubs of Soho to prolong the night and to dance, drink, and socialize in a restrictive but mixed space. After the Café de Paris closed (usually around 1 a.m., or by 2 a.m., when it had been granted an extension), many patrons floated on to the myriad illegal, after-hours clubs of Soho. The most popular resorts were under the control of Mrs. Kate Meyrick, a middle-aged Irish woman of genteel upbringing, who gained notoriety as the "queen of nightclubs."

Proprietors like Meyrick explicitly modeled their Soho establishments on American speakeasies. They duplicated the louche ambience of the clandestine venues of Greenwich Village, Harlem, and the side streets of Midtown, including the spatial arrangements, the band music, the name of establishments (Manhattan, Rector's), the American accents acquired by dance hostesses, and the procedures of gaining entry through locked doors, peep holes, or a heavily guarded elevator. Like New York dives, they were concentrated in a low-rent and unimproved district, relatively immune from careful police surveillance. As in New York, first- and second-generation European immigrants – mostly Jews and Italians – were instrumental in shaping the performance culture and environment of Soho joints.

Meyrick establishments purveyed a culture of risk and danger to attract members of Café society eager for "early morning excitement."[11]

Young elites thrilled at the idea that they might find themselves dancing alongside the free-spending burglars who had broken into their homes. The illegal status of the clubs encouraged other illicit practices: gambling, drugs, cross-class erotic encounters, and, in some venues, the non-conformist sexualities of transvestites, lesbians, and "fairies." Paid dance hostesses decorated the rooms. The conditions of their labor required them to be mercenary "gold diggers," flappers on the make, seducing men out of money by demanding champagne and chocolates. Their grafting helped to "oil the machinery" and "keep the waiters busy."[12]

Augmenting the atmosphere of speed and risk were sporadic gangster and police raids. Interwar Soho was the leisure center for the criminal underworld and the prize location of lucrative criminal protective rackets that targeted nightclubs. Over the years, violence broke out in Soho clubs reminiscent of Al Capone's Chicago and Dutch Schultz's New York minus the machine guns. Like other nightclub proprietors, Meyrick paid protection money to both the police and gangsters. When these intruders showed up at her door, she exercised her charms to manage the situation. She treated disruptive gangsters with fantastic guile, easing them out without raising her voice. She even persuaded police to remove their headgear when they conducted a raid.

The cultural politics of Meyrick's establishments were mixed. While remaining social and political bastions of the Establishment, her clubs also operated as relatively innovative musical spaces for habitués lower down the social order. At the 43, her "mother house," Mrs. Meyrick encouraged musical jam sessions, a practice common in Harlem speakeasies. Around 1925, white American musical celebrities, such as Sophie Tucker and Paul Whiteman, began dropping in and agreed to perform. Meyrick also welcomed jazz-minded Jewish dance musicians, such as Billy Amstell and Harry Gold, who worked in West End bands and were anxious to hear and play with international stars. Mrs. Meyrick allowed them to have a blow, to perform the kind of jazz improvisations that were strictly forbidden in smart places like the Café de Paris.

Racial Politics: Black Clubs and the Popular Front

When black clubs emerged in the late twenties, they replicated Meyrick's template for the successful shady nightclub, but they also reconfigured the political ambience in significant ways. They were densely localized in Soho basements and subject to gangland attacks and police raids. Most of them were furnished with minimal appointments and primitive sanitary facilities. They featured illicit practices – "weeds," prostitutes, and gambling – that accelerated the culture of risk. They charged hefty prices for drinks. They were "expensive" but not "exclusive."[13] Blacks and Jews often teamed up to run these nightspots. All in all, the service staff was drawn from the racial/ethnic mix of the locale, with the added *frisson* of black Britons as entertainers and customers.

Like many other Soho nightspots in the thirties, black clubs operated as bottle parties, pretending to be private parties, where guests reserved bottles of wine and spirits in advance to avoid the restrictions of licensing laws. To the usual list of Soho attractions, black clubs added hot jazz, interracial dancing, and black musicians. Like Meyrick's establishments, their musical scene was enlivened by impromptu jam sessions, often with visiting musical stars from America. The visiting "firemen" at the jam sessions now included black American stars Duke Ellington and Louis Armstrong. While still catering to Guardsmen, visiting businessmen, and the like, black clubs also became informal sites of the Popular Front, a broad-based political alliance of British left-wing groups dedicated to fighting fascism.

Journalist Maurice Richardson captured the distinctive atmosphere of black clubs in his 1937 survey of the "Bottle Party Belt." Richardson praised the Nest, Frisco's, and the Shim Sham, where "injections of negroes and swing have hotted up the night boxes." All sorts of white sophisticates went to these clubs. Tough and noisy, they were full of black bandsmen, music hall performers, students, West Indians, Americans, and Africans, but not many women of color. At these clubs, Richardson confided to readers, "you will find the atmosphere ... friendly, quite democratic, very international."[14]

Other press notices recommended hot dancing in black clubs to white Londoners who wanted to learn Latin and "coloured body movements." *Gramophone* advised readers to drop in one night to the Shim Sham, co-owned by Ike Hatch, where the clientele was "about fifty-fifty White and Negro."[15] Journalists reported that the dancing scene in these clubs tended to be more acrobatic, less couple oriented, and more eroticized than at West End resorts. Dances ranged from a conga line to a Suzy Q that, on one occasion, ended in an "unrehearsed strip tease."[16] Articles on dancing in "negro clubs" continued to spotlight the elite female habitué, the fair girl with the "aristocratic name" whose reckless behavior now extended to visiting a "negro club" and who danced exclusively with "negroes who would dance cheek to cheek with her."[17] Hostile witnesses and undercover police went so far as to condemn the mixed dancing scene as perverse, complaining that indecency extended to men dancing with men, women with women, and blacks with whites. While stereotyped and pejorative, these observations correctly registered the presence of well-heeled female adventurers in the clubs such as Lady Mountbatten or Renée Ayer (white men about town were deemed unexceptional), plus a range of other sexual nonconformists on the dance floor. According to black musicians, some of the interracial encounters had a commercial edge: club owners expected black patrons to fill the "hostess" role, to entertain well-heeled white patrons eager to see how "coloured people enjoyed themselves."[18]

Meanwhile, *Melody Maker* led the musical campaign on behalf of black clubs as centers of hot jazz. As champions of black American music, *Melody Maker* exalted true jazz as the direct expression of African-American race and culture. It had organized British tours for Armstrong and Ellington in the 1930s but only as soloists and entertainers. Its sponsorship of live jazz from America was thwarted by legal restrictions on work visas for American musicians. After 1935, stars like Armstrong could still work in Britain as cabaret or music hall entertainment, but they had to perform with a British band or assemble their own band from musicians in residence. To satisfy increased consumer demand for live black music, the black British community moved in to fill the void, attempting to reinvent themselves as Americans.

Black British musicians were poorly paid, lived hand to mouth, and were pressured by management to eroticize and exoticize their musical performances. Not only were they expected to play jazz like Americans, they also felt obliged to impersonate black Americans, adopting American slang, deportment, and dress, despite the fact that most of them hailed from Cardiff, Africa, and the West Indies. Some of them recalled these impersonations as demeaning. But at a time when there were few opportunities to break into the white dance band ranks, the vogue for black swing, informed as it was by a racialized notion of culture, provided local musicians of color with new opportunities for work of an irregular sort, musical improvement, and professional networking between black and white musicians.

They were a small but diverse group, reflecting varied migration patterns, career paths, musical training, cultural fusions, and political engagement. A few, like Ike Hatch, were African Americans long resident in London. Arriving from New York in 1925, where he had been trained in *bel canto*, Hatch hooked up with African-American pianist Elliott Carpenter to play a minstrel act in music halls, theaters and clubs. By the mid-thirties, Hatch was regularly performing on the BBC, again as part of a minstrel program, recording for Parlophone, and serving as emcee in Soho's black clubs. By contrast, guitarist Joe Deniz, who would join Johnson's orchestra, was a black Welshman of African descent, with very little formal musical training and an attenuated relationship to African-American music. Deniz's first exposure to jazz came from records bought in Woolworth's and visits to the variety theatres in Cardiff.

West Indian musicians often gained musical instruction from the military networks that transported them to London. After arriving in 1920 as a band boy in the West Indian Regiment, Leslie Thompson underwent formal training in military music at Kneller Hall. He went on to play in the pits of West End theatres, record with Spike Hughes's band, and gain standing as a "coloured trumpeter" at Jewish weddings. He perfected his craft during jam sessions with Louis Armstrong in Soho's black clubs. All the while, he was gaining a "colour consciousness."[19] Thompson's political education began in 1921, when a fellow soldier gave him a copy of Marcus Garvey's *Negro World* newspaper; throughout the thirties he often went to hear Garvey, who had been deported from the United States, preach Pan-Africanism in Hyde Park Corner. This political engagement intensified his interest in jazz and in organizing a black band in London.[20]

A combination of political activism and musical entrepreneurship marked the career patterns of other notable black musicians in 1930s London. In 1933, writer Nancy Cunard invited Ike Hatch to serve on the London organizing committee in support of the Scottsboro boys, young black men accused of raping white women in Alabama. Hatch presided over one London gala fundraiser where Ken Johnson displayed his tap dancing skills, while classically trained musician, composer, and conductor Rudolph Dunbar performed clarinet. Historians interpret the 1933 Scottsboro defense campaign as the immediate precursor to the Popular Front. Two years after the Scottsboro campaign, protest against Italy's invasion of Abyssinia became the first international *cause célèbre* of the Popular Front, providing an impetus to new cultural formations and venues for the dissemination of antiracism and antifascism.

One of these new venues was the Florence Mills Social Parlour, named after the great Harlem dancer and singer. It opened in 1936 as a Pan-

Africanist club in Carnaby Street, Soho. Cosponsored by Dunbar and Amy Jacques Garvey, Marcus Garvey's ex-wife, it was intended to serve as a social headquarters "for colored people in the English metropolis" and to further the cause of "swing" music and dancing.[21] The Florence Mills became a regular stop on the nighttime itinerary of West African student Ben Nnamdi Azikiwe, who recalled how he would dine there before he moved on to enjoy the casual "confraternity between blacks and whites" in the nearby black jazz clubs.[22] Writing in *Melody Maker* in 1936 about the newly opened Shim Sham, Rudolph Dunbar also singled out the interracial spectacle of the dance floor as a sign of a "new outlook on the colour question."[23]

Besides dancers, the "confraternity" of blacks and whites extended to musicians. These friendships were both professional and political. Thompson and Joe Deniz had some harsh things to say about exploitative white club owners, but they also recalled friendly encounters with the Jewish sidemen who visited black clubs, although socializing never extended to the home. Like the small black clubs of Harlem, Soho clubs functioned as intimate spaces of "emulation and guildship" where the audience participated in the performance.[24] At the Shim Sham, Deniz made contact with guitarist Ivor Mairants, who told Joe and his brother Frank that they played guitar very well and encouraged them to move beyond the black club scene of Soho. The club attracted other West End musicians, such as Billy Amstell and Harry Gold, who had frequented the 43 in the twenties but now sat in with the black musicians to play improvised small-band swing music. Since their days at the 43, Amstell and Gold had undergone a radical political conversion (as did Ivor Mairants). "I watched the rich patrons of the Café de Paris and thought about it all politically," Harry Gold recalled in his memoirs. "It reinforced my socialist convictions."[25] Also reinforcing their left-wing convictions was the subordinate status they experienced at the swank West End resorts, where they were required to enter separate doors and were proscribed from mixing with guests. Class knowledge and class grievances, as well as anti-Semitism, made such musicians receptive to recruitment into the Communist Party.

Ken Johnson and London's First Swing Band

West End impresarios were far less impressed with the left-wing cultural politics of black clubs than with their commercial success at attracting well-heeled urban sophisticates anxious to hear and dance to black bands. Having already recruited black American stars like Ethel Waters to their cabaret, elite club owners became increasingly receptive to hiring local black talent – at lower wages than white musicians – to stage a West End version of "Harlem in London." When Ken Johnson collaborated with Leslie Thompson to organize an "all-coloured" band, their goal was to establish a black ensemble with the technical proficiency to gain regular employment in the West End clubs.

The son of a prominent Guyanese doctor, Johnson was sent as an adolescent to Britain to be educated and then to study medicine. When Johnson left school, he set his sights instead on entertainment: he took tap dancing lessons from African-American choreographer Buddy Bradley, who had taught Fred Astaire and a host of other Hollywood screen dancers. Johnson also picked up his nickname from Earl "Snakehips" Tucker and established himself as a dancer. Returning from a visit to Guyana in 1934, he stopped by New York, where he gained first-hand knowledge of African-American vernacular dancing, learning to swivel his hips in the manner of his namesake. He visited Harlem's Cotton Club, a mob-owned center of Jim Crow entertainment with a plantation atmosphere, where Ellington, "Cab" Calloway, and other Harlem luminaries performed for white patrons. Calloway inspired Johnson to become a dancing bandleader and to model his signature costume on Calloway's extravagant white suit and tails plus carnation. By emulating Calloway, Johnson joined the ranks of black dandies, embracing a masculine performance style distinguished by sartorial flamboyance, sexual energy, and kinetic exuberance. Remembered for his beautiful, elegant face and restless grace, he presented himself as an object of desire "to be looked at," a self-presentation at some remove from the normative codes of elite white male patrons of nightclubs. Like other dandies, Johnson used attitude and style to command attention "when privileges of birth, wealth and social standing might be absent."[26]

While in New York, Johnson also seems to have learned some dancing moves from the Lindy dancers at Harlem's Savoy Ballroom, an interracial public dance hall that opened in 1926, where swing dance and music evolved together, well before Benny Goodman and his orchestra went on to make swing a national craze for white America in the mid-1930s. On the dance floor, the Lindy complemented the instrumentalist solos of swing bands, allowing for cooperation and self-expression among dancing couples. The Savoy Lindy Hoppers, a team of young Harlem dancers, perfected the Lindy as choreographed swing dancing. They improvised with their feet and hands, even going so far as to break away from their partners, or, in the case of back flips, literally "fly."[27]

Johnson brought that synergy of swing dance and music back to London and packaged it. Upon his return, "Snakehips" persuaded Thompson to join him in assembling an "all-coloured band" that he could front as a charismatic hip-swiveling bandleader. Because he was a dancer and not a musician, Johnson heavily depended on Thompson to arrange the music, recruit a talented group of musicians, and then knock them into shape. Thompson later dismissed Johnson as a "stick wagger," but Johnson's dancing body made a vital contribution to the success of the group.[28] Johnson became London's "ambassador of swing," developing a performance style that advertised hot swing dancing to the public.

Six of the players recruited into the Emperors of Jazz were Jamaicans, but others hailed from different parts of the African diaspora, including Britain. None of them were American. Unable to find sufficiently proficient trombone players of color, Thompson hired two white players to perform in blackface. These musicians could play in a wide range of styles, but Thompson's job was to make them sound American. The partnership did not last; it ended with Thompson and some of the players leaving the band. Johnson quickly recruited another four musicians from the West Indies and renamed the ensemble Ken "Snakehips" Johnson's West Indian Dance Orchestra. Advertised as London's first true swing band, it gained its first West End residency at the Old Florida Club in Mayfair in 1938 before moving on as a ten-piece band plus vocalist to the Café de Paris in 1939. Johnson's band attracted patrons with a "predilection for jitterbugging" who were younger and more socially diverse than the Café's upper-crust regulars of prewar years.[29]

Contemporaries judged Johnson's ensemble to be the best jazz band in London, the "first to swing," thanks to the "lift" of the rhythm section.[30] *Melody Maker* also praised their "dancing inducing quality."[31] According to one dance critic, Johnson set the standard for hot swing dancing, descending from his bandstand to join the dancers, with a "dizzy blond" in his arms, warbling "My heart belongs to Daddy."[32] Today, jazz critics continue to praise "the cohesion, collective ensemble and solo swing" of Johnson's band, while noting a certain hybrid repertoire in the swing music, a "subtle," "barely perceptible" calypso phrasing in the trumpets.[33] Black musicians judged Johnson's achievement to be social as much as musical: for Frank Deniz, Johnson "elevated the colour question – people thought something of him," ultimately inspiring him to organize his own band along similar lines.[34]

Wartime Internationalism

In the immediate aftermath of the Café de Paris bombing, the surviving members of Johnson's band dispersed. Some had been injured, others drafted into the service. A few found a place in white dance bands or gained a new public following from presentations on the BBC and recording deals. One former member of Johnson's band went on to form his own band in 1944, but black ensembles did not reclaim a major residency in the West End during wartime. Nonetheless, black musicians continued to perform in the black clubs of Soho, whose fortunes had been reshaped by the wartime arrival of 130,000 black GIs (American servicemen). Racial tensions in Britain sharpened in 1943 as the number of black troops stationed in Britain swelled. In many dancing venues, the kind of interracial scene lauded by Rudolph Dunbar in 1936 provoked violent reactions from white GIs and some Britons. Black troops found a friendlier reception in Soho's "coloured clubs."

Building on meanings already developed by the Popular Front of the thirties, left-leaning media praised interracial dancing at the clubs as the embodiment of wartime internationalism. *Picture Post*'s 1943 photo essay, "Inside London's Coloured Clubs," displays the attractions of Soho clubs for the soldiers and seamen who swelled "London's coloured population." The article's text firmly locates these Soho clubs as the successors to the defunct black clubs of the thirties, most of them, it claimed, the "casualties of the war" (or, more accurately, wartime police crackdowns). Like their predecessors, the new clubs featured hot jazz and musical improvisation by black entertainers. However, the real stars of black clubs were the new wartime clientele. Images, captions, and text all testify to the liveliness, communal energy, and diversity of occupation, skin color, accents, and nationalities of the "international stream" flowing under "white London."[35]

The photographs represent a young communal throng of black men laughing and dancing with ordinary English girls. This dancing scene embodies the internationalist sentiments of the wartime "dancing front," when progressive organs celebrated jazz and jazz dancing as "a potential weapon, and one we possess and Germany doesn't."[36] A wide rectangular photo spread extends across two pages of the story to illustrate the international stream. The reader is positioned at eye level with interracial couples on the dance floor: the "dark Nigerian" facing the camera is dancing with a white woman; next to them, a blond English woman with spectacles, in ordinary street attire, is laughing and dancing with the "light-skinned Negro" from Chicago.

There is one exception to the upbeat communalism: a cameo portrait of "The White Girl Who Likes Frisco's" (Figure 14). This photograph spotlights the face and shoulders of an elegantly dressed and groomed young woman "from Mayfair." She is looking off into the distance, emotionally detached from her black partner in military uniform, his face and figure in shadows. However much *Picture Post* embraced the internationalism of Soho's "coloured clubs," it still registered anxieties about the boundaries of the race and nation through the figure of the self-absorbed female hedonist. There may have been no color bar at these clubs, but *Picture Post*'s rendering of the scene still fell short of realizing Rudolph Dunbar's utopian dreams of a "new outlook on the colour question."

Conclusion

The "international stream" of interracial couples dancing under "White London" in 1943 and the chaotic wreckage at the Café de Paris in 1941 represent different moments in London's wartime history as well as competitive market niches of the nightclub economy. As cultural representations of the nightclub, they present striking points of convergence and divergence. Both build on long-standing associations of the nightclub as a forcing ground for modern self-actualization and international cultural exchange. Both treat pleasure seeking as a defiant mode of political resistance. Both incorporate some nightclub habitués into a mobile, heterogeneous collectivity while marking off others as socially or morally outside the fold. The elite female hedonist presents one test of communal boundaries, the man of color yet another. In *Picture Post*, the "girl from Mayfair" is a detached narcissist, whereas the bejeweled debutante of 1941 emerges as an improvising home-front heroine who tears up her satin gown to make bandages. Even so, the signs of conspicuous consumption in the Café de Paris wreckage – the champagne, priceless jewels, and satin gowns – challenge the democratizing spirit of the Blitz. They accentuate the social divisions between rich and poor even in wartime, even in death. Finally, both events incorporate members of the African diaspora into the wartime landscape, but once again, in radically different ways. *Picture*

FIGURE 14   "The White Girl at Frisco's," from "Inside London's Coloured Clubs," *Picture Post* (July 17, 1943). Photo by Leonard McCombe/Getty Images

Post celebrates the multiple ethnicities of the international dancing stream, while media accounts of the 1941 bombing tend to marginalize and homogenize the "all-coloured" band of musicians as a backdrop to white pleasure. Only "Snakehips" Johnson stands out as the black British ambassador of swing, fondly remembered as an energizing dandy who broke down barriers to join white Europeans, Canadians, and Britons on the Café de Paris dance floor.

Notes

1   "Bombed Dancers Rescued in Restaurant," *Daily Sketch,* Mar. 10, 1941, 2.
2   Berkeley Ballard, in Joshua Levine, ed., *Forgotten Voices of the Blitz and the Battle for Britain: A New History of the Words of the Men and Women on Both Sides* (New York: Random House, 2010), 400–02.
3   "Night Out," *Time*, Mar. 17, 1941, issue 11, vol. 37, p. 27.
4   Ken Snakehips Johnson, quoted in Val Wilmer, "Johnson, Kenrick Reginald Hijmans (1914–1941)," *Oxford Dictionary of National Biography* (Oxford: Oxford University Press, 2006). Online edn, May 2006.
5   "Dance Band Leader Dead," *Manchester Guardian*, Mar. 10, 1941, 4.

6 "The Profession Mourns," *Melody Maker*, Mar. 15, 1941, 1.

7 Frances Lonsdale Donaldson, *Child of the Twenties* (London: Hart-Davis, 1959), 71.

8 Gilbert Seldes, "Shake Your Feet," *New Republic*, Nov. 4, 1925, 284.

9 Marguerite Strickland, quoted in Gavin Weightman and Steve Humphries, *The Making of Modern London: A People's History of the Capital from 1815 to the Present Day* (London: Random House, 2007), 115.

10 Sid Colin, *And the Bands Played On* (London: Elm Tree Books, 1977), 21.

11 "Mushroom Growth of Bottle Party Resorts," *Melody Maker*, Mar. 30, 1935, 1.

12 Richard Carlish, *King of Clubs. Richard Carlish as Told to Alan Bestic* (London: Elek Books, 1962), 36.

13 Leslie Thompson and Jeffrey P. Green, *Leslie Thompson, an Autobiography* (Crowley, UK: Rabbit Press, 1985, 87.

14 Maurice Richardson, "The Bottle Party Belt," *Night and Day*, July 1, 1937, 23.

15 Edgar Jackson, "Hot Dance Bands," *Gramophone*, May 1935, 500.

16 Jack Glicco, *Madness after Midnight* (London: Elek Books, 1952), 132.

17 Hugh Ross Williamson, "In a Negro Night Club," *Listener*, July–Dec. 1936, 250–51.

18 Louis Stephenson, interview, Oct. 28, 1987, London, "Oral History of Jazz in Britain," C122, British Library Sound Archive.

19 Thompson, *Leslie Thompson*, 36.

20 Wilmer, "Johnson."

21 Franklyn Frank, "London Pair Name New Club after the late Florence Mills," *Afro-American*, Aug. 1, 1936, 11. Web version.

22 Nnamdi Azikiwe, *My Odyssey: An Autobiography* (New York: Praeger, 1970), 203.

23 Rudolph Dunbar, "Harlem in London: Year of Advancement for Negroes," *Melody Maker*, Mar. 7, 1936, 2.

24 John Weldon Johnson, quoted in Shane Vogel, *Scene of the Harlem Cabaret: Race, Sexuality, and Performance* (Chicago: University of Chicago Press, 2009), 84.

25 Harry Gold, *Gold, Doubloons and Pieces of Eight: The Autobiography of Harry Gold*, ed. Roger Cotterrell (London: Northway, 2000), 52.

26 Monica Miller, "The Dandy as Bad Modernist," in Douglas Mao and Rebecca L. Walkowitz, eds. *Bad Modernisms* (Durham: Duke University Press, 2006), 182.

27 Lewis A. Erenberg, *Swingin' the Dream: Big Band Jazz and the Rebirth of American Culture* (Chicago: University of Chicago Press, 1998), 49–50.

28 Thompson, *Leslie Thompson*, 91.

29 Josephine Bradley, "Random Reflections: War-time Dancing," *Dancing Times,* Feb. 1940, 192.

30 Les Leston, to the Editor, *Daily Mirror*, Dec. 22, 2012. Web version.

31 Andy Simon, "Black British Swing: The African Diaspora's Contribution to England's Own Jazz of the 1930s and 1940s," Dec. 22, 2012. Web version.

32 Bradley, "Random Reflections."

33 Alyn Shipton, *A New History of Jazz* (London: Bloomsbury, 2004), 268; "Swinging into the Blitz: A Culture Show Special," BBC 2, uploaded on YouTube, June 25, 2013.

34 Frank Deniz, quoted in Val Wilmer, "First Sultan of Swing," *Independent*, Feb. 24, 1991, 10.

35 "Inside London's Coloured Clubs," *Picture Post,* July 17, 1943, 19–21.

36 Tom Harrisson and Charles Madge, eds., *War Begins at Home* (London: Chatto & Windus, 1940), 250.

11

Sport

Sports are a human universal that assumes culturally specific forms. During the era of literary and artistic modernism, from 1890 to 1940, sports pervaded Western society thoroughly as in Greek antiquity. During these years, moreover, sports and body image were more closely related than at any time since Christian asceticism put an end to pagan athletic festivals. The ideal body for young men and – to a lesser degree – young women was the body capable of, trained for, and physically shaped by sports.[1]

I

The Uniqueness of Modern Sports

Modern sports are fundamentally different, spatially, temporally, and conceptually, from premodern physical contests. Spatial differences are the easiest to understand. Premodern sports such as Nuba wrestling and Cherokee stickball were local; modern sports are global. Although the athletic festivals of Greek antiquity flourished throughout the Mediterranean littoral, they were narrowly confined in comparison to modern sports such as soccer (football). A second fundamental spatial difference has to do with venues. Premodern sports customarily took place in the unbuilt natural environment, but modern sports sites are purpose built and sport specific. There are of course exceptions to both halves of this generalization. Roman chariot races, which were unquestionably premodern, took place in purpose-built, sport-specific facilities, the "circuses" that the poet Juvenal had in mind when he condemned "bread and circuses"; most modern rowers train and race on rivers or lakes rather than in a constructed basin of water.

Modern purpose-built, sport-specific facilities vary in countless ways. No one ever mistook Lord's Cricket Ground for Madison Square Garden. While some sport-specific sites, such as golf courses, mimic the natural environment, most do not. Most modern sports are played on rectangular or (less often) elliptical surfaces whose dimensions have been standardized by national or international sports federations. Baseball is unusual in that the infield is diamond shaped and the outfield is unbounded, and the players' movement is circular. Untouched by a retrieved ball, successful batters *round* the bases. In nearly every other modern ballgame, the movement of the players and/or the ball is back and forth.

Modern ludic (from *ludus*, "game") space also differs from premodern in that distances are precisely measured in standardized units. The shortest race at Greek athletic festivals was from one end of the stadium to the other, but stadiums were of various sizes, which meant that the length of the *stade* race varied from site to site. Comparability was clearly a problem, which is why no comparisons have come down to us.

Modern sports are also temporally different from premodern sports. The latter were often associated with religious ritual, which meant that they occurred at irregular intervals dictated by the lunar or – less commonly – the solar calendar. Premodern sports that were *not* seasonal in this sense often took place to celebrate an important political event or in response to a challenge. Examples are the tournament given by Henry VIII in 1511 to celebrate the birth of a son by Katharine of Aragon and the grand intercity match staged by Strasbourg in 1575 to demonstrate the superiority of its crossbow archers. For such competitions, there was obviously no calendar of events.

Although we still continue to speak of summer games and winter sports, modern sports are not strictly seasonal. The entrepreneurs who control modern professional sports schedule as many contests as they possibly can, which means that there is in fact scarcely a day in the year when two or more major sports are not simultaneously vying for the fans' attention. Baseball, the archetypical "summer game," often begins before the last snowbanks have melted away and ends after the first fall freeze. The National Hockey League, which now has franchises as far south as Florida, has extended its season into May.

Modern sports are temporally different in other, less obvious ways. Nature set limits to the duration of premodern sports events. Ballgames often began by dawn's early light and ended when there was a winner or when play was halted by darkness. Modern ballgames begin, typically, "on the hour" and last a predetermined number of minutes or until one side or another has scored a predetermined number of points or goals. When "clocked time" differs from "natural time," as it does in American football, a sixty-minute game can last for several hours. Baseball is, once again, an anomaly. Each of the game's nine innings lasts until each of the two sides has had three of its nine players put out, which means, theoretically, that a game can last forever while an immensely superior team scores an infinite number of runs.

Temporal difference also appears in a more abstract form. Given the tools for measurement available in antiquity, it was at least theoretically possible to determine the length of a footrace in local feet (which varied from city to city). It was utterly impossible, given the state of ancient chronometry, to measure the victor's time. The best that the ancients were able to say was "fast, faster, fastest," and that was all they cared about. Modern runners and swimmers (and horses) have their times measured to the hundredth of a second.

The precise measurement of distances and times gave birth, in the late nineteenth century, to the concept of the sports record. Within the context of premodern sports, there was no way to express this concept (other than to say that a wrestler or a chariot driver had won more times than anyone else). There seems to be no way to talk about modern sports without the "stats" and the records for which the "stats" are a logical sine qua non. An obsession with quantified records is, indeed, one of the hallmarks of modern sports.

Modern sports are also conceptually different. They are shaped by what Max Weber called "instrumental rationality," the use of reason to determine the most efficient means to any given end, and by what Michel Foucault called "the technology of the body." Combining both concepts, we can speak of ludic technology, by which we mean the scientific search for equipment and training that will enable an athlete to achieve his or her optimal performance. By 1890, ludic technology had transformed competitive rowing from awkward efforts in clumsy boats to the disciplined movements of trained bodies in scientifically designed lightweight "shells" equipped with iron outriggers and sliding seats. It had also transformed the backyard hurdler's leafy hedge into the track athlete's lightly constructed portable rectangles placed at precisely measured intervals on a 440-yard elliptical track. Unfortunately, ludic technology was also well on its way to the widespread production of performance-enhancing drugs. Thomas Hicks won the 1904 Olympic marathon with the aid of two milligrams of strychnine and a glass of brandy.

The best example of ludic technology, however, is the invention of a wholly new sport. Basketball has no recognizable ludic antecedents. It was invented by James Naismith on December 21, 1891, at the YMCA's School for Christian Workers in Springfield, Massachusetts. Naismith described his invention as "a modern synthetic product of the office. The conditions were recognized, the requirements met, and the rules formulated ... before any attempt was made to test its value." He recalled, in an article published in the *American Physical Education Review* (1914), that he had been challenged by the school's superintendent to create an indoor game "for the winter season ... that would have the same interest for the young man that football has in the fall and baseball in the spring." In his article, Naismith reconstructed the sequence of logical steps that led to the solution of his problem. Perhaps the best indicator of his instrumentally rational approach was the placement of the goal. Fearful of potential injury from balls hurled forcefully at a ground-level vertical goal (like soccer's), Naismith elevated the goal above the players' heads and designed it so that its aperture was horizontal and narrow. The ball *had* to be propelled softly – in those pre–dunk-shot days – if its arc was to pass through the center of the basket. Constructed rule by rule, basketball represents rational design.

Naismith's rules were continuously reshaped by various national and international organizations anxious to perfect the game and to enhance its attractiveness and profitability. One result of this instrumentally rational approach to play is that historians can chronicle the development of the rules in the minutest detail. The pivot was allowed in 1893, the dribble in 1896. At first, fouls were penalized by points, but the free throw was introduced in 1894 as an added element of suspense. Naismith began with nine players to a side (because his YMCA class consisted of eighteen men), but the Amateur Athletic Union reduced teams to five in 1897. The peach-basket goals of the first game made retrieval of the ball something of an inconvenience. The problem solvers knocked out the basket's bottom. The modern net, "basket" in name only, was introduced in 1906. The out-of-bounds rule was imposed in 1913 to end mad scrambles for loose balls, and the jump for the ball that followed every basket was eliminated in 1937. This innovation quickened the pace of the game and satisfied, for the moment, the demands of ludic technology.

II

The Development of Modern Sports

Team Sports: Cricket

The earliest reference to the iconically English game of cricket is from the late thirteenth century, but the transition from premodern to modern ludic forms began in the eighteenth century, when, for instance, the dimensions of the bat and the pitch were determined and niceties like the leg-before-wicket prohibition were mentioned. The first complete set of rules appeared in 1744, which was also the first year from which we have records of a fully scored match. The Marylebone Cricket Club (MCC), which became the game's most hallowed, most authoritative institution, was established in 1787.

Although the titled aristocrats who controlled the MCC were status conscious enough to distinguish "gentlemen" cricketers from mere "players," they were egalitarian enough to allow the latter to join the former on (but not off) the field. The gentleman-player distinction was less extreme than the Henley Regatta's amateur rule, which excluded not only athletes who competed for money or material prizes but also anyone who had *ever* been employed in manual labor of any sort whatsoever. In the course of the nineteenth century, occasional cricket matches on village greens evolved into a national system of county cricket and a series of international Tests that matched English teams against teams from the Dominions and the colonies.

For the years 1890 to 1940, Australian Tests were the most important. Cricket clubs had been formed in Sydney (1826) and Melbourne (1838). Regular steamship voyages between Britain and its colonies made international matches possible, and newspapers were eager to report if not to sponsor them. Rivalry for the "Ashes," the terracotta urn that has since 1882 symbolized cricket supremacy, was so intense and the controversies that surrounded the MCC's 1932–1933 Australian tour were so rancorous that diplomats from both countries had to intervene and an English player commented lugubriously, "Well, we shall win the Ashes – but we may lose a Dominion."

W.G. Grace, a Gloucestershire medical practitioner, was nineteenth-century county cricket's brightest star. In English poetry, he *was* England. Early in the twentieth century, he was rivaled by a Cambridge-educated Indian, K.S. Ranjitsinhji. In the 1920s and 1930s, the Australian batsman

Donald Bradman eclipsed all other cricket stars. Popular novels and poems about cricket abound, but not in the modernist canon.

Team Sports: Football

The iconography of cricket has been nostalgically pastoral. "The cricket pitch, nestling among mature trees with the Norman church and half-timbered pub nearby," writes John Bale, "is, to many, the quintessence of rural England." The iconography of soccer has been decidedly different. Pictured in our imagination against a background of coal mines and steel mills, the football pitch is an emblem of the industrial age.

The modern game evolved from medieval sports such as English folk-football and French *soule*. The medieval rules were simple. Kicking, throwing, and carrying the ball, villagers made their way across fields, through hedges, over streams, and down narrow streets until they were able to propel the ball into the portal of the opposing villagers' parish church. It was a rough game that the sixteenth-century Puritan moralist Philip Stubbes found lamentably conducive to "fighting, brawling, contention, quarrel-picking, murther, homicide, and great effusion of blood."

A somewhat less violent version of football was born in 1848 when fourteen students of Trinity College, Cambridge, agreed upon a single set of rules for the many different football codes that they and their Oxford counterparts had played at Eton and other "public" schools. Fifteen years later, on October 26, 1863, a group of Londoners, mostly graduates of Oxford and Cambridge, founded the strictly amateur Football Association (from which soccer took its name). They were elitists who intended to keep the game to themselves. *The Times* approved, opining that thoughtless gentlemen who stooped to compete with "artisans, mechanics, and such like troublesome persons" contributed to the "social degradation" of amateur sports. Unfortunately for the "old boys," the desire to win trumped class prejudice. Clubs began to accept working-class members as long as they scored goals and renounced the taint of cash payment.

The workers took over the game. Manchester United, the world's best-known soccer club, began as Newton Heath FC, founded in 1878 by railroad workers. Coventry City FC had its start as a club organized by the workers at Singer's bicycle factory. In 1895, laborers at the Thames Iron Works founded a team that became West Ham United FC.

When soccer spread to the European continent in the 1870s and 1880s, the game's social composition changed in exactly the same way. Upper-class schoolboys were the first to emulate their English coevals, but miners and factory workers were quick to follow. Diffusion to Latin America took the same course. Argentine schoolboys were the first to play, but employees of British-owned railroads soon founded a number of working-class soccer clubs, typical of which was Rosario Central (1889). By 1930, the Latin American game had developed so rapidly that football-mad Uruguay was able to host and win football's first World Cup. (The runner-up was Argentina.)

The Football Association's trepidation about including working-class players was a realistic assessment of the danger of professionalization (understood in the everyday sense of "play for pay"). Harkening to the clubs' lament that they *needed* some factory hands to compete against their rivals' factory hands, the FA reluctantly agreed that clubs might reimburse players for their travel expenses, but believers in amateurism drew the line at payments for "broken time" (time lost from work). It was a lost cause. Under-the-table payment became so common and so embarrassing that the FA's directors capitulated in 1888 and accepted the establishment of openly professional teams.

The Football League began with twelve teams, six from the North of England and six from the Midlands. Four years after its birth, FL expanded into a First and a Second Division. By century's end, teams from the Midlands and the North, Britain's most industrialized areas, dominated the game. By the 1920s, the working-class stamp was so strong that British football grounds were said to be the site of "the Labour party at prayer."

Football grounds were not, however, hospitable to women at play. A few hardy women played soccer in the Victorian era and somewhat more sustained involvement began during World War I when Grace Sibbert formed a women's team from employees of Dick, Kerr & Company, an engineering firm. After the war, the Dick, Kerr's Ladies played four matches against a team formed from nine French sports clubs. In 1921, twenty-five English teams formed a Ladies' Football Association, but the FA banned use of its grounds.

The FA was similarly uncooperative when it came to foreign clubs. In 1903, Robert Guérin, a French sports official, suggested to the FA that an international federation be formed to propagate the game. The English were not interested and Guérin characterized his efforts to persuade them as "like beating the air." Undeterred, he went ahead with his plans and the *Fédération Internationale de Football Association* (FIFA) was formed on May 21, 1904, by representatives of France, Belgium, Denmark, Holland, Spain, Sweden, and Switzerland. The four British soccer federations, whose members far outnumbered those of any continental nation, boycotted the organization.

Rugby's history is similar. It evolved from medieval folk-football, achieved its more-or-less civilized form in 1871 with the establishment of Rugby Football Union (RFU), and spawned an openly professional league in 1895 when eleven clubs from Yorkshire, nine from Lancashire, and two from Cheshire withdrew from RFU and formed the Northern Rugby Football Union, which allowed compensation for wages lost when players missed time at work. RFU's reaction was to expel clubs whose members played with or against a Northern RFU club.

The amateur version of the game, which flourished in Wales, the Southwest of France, and New Zealand, underwent an unexpected transformation in the United States, where it arrived on May 15, 1874, when students from Montreal's McGill University competed against a novice squad from Harvard. Rugby proved to be immensely attractive to upper-class American youths uncertain of their masculinity and seeking to demonstrate the manly courage that their elders had recently proved on bloody Civil War battlefields. Two years later, representatives from Harvard, Columbia, Princeton, and Yale, meeting in Springfield, Massachusetts, founded the Intercollegiate Football Association (IFA).

The IFA initially adopted RFU rules, but they were quickly modified. The impetus behind most of the rule changes came from a single man. For forty-six years, Walter Camp, who had played the game for Yale, was the dominant force on the Rules Committee that transformed rugby into American football. Camp, who worked for a clock manufacturer, approached the game with an engineer's commitment to instrumental rationality. He was responsible for the reduction of the team from fifteen men to eleven. More importantly, he replaced the chaotic shoving and pushing of the rugby scrum with the static line of scrimmage. Both innovations were introduced in 1880. After dogged possession of the ball turned the 1882 Yale-Princeton game into a scoreless tie, Camp required the offensive team to gain five yards in three tries ("downs") or to surrender possession of the ball. That rule required a field marked with lines of chalk. The look of the lined field gave the game its nineteenth-century name: gridiron football. Like Frederick Winslow Taylor of scientific-management fame, Camp understood the advantages of specialization. "Division of labor," he wrote, "has been so thoroughly and successfully carried out on the football field that a player nowadays must train for a particular position." That Camp was not prophetic enough to foresee that specialization would eventually lead to entirely separate offensive, defensive, and "specials" teams does not detract from his insight.

American football's success narrative was interrupted by violence. Soccer has always been plagued by rowdy fans scorned as "football hooligans," but gridiron football's violence was committed by the players. By 1905, the problem of on-field violence was so serious that 18 players were killed and 159 were seriously injured. When the Rules Committee failed to take remedial action, representatives from thirty-eight schools met early in 1906 and established the Intercollegiate Athletic Association, or IAA (renamed National Collegiate Athletic Association in 1910). The IAA acted on its mandate to reform the game. New rules specified that ten yards were required for a first down (instead of five) and four downs were allowed (instead of three), but changes of this sort did little to diminish the violence that was the organization's original *raison d'être*. In fact, the number of those fatally injured rose to thirty in the fall. Meaningful reform came when the Rules Committee decided the following spring to remove the fifteen-yard penalty for an incomplete forward pass. This opened the game and encouraged throwing the ball rather than running with it. Biomass ceased to be decisive – at least until later in the century, when anabolic steroids and year-round training produced a new breed of brobdingnagian players.

That references to and interpretations of these three football codes – soccer, rugby, and American football – permeated twentieth-century popular music, realistic fiction, and applied art is well known, but few cultural historians have noted rugby's importance as a modernist topos in music and the visual arts. In 1929, Arthur Honegger composed symphonic music to what he called "the savage, brusque, disordered, struggling rhythm of rugby." Henri Rousseau's *Rugby Players* (1908) can be labeled primitivist rather than modernist, but there is no doubt about the modernism of Robert Delaunay's *The Cardiff Rugby Team* (1912–1913), André Lhote's *Rugby* (1917), and Max Beckmann's *Rugby Players* (1929). Why soccer and American football were not equally prominent in the modernist movement is an unanswered question.

Team Sports: Baseball

Credit for the innovations that transformed traditional English bat-and-ball games into American baseball is usually given to the

Knickerbocker Base Ball Club, organized on September 23, 1845, by Alexander Joy Cartwright and other youths from New York's mercantile class. The following June, the Knickerbockers lost to the New York Nine, by the embarrassing score of 23–1, after which the team seems to have dissolved. They were replaced by the New York Gothams (1850), the Excelsiors (1854), and a number of other middle-class teams. The first viable blue-collar clubs were the Eckfords of Greenpoint and the Atlantics of Jamaica, both founded in 1856. It was they – the dockworkers, teamsters, bricklayers, and carpenters, not the merchants and young professionals – who became the new sport's typical players.

By 1858, baseball was popular enough for twenty-two clubs to form a National Association of Base Ball Players. Among the organization's contributions were the nine-inning format and the called strike. Contrary to what one might have expected, the Civil War advanced rather than hindered the diffusion of the game. Union soldiers from the Northeast taught the game not only to the men of Midwestern regiments but also to Confederate troopers with whom they fraternized in prisoner-of-war camps.

Openly professional baseball began in 1869 when Harry Wright's Cincinnati Red Stockings toured the Northeast, won every game, and earned the handsome sum of $9,400. Wright then enrolled the team in a National Association of Professional Base Ball Players, which began play in 1871. Each team agreed to play every other team five times, but there was no gate sharing and the teams were unable to agree on a fixed schedule. Instrumental rationality came to the rescue in 1876, when Wright banded together with William A. Hulbert and A.G. Spalding to create an eight-team National League of Professional Base Ball Clubs. Their canny rationalization of the game required every team to play every other team a set number of times according to a set schedule devised by the owners. Rail transportation was advanced enough to make it quite practical for geographically distant teams to compete on a regular basis. Journalists traveling with their local teams quickly learned telegraphic English: "New York will be in Boston tomorrow."

Operating as a cartel, the National League attempted to monopolize baseball, but the game's profitability inspired competition. The American Association was formed in 1881 by a group of Midwestern entrepreneurs – mostly German-American brewers – who enticed crowds with twenty-five-cent ticket prices, Sunday games, and foaming mugs of beer. After the 1891 season, the National League absorbed four of the American

Association's teams and then used its monopolistic power to raise ticket prices and reduce players' salaries. Keen competition from the American League, formed in 1900 by Byron Bancroft Johnson, forced the National League, in 1903, reluctantly to accept the newcomer as an equal partner. Until this moment, baseball had been in constant flux. Between 1876 and 1900, teams representing twenty-one different cities had National League franchises. The sixteen teams party to the 1903 agreement stayed where they were for the next half-century.

Talented black baseball players had seemed on the verge of a significant breakthrough in 1884, when Oberlin-educated Moses Fleetwood Walker and his brother Weldy played for Toledo in the American Association. Unfortunately, racists such as the Chicago White Sox's Adrian "Cap" Anson felt that the presence of black players was an intolerable affront. African-American players were forced from major-league baseball and Anson was doomed to be remembered less for his great skills than for his infamous shout, "Get that nigger off the field!"

By the end of the century, black players were gone from the major leagues but not from baseball. Thanks largely to the efforts of Cumberland Posey and William A. "Gus" Greenlee, a Negro National League was established in 1920. Playing unofficial games against white teams wintering in Cuba, African Americans such as Josh Gibson and James "Cool Papa" Bell proved that they were as good at baseball as the major leagues' best.

Just as black players were forced out of major-league baseball, Irish and German Americans were welcomed in. "German and Irish players so dominated some rosters," writes Larry Gerlach, "that teams on St. Patrick's Day staged intrasquad games between the two ethnic groups." Ironically, the greatest German-American player was never perceived in ethnic categories. George Herman "Babe" Ruth was worshipped as a representative American rather than as an ethnic hero.

Americans who marvel at Ruth's contributions to the "golden age" of American baseball seldom realize that he was also godfather to Japan's first professional sports league. Baseball arrived in Japan in the 1880s and became a national passion in the 1920s. In 1934, Shôriki Matsutarô, owner of Tokyo's *Yomiuri Shimbun* newspaper, invited Philadelphia Athletics owner Connie Mack to come to Japan with an exhibition team. One hundred thousand fans stormed Tokyo's Meiji Stadium in order to see Ruth and Gehrig. The Japan Professional Baseball League was born two years later. Its seven teams were financed by three railway companies and four newspapers. Thus Japan's emblematically modern sport was sponsored by enterprises symbolizing modern transportation and communication.

Images of baseball players, ubiquitous in popular culture, appeared in modernist art as well. The multiple perspectives of James Henry Daugherty's Cubist *Three Base Hit* (1914), the grotesque foreshortening of Philip Evergood's Expressionistic *Early Youth of Babe Ruth* (c. 1939), and the contortions of Jacob Lawrence's *Strike* (1949) are good examples. As for modernist poetry, Marianne Moore's "Baseball and Writing" is unbeatable.

Individual Sports: Athletics

From Athens in 1896 to Berlin in 1936, Olympic runners and swimmers had their quadrennial week in the sun. In the 1920s and 1930s, extraordinary track-and-field athletes such as Paavo Nurmi, Mildred "Babe" Didrikson, and Jesse Owens briefly captured the world's attention, but team sports were always more popular with participants and spectators than individual sports were. As if in compensation, the latter were prominent in modernist art and literature. Paintings by Robert Delaunay (*Runners*, 1926) and Willi Baumeister (*Runner II*, 1927) and novels by Henry de Montherlant (*Le Songe*, 1922; *Les Olympiques*, 1938) are prime examples of modernist fascination with athletics. But the most impressive modernist treatment of individual sports is Leni Riefenstahl's technically innovative, visually awesome, politically questionable two-part documentary film, *Olympia* (1938). Viewing the introductory collage of Greek statuary, the morphing of Myron's discus thrower into his modern counterpart, the spliced images of the divers, and the fencers' surrealist shadows, one has to conclude that Riefenstahl's film is the most spectacular and most memorable twentieth-century aestheticization of sports. (The 1936 Olympics were also memorable for a breakthrough in communications technology. Televised images of the competition were visible in a number of Berlin *Fernsehstuben*.)

Individual Sports: Tennis and Golf

The Renaissance game of court tennis, a favorite of Henry VIII, adopted its simpler modern dress in 1874 when Walter Wingfield received a patent for Sphairistike, a racquet-and-ball game played on a portable hourglass-shaped court. Three years later, the court was rectangular and the sport was lawn tennis. Two years after that, the All-England Croquet Club, located in Wimbledon, staged its first (men-only) tournament.

British players dominated until the 1920s, when flamboyant Suzanne Lenglen overwhelmed her ladylike opponents and her countrymen – Jean Borotra, Henri Cochet, and René Lacoste – battled the American William Tilden for supremacy in the men's game. Throughout the *entre deux guerres* period, tennis remained very largely a country-club sport. The same can be said of the game of golf, whose rules were formulated by the Royal and Ancient Golf Club of St. Andrews in 1754. In both tennis and golf, the country of origin quickly lost its ludic hegemony. British golfers won most of the pre-1914 tournaments, but the brightest stars of the 1920s were the Americans Glenna Collett and Robert Trent "Bobby" Jones.

Throughout the 1920s and 1930s, countless images of golfers and tennis players appeared in daily newspapers and in the sport-specific weekly journals that sprang up wherever the seeds of modernity took root. Although golfers and tennis players seldom figure in the work of modernist painters, Childe Hassam did place a single tiny figure in the Impressionist landscape of *The Dune Hazard* (1922), and tennis players are the subject of Fernand Khnopff's Symbolist *Memories* (1889), Max Liebermann's Impressionist *Tennisplayer at the Seaside* (1901), Marcel Gromaire's cartoonish *Tennis devant la Mer* (1928), and – most impressively – in Willi Baumeister's totally abstract *Tennis Player in a Blue Oval* (1935).

Individual Sports: Boxing

By 1892, when John L. Sullivan lost the heavyweight championship to James "Gentleman Jim" Corbett, boxing had become a somewhat modernized version of bare-knuckles brawling, which went on until one of the two combatants was too battered to "come up to scratch." The Sullivan-Corbett bout was a gloved contest conducted by the Marquess of Queensberry Rules (1867), which specified three-minute rounds with one-minute rests in between. In 1910, the London-based National Sporting Club carried ludic technology a step farther by dividing boxers into eight weight classes. That boxers were able to win on points rather than by a knockout mollified but did not eliminate boxing's savagery.

From 1908, when Jack Johnson became the first black heavyweight champion, until 1938, when Joe Louis reclaimed the title from Max Schmeling, boxing was a stage for the racially inflected performance of masculinity. Popular culture was rife with references to and images of champion boxers. Boxing figured in realistic fiction such as Louis

Hémon's *Battling Malone, Pugiliste* (1925) and in the figurational art of Thomas Hart Benton and dozens of lesser artists. George Bellows was unquestionably the modernist painter most enthralled by men reduced to their most primitive selves, but he was definitely not alone.

Technological Sports

Modernity brought not only a reconceptualization of the technologies of the body but also wholly new technological sports such as bicycle, automobile, and airplane racing.

Cycling has numerous technical terms taken from French rather than English – *péleton, derailleuer, domestique* – because it is the only globally popular modern sport with French rather than British or American origins. As early as 1868, there were bicycle races in Paris and in Bordeaux. In 1891, clubs from Bordeaux (*Le Vélo*) and Paris (*Véloce Sport*) sponsored a race from Bordeaux to Paris. It was won by an Englishman, George Pilkington Mills, who traversed 560 kilometers in fourteen hours. In the 1890s, Paris was dotted with more than three hundred built-to-purpose velodromes, symbols of the *La belle époque sportive*. Among them was the famed *Vélodrome Buffalo*, frequented by Henri de Toulouse-Lautrec (who picked up a few extra francs painting bicycle advertisements). The *Tour de France* (1903) was and still is cycling's most important competition. It was the inspired invention of Henri Desgranges, cyclist, velodrome manager, sports journalist, and editor-in-chief of *L'Auto*. (The jersey worn by the leader of the race is yellow because that was the color of *L'Auto*'s cover.) The inaugural tour, which lasted nineteen days, consisted of six stages and a mere 2,408 kilometers. The weary victor, Maurice Garin, pocketed 6,125 gold francs and the circulation of *L'Auto* more than doubled. Italy's great tour, the *Giro d'Italia*, began in 1909. The leader wears a rose-colored jersey because the *Gazzetta dello Sport*, which sponsored the race, appeared on rose-colored paper. The most successful Italian cyclist was Gino Bartali, who won the *Giro* in 1936 and 1937 and the *Tour* in 1938.

The *Tour de France* continues to fascinate millions, but automobiles quickly displaced bicycles as emblems of ludic modernity. The first major automobile race, sponsored in 1894 by *Le Petit Journal,* was from Paris to Rouen. A year later, a pair of French counts formed the *Automobile-Club de France* and staged the first Paris-Bordeaux-Paris automobile competition, sending a wave of excitement across the continent. Tracks were constructed by the French at Le Mans (1906), the British at Brooklands (1907), and the Americans at Indianapolis (1911).

Although airplane pilots competed to fly the fastest, the farthest, and the highest, the most memorable flights, for Americans, were Charles Lindbergh's transatlantic solo flight to Paris (1927) and Amelia Earhart's disappearance somewhere over the Pacific (1937). The French focused on Louis Blériot's historic 1909 flight across the English Channel.

Modernist artists and writers responded to the gamut of modern sports, but their most intense and sustained engagement was – not surprisingly – with the technological sports created during and emblematic of modernity. Modernist painters were mesmerized by cycling. Lyonel's Feininger's *Bicycle Race* (1912), Umberto Boccioni's *Dynamics of a Cyclist* (1913), and Natalia Goncharova's *Cyclist* (1913) are clearly Futurist, while Jean Metzinger's *Racing Cyclist* (1914) is just as clearly Cubist and Lazlo Moholy-Nagy's *Bicycle Racer* (1919) is unmistakably Bauhaus. All five painters evoke the thrill of mechanized velocity. Their paintings are clearly affirmations of the sport and of the modernity it symbolizes. Modernist writers were also pulled along by the cyclists' draft. Georg Kaiser's Expressionist *From Morning to Midnight* (1911) includes a six-day bicycle race. That Ernest Hemingway's *The Sun Also Rises* (1926) contrasts the nobility of bullfighting, a premodern survival, with the commercialism, dishonesty, and sheer vulgarity of bicycle racing, is no surprise, but the depiction of Albertine as an avid cyclist in Marcel Proust's exquisitely nostalgic search for lost time is rather unexpected.

Futurist painters attentive to Filippo Tommaso Marinetti's innumerable manifestos also attempted to translate the rush and roar of automotive *velocità* into abstract art, but Luigo Russolo's *Dynamism of an Automobile* (1911) and Giacomo Balla's *Automobile Race* (1913) failed to accomplish what is, finally, impossible. Although words on a page might seem even less likely than pigments on a canvas to capture the excitement of an automobile race, Kasimir Edschmid's *Sport um Gagaly* (1928) comes close. Cesare Passari, the novel's hero, whom we meet at the wheel of a Lancia, is an ardent *automobilista*, a daring driver whose state-of-the-art Fiat leaves Peugeot drivers in the dust.

Robert Delaunay's modernist festival of circular color, *Hommage to Blériot* (1914), was obviously inspired by Blériot's cross-channel flight. Futurist painter Mario Sironi followed with *Yellow Airplane and a View of the City* (1915). In addition to Kasimir Edschmid, whose Cesare Passari is an airplane pilot as well as an automobile racer, at least one other modernist novelist responded to the Futurist call for fiction appropriate to modernity. William Faulkner, famed as the chronicler of Yoknapatawpha County, also published *Pylon* (1935), a modernist take on the thrill of airplane races.

III

The Modern Body

Modern sports began in England, but modern conceptions of physical education and fitness derive very largely from the gymnastic traditions of eighteenth-century Germany and nineteenth-century Scandinavia. From their origins until the 1940s, German and Scandinavian gymnastic organizations were at odds with rather than enthusiastic about modern sports, which they considered more harmful than beneficial to one's health. The criticism of sports was most emphatically expressed by Europe's largest and most influential gymnastics organization, *Die Deutsche Turnerschaft*, established in 1868. The *Turner* roundly condemned modern sports, which they considered to be individualistic and competitive rather than collective and cooperative. They argued that gymnastics exercised the entire body while modern sport's specialized movements resulted in asymmetrical and unhealthy physiques.

Gymnastics and related forms of exercise such as calisthenics and military drill had one insurmountable problem: boredom. While educators preached health and hygiene, their students rushed to experience the physical and psychological excitement of sports competition. In Europe, the conflict between physical education and sports was resolved by amiable divorce: school curricula required gymnastic sessions; private clubs offered sports. In the United States, however, physical-education classes evolved into a system of intercollegiate sports that by 1929 had become so professionalized that the Carnegie Foundation warned (vainly) about the degradation of American higher education.

Turn-of-the-century fitness reformers such Eugene Sandow and Bernarr Macfadden thought of themselves as educators. Their fitness agenda, propagated by posing performances, beauty contests, and magazines such Macfadden's *Physical Culture*, was motivated by aesthetic rather than athletic considerations. While weightlifters strained to hoist the heaviest possible barbell, Sandow flexed to display the perfect body.

Ideas about what that perfect body should look like varied with social class. Not surprisingly, the ideal for working-class men was a robust

FIGURE 15 "The Coming Game: Yale Versus Vassar," *Colliers Weekly* (1895)

body fit for manual labor; for their wives, the ideal was a body capable of hard work and frequent childbirths. In the 1890s, men and women of Thorstein Veblen's leisure class began to alter their notions of physical attractiveness. The heavy body that signaled wealth enough to sit down for a five-course dinner – conspicuous consumption indeed! – became less prestigious than the body fit for and formed by modern sports. This was somewhat truer for men than for women because a vocal minority of nineteenth-century medical experts wrongly believed that strenuous physical activity damaged the reproductive organs of middle- and upper-class women. Their exaggerated fears were ineffective. The 1890s were, after all, the era of the "Gibson Girl," whose iconic attributes were bicycles, tennis racquets, and golf clubs (see Figure 15).

The director of Harvard's Hemenway Gymnasium, from 1879 to 1919, was Dudley Sargent, a reformist proponent of German and Swedish gymnastics. One of his projects was to determine the ideal body, which he did by systematically measuring the bodies of male and female students. When he averaged the measurements, he found that the composite body, for girls as well as boys, had proportions remarkably similar to those of Greek athletic statues. Small wonder, then, that Sargent hailed Sandow, whose most famous pose imitated the Farnese Hercules, as the world's most perfectly developed man.

By the 1920s and 1930s, however, sports rather than calisthenics and drill were the preferred path to physical fitness and the ideal body for everyone not employed as a physical-education teacher. European and

American filmmakers flooded the market with sports films. Arnold Fanck sent Leni Riefenstahl up and down snow-covered mountains in *The White Hell of Pitz Palu* (1929) and three other feature films. Three-time Olympic champion Sonja Henie skated gracefully through no fewer than seven films between 1936 and 1939. Riefenstahl and Henie had plenty of company. When Hollywood producers replaced magazine illustrators as arbiters of male and female physical beauty, they looked surprisingly often not only for athletic men and women such as Douglas Fairbanks and Katharine Hepburn but also for actual Olympic champions such as Johnny Weissmuller and Eleanor Holm. German filmmakers were even more explicit. Wilhelm Prager's 1925 documentary, *Paths to Strength and Beauty*, reverting to Sandow's Hellenizing poses, drew a parallel between the naked bodies of ancient and modern athletes. The athletic body was not as perfectly proportioned as the body developed by gymnastics, but it was good enough for the ancients and good enough for modern men (and women).

Notes

1 The sources for all the quotations and for all the factual information pertaining to sports history are indicated in the notes to my books: *Games and Empires* (New York: Columbia University Press, 1994) and *Sports: The First Five Millennia* (Amherst: University of Massachusetts Press, 2004).

12
_____

Travel

Modernity's rapidly changing technology, Walter Benjamin argues in "Some Motifs in Baudelaire," has transformed not only the practice and practicalities of modern living but human sensibility as well. From the invention of the match to the "shocks and collisions" of urban traffic, "technology," he suggests, "has subjected the human sensorium to a complex kind of training."[1] In recent years, a number of modernist scholars have looked at the way rapid technological change shaped subjectivity, modes of perception, and aesthetic form in the late nineteenth and early twentieth century and how writers and artists of the period registered these changes in their creative work. Photography, film, x-rays, the phonograph, the telephone, the telegraph, the gramophone, the radio, even the typewriter all had far-reaching influence on society and the arts.[2] Yet perhaps there was no technological advance that had such profound effects on life and art in those years as the increasing speed, availability, and (comparative) comfort of modes of travel. Modernist art and literature sprang up in the great metropoles, which had become international hubs, centers where numerous routes met. As Raymond Williams has argued, it was the very "miscellaneity of the metropolis" that made its contacts so productive and produced the fractured, multifaceted, heterogeneous creative forms we know as modernist art.[3] Modernism was cosmopolitan; provincialism was, as the title of a famous essay by Ezra Pound puts it, "the enemy."

The increasing efficiency of modes of transport had been driven largely by the desire for trade and empire. Although there was enormous public interest in the exploits of explorers and in the lands that they were credited with opening up, the money behind them was largely put up because of hopes of commercial gain and of what was believed to be its facilitator, colonial expansion. With increasingly sophisticated methods of transport, both trade and colonial despoliation brought new commodities, artefacts, and skills into mainland Europe, and the search to find fresh markets and possessions took Europeans round the world. Yet these improvements in travel also made possible an exponential expansion of knowledge of other cultures, other arts, other ways of being, understood often in mistaken and ethnocentric terms but crucial to the new art forms that questioned European traditions. Modernism, it has long been realized, was international, writers and artists moving between London, Paris, Munich, Berlin, Moscow, New York, Rome, and more; but now the extent to which it was *transnational* seems increasingly significant, modernist forms from one culture transforming and being transformed by others through the cultural contact that modern travel in one way or another made possible.[4]

One factor that made travel so central to the development of modernism was that transport was not only more efficient; it was cheaper. The Grand Tour had been the finishing school for the sons of English gentlemen, but travel of that sort was available only to the rich. By the 1880s, Karl Baedeker's famous guidebooks, with their authoritative recommendations of important sights and practical advice on available accommodation, had been in existence for fifty years and Thomas Cook in business since the 1840s. Baedeker's handbooks and Cook's tours were there to cater to a new market of middle-class travelers, anxious to visit the cultural shrines previously only seen in etchings or daguerreotypes. But travel was not just easier for tourists (as they were disparagingly called) out for an improving holiday, like Lucy Honeychurch in E.M. Forster's *A Room with a View*, or for a brief escape from routine. It made realizable the dream of a new life for European workers and peasants, as they joined the waves of immigration that crossed the Atlantic to build up a transformed United States, a haven, they hoped, for political and economic refugees from the old world. It brought to Britain East Europeans and Russians fleeing pogroms or Tsarist autocracy, and later Jewish refugees from the Nazis. And for many writers and artists in the modernist period, this comparative cheapness of travel meant that it was much easier for the restless young to try the expatriate life, perhaps living first in one place, then another, or moving backward and forward between them. So much of modernist literature and art was created by those working in countries far from their original homes, in heterogeneous, changing clusters of fellow artists. Imagism emerged in London, the *Blaue Reiter* group in Munich,

Cubism in Paris, Dadaism in Zurich, in each case from a group of mixed nationalities rather than simply from those native to the city. To return to Raymond Williams again, he comments, "It is a very striking feature of many Modernist and avant-garde movements that they were not only located in the great metropolitan centres but that so many of their members were immigrants into these centers, where in some new ways all were strangers."[5] Modernism grows out of this transcultural interchange; as Michael North says of Williams's analysis, he posits modernism as "a social formation," the "key to which [was] geographical mobility."[6]

Transporting Travelers

As developments in transport in the late nineteenth century and early twentieth century accelerated, travel was increasingly available for a new mass market. The first steamship to cross the Atlantic had been the Cunard Line RMS (Royal Mail Steamship) *Britannia* in 1840, sailing from Liverpool to Boston; by the 1870s, regular passenger steamships were an economic possibility and, indeed, financial opportunity. The liners' different sections and levels of accommodation might parallel and reinforce the social class divisions of the old world, but they could propel the owners of steamship companies from relatively modest backgrounds into the opulent riches that shipping magnates came to enjoy. Sir John and Lady Ellerman, the parents of the writer Bryher, were a case in point. Affordable transatlantic travel was foundational for the development of Anglo-American modernism, though also a painful rite of passage for those who had to travel in the cheapest class. As Pound would write to Margaret Cravens in 1910, "the Lusitania had delirium Tremens in the end of it I used."[7] Railways had already transformed nineteenth-century life, but by the 1880s, when the vast railroads like the American Transcontinental Railway and the Trans-Indian Peninsular Railroad had been built, and the Suez Canal opened, the global nature of communications made imperative a new, internationally agreed time system, with, Stephen Kern has argued, profound effects on contemporary perceptions of time. The insensitive, bullying doctor, Sir William Bradshaw, in Virginia Woolf's *Mrs Dalloway* significantly shares the name of Bradshaw with the annual railway timetable directory, with its rigid mechanistic, autocratic clock time. If one accepts A.P.J. Taylor's view that World War I was the result of the unstoppability of railway timetables, they profoundly changed history as well.

Yet as well as these vast overland projects, work was also beginning on the complex underground network of trains that would transform travel within the great metropoles. In London, the tube network began with the Metropolitan line in 1863, the Circle line in 1884, and four more between 1890 and 1904. The Metro in Paris opened its first line in 1900, the U-Bahn in Berlin in 1902, and the subway in New York in 1904. The entrances to the Paris Metro stations, with their magnificent art-nouveau ironwork arches, designed by Hector Guimard, brought glamour to everyday travel, as if the descent to the depths was through an enchanted liminal space. One of the most famous modernist poems is set "In a Station of the Metro":

> The apparition of these faces in the crowd;
> Petals on a wet, black bough. [8]

The crowd scene, the mise-en-scène of all urban living, magically transformed: this "hokku-like" poem, as Pound describes it, brings together East and West, Greek myth and modern living, the underworld and modernity, death and life, making this iconic scene symbolic of the metropolitan artist's transnational, transhistoric imagination. But more negatively, underground travel could exacerbate the sense of alienation within the crowd so omnipresent in accounts of modern cities, so physically close to strangers, so psychically apart, the recurrent mistrustful unease of urban living. Richard Aldington has a particularly disturbing version of this rumbling hostility in his poem "In the Tube," where the speaker looks at "A row of hard faces / Immobile ... A row of eyes ... immobile":

> Antagonism,
> Disgust,
> Immediate antipathy,
> Cut my brain, as a dry sharp reed
> Cuts a finger.
> I surprise the same thought
> In the brasslike eyes:
> "What right have you to live?" [9]

"In a Station of the Metro" was written in 1913, "In the Tube" in 1915 under the shadow of World War I. Aldington, as a young man not in uniform, was constantly subject to disapproval, though here the antipathy is mutual, and the visceral response to the mute tube travelers depicted in the poem hovers somewhere between modernist scorn for the ordinary man and urban paranoia. The great sociologist Georg Simmel had written in his 1903 essay on "The Metropolis and Mental Life" that the problem of the individual in the modern metropolis was that "some modicum of self-esteem" could only be achieved "through the awareness of others," yet the "brevity and scarcity of the inter-human contacts granted to the metropolitan man" makes it difficult to find "an unambiguous image of himself in the eyes of others."[10] Modern travel can breed fear and alienation as well as offering contact.

Other modern technological advances offered possibilities of more individual travel. In the later nineteenth century, the form of transport to have the most profound and positive transformative effects on social being was the bicycle. The geneticist Steve Jones argues that the bicycle brought about one of the most dramatic improvements in public health in the modern period: if young people from one village could socialize with the young from the next, the close inbreeding of country villages was no longer inevitable. And if the bicycle brought more freedom to young people in general, its role was particularly liberating for young women. The penny-farthing of the 1870s had been the preserve of young men. That changed dramatically when the "safety bicycle" appeared in the mid-1880s, with the welcome addition of pneumatic tires from 1888. As John Galsworthy writes, the bicycle

> began to be a dissolvent of the most powerful type when accessible to the fair in its present form. Under its influence, wholly or in part, have wilted chaperons, long and narrow skirts, tight corsets, hair that would have come down, black stockings, thick ankles, large hats, prudery and fear of the dark; under its influence, wholly or in part, have bloomed week-ends, strong nerves, strong legs, strong language, knickers, knowledge of make and shape, knowledge of woods and pastures, equality of sex, good digestion and professional occupation – in four words, the emancipation of women.[11]

Depictions of the New Woman are rarely without a bicycle.

Bicycles were used by all classes. Motorcars were a different story; even though Ford Model Ts began production in 1909 in the United States, and in Britain in 1910, before World War I, motorcars were largely the preserve of the rich. In *The Wind in the Willows* (1908), it's the noisy, nouveau riche Mr. Toad who develops a passion for cars. In E.M. Forster's *Howard's End*, to impecunious clerks like Leonard Bast, the car's only contribution to London life is the smell of petrol and increasing difficulty in crossing the road: it's the wealthy Mr. Wilcox who has a motorcar and chauffeur. Mr. Wilcox also gives a car as a wedding present to his son Charles, whose reckless driving emblemizes his brutal lack of consideration for others; Margaret Schelgel, for her part, hates driving, worrying about the safety of chickens and children on the road. In *The Great Gatsby*, fifteen years later, Tom and Daisy Buchanan's reckless driving again exemplifies the way their money makes them indifferent to their destruction of other lives. Not all literary figures were opposed to the car. The novelist Edith Wharton, well to do herself, adored motorcars, and in her travel book, *A Motor-Flight through France* (1908), she writes that the "motor-car has restored the romance of travel."[12] (It is striking, incidentally, how many modernist novelists were also travel writers.)[13] The poet Amy Lowell, when she crossed the Atlantic to meet up with the Imagists in July 1914, brought her maroon-colored Pierce-Arrow and a maroon-liveried chauffeur to match, causing something of a sensation. She was one of the wealthy Boston Lowells; none of the other, largely impecunious Imagists owned a car. Yeats had hired one in January that year so that he and Ezra Pound could be driven from Stone Cottage to William Scawen Blunt's country estate, Newbuildings, where he entertained them with a magnificent peacock dinner. But motoring could still be a testing experience in winter; Pound was excited but wrote apprehensively to Dorothy Shakespear the week before: "if it's as dammmmM cold sunday next as it is now we'll arrive like a box of marrons glacés."[14]

For some like Forster, the motorcar is a symbol of greed and destruction: for others, it embodied new possibilities and new pleasures. Andrew Thacker quotes a poem by John Davidson, published in 1908, which celebrates the car in Nietzschean terms for its "Will to be the Individual" in contrast to the train's "Will to be the Mob."[15] For the Futurists, however, the car was the dynamic essence of the modern age. The year before *Howard's End* came out, the Italian F.T. Marinetti had published the first Futurist manifesto in *Le Figaro* in Paris, in which Futurism springs to life out of the rapture of a car drive and a climactic, orgasmic crash: "the raging broom of madness swept us out of ourselves and drove us through streets as rough and deep as the beds of torrents ... on we raced, hurling watchdogs against doorsteps, curling them under our burning tyres like collars under a flatiron," until they end upside down in a muddy, sludge-filled ditch. So with "faces smeared with good factory muck ...

we ... declared our high intentions to all the *living* of the earth." Central to the manifesto is the motorcar:

> We affirm that the world's magnificence has been enriched by a new beauty: the beauty of speed. A racing car ... A roaring car that seems to ride on grapeshot is more beautiful than the *Victory of Samothrace* ... We want to hymn the man at wheel, who hurls the lance of his spirit across the earth, along the circle of its orbit.[16]

For the Futurists, the potential for destruction in the car is an exhilarating part of its glory; destruction is essential to their mission, the sweeping away of existing museums, galleries, and libraries – in short, of established art and culture.

The Vorticists, however, in spite of their considerable debts to Futurism, wanted a new art that channeled primitive energies rather than the destruction of past art – indeed, although their short-lived periodical *Blast* expressed admiration for the Suffragettes, it begged them to stop destroying works of art. They had only scorn for the Futurists' admiration for cars, describing it derisively as "automobilism"; instead, the Vorticists commended ships. And by the postwar years, the pretensions and banality of the motorcar were being mocked, as by T.S. Eliot in *The Waste Land*:

> But at my back from time to time I hear
> The sound of horns and motors, which will bring
> Sweeney to Mrs Porter in the spring. [17]

In *Mrs Dalloway* (1925), the London pedestrians look with awe, loyal respect, or irritation at the imposing motorcar, "with its blinds drawn and an air of inscrutable reserve," that may or may not be carrying the queen, or the prime minister, or possibly the Prince of Wales; nobody knew, but "there could be no doubt that greatness was seated within."[18]

Mrs Dalloway also famously includes an airplane, skywriting as an advertising gimmick, tracing out Kreemo or Glaxo or Toffee, no one is sure which. But although the Channel was first crossed in a plane by Louis Blériot in 1909, the same year as the publication of that first Futurist Manifesto, the airplane did not contribute in any substantial way to civilian travel during the modernist period. Commercial air travel grew mainly after World War II, though the first commercial passenger airplane, the Boeing 247, went into service in 1933, taking twenty hours with seven stops to fly between New York and Los Angeles.

Aviators like Charles Lindbergh became famous as they set new records, but much of aviation development was military. Vorticism's dismissal of the Futurists' enthusiasm for cars was posited on the view that Italy, unlike Britain, was a novice in the development of machines, hence their unseemly excitement over motoring, but in fact Italy achieved the dubious distinction of inflicting the first ever aerial bomb raid, on Libya in 1911, and the highly successful Italian writer, Gabriele d'Annunzio, became an equally fêted fighter pilot during World War I. The twelve airplanes that interrupt the Rev. G.W. Streatfield's speech in *Between the Acts*, as they fly "in perfection formation like a flight of wild duck" – that is, in battle formation – are an intimation of World War II, not yet come in the novel but all too present for Virginia Woolf and for the first readers of the book.[19]

Traveling Writers, Traveling Lives

One of the most striking facts about modernist writers is how many of them were on the move, exhibiting that "geographical mobility" that Raymond Williams saw as so formative for modernism; they lived, as Max Saunders puts it, "peripatetic lives." Saunders cites in particular Ford Madox Ford, who himself confessed to his "always migratory life," being, as Saunders says, continually on the move "between London, and the South Coast of England, and Germany and France, and increasingly towards the end of his life, the United States." Ford's writings, Saunders suggests, whether his fiction or travel writing, are studies of what Ford himself called "mental travel," which Saunders paraphrases as "psycho-geography," people and places in transit, transformed through travel and travelers.[20] Ford's friend and collaborator, Joseph Conrad, had himself been born Józef Teodor Konrad Korzeniowski in Poland, then divided among Prussia, Austria, and Russia. Because of his father's exile for nationalist resistance and his early death, the young Conrad had to move repeatedly around different parts of Poland and Ukraine as he grew up; he spent time in France before coming to England and embarking on twenty years as a merchant sailor; only after his time at sea did his writing career begin. His books are set in the Dutch East Indies, South America, the Congo; even a London-based novel like *The Secret Agent* centers on the foreigners and immigrants circulating in the city. Conrad's novels are fascinated by cultural difference: the modernist novel in his hands began, as Edward Said among others has noted, with the observation of the mix of races, cultures, and languages in the often corrupt and compromised outreaches of European colonialism before observing such complex mixing in the great metropoles.

Henry James, whose work, particularly his later novels, was so influential in the development of modernist fiction, was not so widely traveled, nor quite so peripatetic, but he was an American émigré who settled in England, even there moving frequently between London and Rye and often traveling in France and Italy. He too was preoccupied with cultural difference, making his life work the tracing of the interactions, misunderstandings, and accommodations among American, British, and continental European culture. Ezra Pound was born in the American Midwest and transported to Philadelphia at the age of eighteen months; he had had three visits to Europe (one that extended to North Africa) by the time he moved to Europe in early 1908 at the age of twenty-two. Settling in London, he had one visit home to America and several to Italy and France before he left for Paris in late 1920, moving on to Rapallo in Italy in 1925, though with frequent journeys away, including back to the States in 1939. His involuntarily return there in 1945 as an American prisoner of war was of a rather different order, but once released, he traveled back to Europe. Pound's development as a poet was powerfully influenced by other travelers that he met: his brief but formative association with the Bengali poet Rabindranath Tagore; his crucial meeting in 1913, in the London house of the Indian poet, Sarojini Naidu, with the American Mary Fenollosa, who passed on to him her dead husband's notebooks on Noh drama and Chinese poetry, compiled during his fifteen years in Japan; his friendship with the French sculptor Henri Gaudier-Brzeska; and his meeting with the Japanese Michio Ito, with whom he and W.B. Yeats worked on Noh drama. From the beginning, Pound's poetry disconcerted his readers with its polyglot, macaronic forms (many of Conrad's novels could be called macaronic too, as might Eliot's *The Waste Land*). Pound's *Cantos* bring together many periods and cultures, and if Douglas Goldring once described his poetry as "stuffed" with "Grand Tour" "bric-à-brac," it was a wider Grand Tour than the traditional European one.[21] Pound had in fact originally come to Europe in 1908 to learn about poetry from the Irish Yeats, who was himself constantly on the move between Dublin, Paris, and London, and later Italy, with several extended visits to the United States. Yeats's flat in Woburn Buildings was presumably chosen for its closeness to Euston station, from which he could get the boat train for Dublin. In 1913, Pound was to comment that the "finest authors" in England were all foreigners.[22]

In the United States, the Harlem Renaissance took its name from the area of New York to which so many southern African Americans had traveled to escape the intense racism and poverty of the southern states; most of the writers associated with it had come to New York from elsewhere, some from the Caribbean, and many would at some stage travel to Europe – in fact, many of those associated with Harlem spent a good deal of time elsewhere. Claude McKay, for example, was born in Jamaica but in 1912, at the age of twenty-three, remarkably managed to get two books of poetry published in London, one of which gained him an award that enabled him to attend the all-black Tuskegee Institute in Alabama. He then moved to New York but spent from 1919 to 1921 in Europe (Holland, Belgium, and England). In 1922, he visited the Soviet Union and then spent eleven years traveling and writing in Europe and North Africa. Langston Hughes, thirteen years younger, came originally from Missouri, although he had lived in six different American cities by the time he was twelve, and later for a while in Mexico, before coming to New York and discovering Harlem; he too traveled extensively, in France, Holland, Italy, the Azores, Canary Islands, and West Africa. Zora Neale Hurston came originally from Eatonville, Florida (which she writes about in *Their Eyes Were Watching God*), but moved frequently before coming to New York in 1925 to study anthropology with Franz Boas at Barnard College and to play a flamboyant role in Harlem cultural life. She later traveled in the American South and the Caribbean, her anthropological research revealing the complex transformations and adaptations of African cultural forms in African American traditions. As Toni Morrison points out, "modern life begin with slavery"; African Americans experienced the transcultural early and painfully.[23] That African-American dual heritage and double consciousness (in W.E.B. Du Bois's phrase) is explored in much Harlem Renaissance work, which can be seen, Rachel Farebrother suggestively argues, as working though a form of collage, or, as Zora Neale Hurston herself puts it, "the rhythm of segments."[24] Farebrother draws here on James Clifford, who earlier argued that a kind of collage technique, "an aesthetic which values fragments, curious collections, unexpected juxtapositions," was the fractured form used by the surrealists to convey the cultural mélange, the constant "irruption of otherness," including both travelers' trophies and detritus, that characterize the modern metropolis, an aesthetic that underlies much other modernist art and culture besides.[25]

Hurston's early travels had been driven by financial necessity, though some of her later traveling was subsidized by her problematic patron, Charlotte Osgood Mason, who also supported Hughes. Other women modernists were on the move as well, though most, but not all, traveled in more affluent circumstances. Paris in the modernist years became a Mecca for artists from around the world, particularly for both black and white Americans, men and women. Ernest Hemingway gives his own mythologizing, masculine take on this in his memoir, *A Moveable Feast*, but Shari Benstock has more recently focused attention on the number of women – Edith Wharton, Natalie Barney, Gertrude Stein, Djuna Barnes, and many more – who found a home on the Left Bank. If the bicycle had been so liberating for the generation of the New Woman, by the beginning of the twentieth century, international travel was becoming much more possible for adventurous young women. Well-to-do American women, as the novels of Henry James make clear, had regularly visited Europe and sometimes beyond in the nineteenth century, though largely well chaperoned: think of the fate of a Daisy Miller, dying of "Roman fever" for defying the rules. By the early twentieth century, crossing the Atlantic, in either direction, to start a different life and find a freedom impossible in home surroundings became increasingly attractive and attainable. H.D., born in Bethlehem, Pennsylvania, came to Europe in 1911, in the first instance for a holiday with Frances Gregg and her mother, and made her name as an Imagist poet there; she stayed on in England after spending almost a year in Italy, marrying the English Richard Aldington. After World War I, she visited Greece and Egypt with Bryher and moved between England and the Continent. Like Pound, she turned to the work of another culture for her poetry, in her case the Greeks, not as understood by Victorian Hellenism but the more archaic, female-inflected, Eastern version of the early Greeks developed by scholars like Jane Harrison, made possible through the work of another set of travelers, the archaeologists, who were transforming the understanding of earlier cultures for the modernist generation. For many of her contemporaries, H.D. "invented" Greek poetry, much as Eliot suggests that "Chinese poetry, as we know it today, is something invented by Ezra Pound."[26]

Gertrude Stein had come to Paris in 1903 with her brother Leo, beginning their great collection of modernist works and the salon that she would continue with Alice B. Toklas. The friendship that developed in Paris between the American Stein and the Spanish Picasso was one of modernism's most productive transatlantic encounters; Michael

North suggests that Picasso's painting of her portrait in 1906, just at the time she was working on her short story "Melanctha," was a pivotal moment in both their work and in the emergence of modernism. In the mask-like portrait of Stein that Picasso paints, he draws on the ancient Iberian reliefs he had seen in the Louvre, from which he would move on to incorporate the African masks he saw at the Trocadéro into his famous 1907 *Les Demoiselles d'Avignon*. In Stein's "Melanctha," in which she claimed she took "the first step away from the nineteenth century into the twentieth century in literature," she finds a way of writing through a similar mask, that of a black Baltimorean, reworking her failed attempt in *Q.E.D.* to describe her unhappy lesbian affair: through this masking, North writes, "Stein and Picasso take the first steps into cubism and literary modernism."[27] There is, he acknowledges, a problematic primitivism involved here; in both "Melanctha" and *Les Demoiselles d'Avignon*, Africa makes the figuring of sexuality possible. White modernists' fascination with black culture was not necessarily free from racism. Yet these works also illustrate how modernism emerged out of the cross-cultural contacts that made it imperative to go beyond traditional Western forms to express their diverse, transcultural world.

Traveling Cultures

James Clifford, looking at this shifting cultural scene in a famous essay titled "Traveling Cultures," suggests that the hotel, "a place of transit, not of residence," as Claude Lévi-Strauss puts it, could be seen as a chronotope of this period.[28] The importance of the hotel as an exemplary transitional place was suggested to Clifford by his work on the Surrealists, so many of whom "lived in hotels, or hotel-like transient digs, moving in and out of Paris," "homes away from homes … launching points for strange and wonderful urban voyages: *Nadja, Paysan de Paris*. Places of collection, juxtaposition, passionate encounters." The hotel, a place of chance meetings, sometimes fleeting, sometimes life changing, is, Clifford suggests, emblematic of the modernist artist's unsettled existence. The hotel can offer an image of all that is positive in modern travel, "exploration, research, transforming encounter": André Breton, for example, in l'Hotel des Grands Hommes, encounters Louis Aragon and Philippe Soupault and there invents Surrealism. But the hotel can also embody modern travel's negative aspects, "transience … exile and rootlessness" – Clifford quotes Conrad in *Victory*, where the hotel becomes an image of the "age in which we are encamped like bewildered travelers in a garish unrestful hotel."[29] Or one could cite Jean Rhys in *Good Morning, Midnight*, where the anonymous, unhomely hotel room epitomizes urban anomie:

> Back to the Hotel of Arrival, the Hotel of Departure, the Hotel of the Future, the Hotel of Martinique and the Universe … Back to the hotel without a name in the street without a name. You press the button and the door opens. This is the Hotel without a name, and the clients have no names, no faces. You go up the stairs. Always the same stairs, always the same room.
>
> The room says: "Quite like old times, Yes? … No? Yes."[30]

Clifford is aware of the limitations of the hotel as symbol for this medley of encounters, with its connotations of "gentlemanly occidental travel," of wealth and leisure, commodities that many travelers in the modernist period singularly lacked. But what he wants to stress is the cultural exchange that takes place in these encounters, in this to-ing and fro-ing, or as he puts it, following Édouard Glissant, detours and returns. Clifford cites the example of the Cuban writer Alejo Carpentier, who came to Paris in 1928 and became closely involved with the Surrealist movement. When he moved back to Cuba eleven years later, Surrealism was reborn in his writing as that very Latin American literary practice, *lo real maravilloso*, "Surrealism, with a difference," as Clifford puts it.[31]

Such serendipitous meetings in the course of travel were central to modernist art and literature. Clifford, however, is also arguing that through travel, not only do individuals meet, but ideas, art practices, creative forms, and cultures are enmeshed with one another and give rise to new and varied cultural fusions. Anthropologists, he notes, used to represent the groups they studied as discrete entities; now they realize that's not possible. Clifford quotes James Boon's comment on Bali: "What has come to be called Balinese culture is a multiply authored invention, a historical formation, an enactment, a political construct, a shifting paradox, an ongoing translation, an emblem, a trademark, a non-consensual negotiation of contrastive identity, and more."[32] All that could stand *a fortiori* for the modernist city, where travel transformed literary and artistic culture, not just through the travel of the individual artist, not just through the chance meetings travel throws up, important though those are, but through what has already reached the metropolis though earlier travels, the artefacts and knowledge that had already been on the move. Traveling objects communicate, as do texts and people, though all are subject to "ongoing translation." Museums, for example, played a key role in modernism. Picasso had, as I noted, discovered African art in the Trocadéro, as had Matisse before him; so did the art critic Wilhelm Worringer, whose seminal book *Abstraction and Empathy* was researched there, although he, like the Surrealists, was fascinated by the whole range of non-Western art. Ezra Pound had been attracted by the Chinese art in the Britain Museum before he read their poetry; Wyndham Lewis was alerted to the possibilities of a new kind of art by its Benin sculptures. Jacob Epstein and Gaudier-Brzeska learned much from the formal properties and power of its Assyrian and other holdings. Much of this was looted in one colonial war or other: the holdings were imperial plunder, morally tainted acquisitions, and out of context, but they were paradoxically to help to make a critique of that imperial world possible.

I mentioned earlier the impact of archaeology, which was revisioning the ancient world. Heinrich Schliemann's excavation of Troy in 1873 had caused a worldwide stir and renewed interest in the Homeric narratives, helping to stimulate, for example, Victor Bérard's *Les Phéniciens et l'Odyssée* (1902), whose reading of *The Odyssey* as a map of Semitic trading routes proved so suggestive for James Joyce's *Ulysses* itself. The ongoing discoveries of Sappho fragments were a powerful impetus to Imagism and later modernist poetry. Anthropology, so influential in the modernist period, was also dependent on travel; even "armchair" anthropologists like James Frazer, whose *Golden Bough* stimulated so many modernist writers, needed their traveling informants. Franz Boas's antiracist cultural anthropology, which did rely on personal contact, was deeply important to the Harlem Renaissance writers. Lawrence (one of the most restless of modernist travelers), Eliot, Pound, H.D., and Virginia Woolf were all intrigued by different aspects of anthropology; to understand the modern world, it was now imperative to look beyond what had been thought civilization, though doing so, as in *Heart of Darkness*, might only serve to illuminate the savagery at home.

Modernist Travel: Catastrophe to Blitzkrieg

During 1912, the possibilities that were opening up for mastery of the world through travel met two particularly dramatic reversals for the British. The first was, famously, the sinking of the *Titanic*; the hubris and commercial greed that led to this disaster struck many immediately. The second, news of which did not reach England until 1913, was the death of

Captain Scott and four other Antarctic explorers as they tried to make their way home, having discovered to their bitter dismay that they had failed to be the first to reach the South Pole. Scott was at the time acclaimed as a courageous hero and English gentleman; it was only later that questions were raised about his contribution to his own and his companions' deaths through his stubborn insistence on using ponies in a traditional British way instead of dogs, as the Inuits did and as other nations had realized was essential. The belief in Western superiority was already under question before World War I, but with the horrors of the trenches, the sense of living in "a botched civilization" became widespread.[33]

On the positive side, Michael North has argued in *Reading 1922*, with more travel and travel mediated by books, photography, and film, there was an increasing interest in the rest of the world, a growing sense in both popular culture and modernist works of living in a global world, what we might now call a planetary consciousness. Both the establishment of the League of Nations and the October Revolution's international socialism reflect this in very different ways, even if eventually the Soviet Union proved another imperial power. Fascism, in contrast, whose attack on the failings of traditional Western capitalist systems awoke wide support, espoused myths of blood and soil, so that a new and deadly kind of exclusionary nationalism was born. Train journeys would take on more sinister meanings. Bliztkrieg would be born, in pursuit of a different kind of imperium. Like others, some modernists moved to the right; some did not. Modernism began to become an orthodoxy in those years, with critics recognizing only its white male practitioners. In the immediate postwar years, indeed until the 1980s, modernism's politics and its sometimes problematic fascination with other cultures were rarely discussed. That has dramatically changed in the wake of feminist, postcolonial, and new modernist criticism, which has expanded and interrogated the field. Looking at the role of travel in modernist culture, at how a new consciousness of other cultures and their "ongoing translation" was central to so much modernist creativity, is one way of making "a return to the scene of the modern," as Michael North puts it, the aim of all this volume.

Notes

1 Walter Benjamin, "Some Motifs in Baudelaire," *Illuminations* (London: Fontana, 1968/1973), 177.
2 See Chapter 2 in this volume.

3 Raymond Williams, *The Politics of Modernism: Against the New Conformists* (London: Verso, 1989), 45.
4 For example, see the introduction to *Geographies of Modernism: Literatures, Cultures, Spaces*, ed. Peter Brooker and Andrew Thacker (London: Routledge, 2005).
5 Williams, 77.
6 Michael North, *Reading 1922: A Return to the Scene of the Modern* (Oxford: Oxford University Press, 1999), 11.
7 Omar Pound and Robert Spoo, eds., *Ezra Pound and Margaret Cravens: A Tragic Friendship* (Durham: Duke University Press, 1988), 40.
8 Ezra Pound, *Selected Poems* (London: Faber & Faber), 113.
9 *The Egoist* 2.5 (1915), 74.
10 David Frisby and Mike Featherstone, eds., *Simmel on Culture: Selected Writings* (London: Sage, 1997), 183.
11 John Galsworthy, *On Forsyte 'Change* (London: Heinemann, 1930), 207.
12 Edith Wharton, *A Motor-Flight through France* (New York: Charles Scribner's Sons, 1908), 1.
13 I discuss this in "Modernism and Travel, 1880–1940," in *The Cambridge Companion to Travel Writing*, ed. Peter Hulme and Tim Youngs (Cambridge: Cambridge University Press, 2002), 70–86.
14 Omar Pound and A. Walton Litz, *Ezra Pound and Dorothy Shakespear: Their Letters 1909–1914* (London: Faber & Faber, 1984), 297.
15 Andrew Thacker, *Moving through Modernity: Space and Geography in Modernism* (Manchester: Manchester University Press, 2003), 85.
16 Umbro Apollonio, ed., *Futurist Manifestos* (London: Tate Publishing, 2009), 20–21.
17 T.S. Eliot, *The Complete Poems and Plays* (London: Faber & Faber, 1969), 67.
18 Virginia Woolf, *Mrs Dalloway* (London: Penguin, 1925/1991), 17.
19 Virginia Woolf, *Between the Acts* (London: Penguin, 1941/1992), 114.
20 Max Saunders, "Ford Madox Ford and Nomadic Modernism," in *Transits: The Nomadic Geographies of Anglo-American Modernism*, ed. Giovanni Cianci, Caroline Patey, and Sara Sullam (Oxford: Peter Lang, 2010), 77.
21 Douglas Goldring, *Odd Man Out: The Autobiography of a "Propaganda Novelist"* (London: Chapman & Hall, 1935), 121.
22 "Through Alien Eyes: 3," *New Age* 12.13 (January 30, 1913): 300. Pound cites Yeats, James, Hudson, and Conrad.
23 Quoted in Paul Gilroy's *The Black Atlantic: Modernity and Double Consciousness* (London: Verso, 1993), 221.
24 Rachel Farebrother, "'The Rhythm of Segments': Zora Neale Hurston's Collage Aesthetic," *Women: A Cultural Review* 22.4 (2011), 328–44; see also her *The Collage Aesthetic in the Harlem Renaissance*, (Farnham: Ashgate, 2009).
25 James Clifford, "On Ethnographic Surrealism," in *The Predicament of Culture: Twentieth-Century Ethnography, Literature and Art* (Cambridge: Harvard University Press, 1988), 118.
26 T.S. Eliot, "Introduction: 1928," in Pound, *Selected Poems*, 15.
27 Michael North, *The Dialect of Modernism: Race, Language and Twentieth-Century Ethnography* (Oxford: Oxford University Press, 1994), 61.
28 James Clifford, "Traveling Cultures," in *Routes: Travel and Translation in the late Twentieth Century* (Cambridge, MA: Harvard University Press, 1997), 17. A chronotope, a concept taken from Einstein's time-space continuum, is Mikhail Bakhtin's term for a literary image or motif that fuses time and space, like the road in the picaresque novel.

29 Clifford, "Traveling Cultures," 30, 31,17. *Nadja* (1928) is a novel by André Breton; *Paysan de Paris* (1926) is by Louis Aragon.

30 Jean Rhys, *Good Morning, Midnight* (Harmondsworth: Penguin, 1939/1969), 120.

31 Clifford, "Traveling Cultures," 31, 30.

32 Clifford, "Traveling Cultures," 24.

33 Pound, *Selected Poems*, 176.

13
———————

Popular Theater

The construction of canonical modernism has often involved erasing much of what was once genuinely significant. In terms of popular theater, influential progressivist historiographies ensured that genres like melodrama were marginalized as staging posts on the way to fully fledged art forms – European naturalism, say, or American realism. According to this version of things, the popular playwrights of the nineteenth and early twentieth centuries were not without talent, but, "like television writers," they were likely to be perceived as "artisans skilled at producing the entertaining effects that audiences wanted." True, transcendent, cultural value awaited the arrival of the modern genius, a figure like Henrik Ibsen or Eugene O'Neill, "looking to illuminate the human condition or challenge received values."[1] Musical theater was typically subject to the same mysterious evolutionary process. Early musical comedy, burlesque, revue, and vaudeville were often seen as developmental, flawed products, "one- or two-dimensional at best" and important only insofar as they led to the great flowering of the integrated American book musical heralded by *Showboat* (1929) and culminating in the 1940s and 1950s with shows like *Carousel* (1945), *Oklahoma* (1949), *South Pacific* (1949), and *Guys and Dolls* (1950). In some intellectual cultures, such shows now take on the reified dimensions of the classic art object.[2]

In an essay titled "From Melodrama to Realism: The Suspect History of American Drama," the theater historian Tom Postlewait explored what he saw as the pervasiveness of these marginalizing, "teleological narratives," evident not least in anthologies and collections of historical documents. He observed, somewhat wryly, that such narratives were "hard to suppress,"[3] although by 1996, when Postlewait's essay was published, ideas about cultural value, still extant and carrying authority in some quarters, had already been seriously unraveled in others. Long before the mid-1990s, progressivist historiography generally had been wrecked by poststructuralism. Moreover, postmodern art practices in such fields as architecture, literature, film, television, advertising, music, and comic-book culture had substantially blurred the high/low culture divide. For many, that antithesis, however embedded it once may have been, was quite simply no longer viable. At the same time, the concept of modernism became hugely problematized, subject to endless reconfigurations as traditional formulations became "deconstructed." One-time universal artists and art products now became masculinist, Eurocentric, Westernized, or otherwise constructionist and exclusionary. From both sides of things, serious pressure was brought to bear as high modernism struggled to preserve its traditional authority and popular culture extended its range of signification. Cultural studies flourished in this context, if on problematic and unstable footings, with the result that a popular theater form like melodrama could no longer be seriously maintained as the Other of legitimate theater culture. An abundance of intellectual equipment now at the disposal of theater historians meant that the license to study popular theater on its own terms could hardly be in doubt, although the question of what to do with that license remained a complex and controversial one.

Theater historians like Michael R. Booth (melodrama), Jacky Bratton (melodrama, music hall, and pantomime), Peter Bailey (musical comedy), Peter Jelavich (cabaret), Marlene Otte (revue, circus, and *jargon* theater), and many others[4] have sometimes been quite prickly about the traditional marginalization of popular theater cultures. On the whole, however, such scholars have been careful to avoid the mistake of attempting to oust the likes of Ibsen, Strindberg, Shaw, Jerome Kern, and the Gershwins with an alternative canon composed of such figures as the Melville brothers, Jimmy Davis ("Owen Hall"), Lionel Monckton, and Paul Rubens.[5] Their research has instead sought to complicate historical narratives, emphasizing the crossovers between the "high" and "low" and illustrating just how rich and complex these popular theater cultures really were in their own right. As a result, and although a great deal more work still needs to be done, we now have quite sophisticated maps of popular theater in the nineteenth and early twentieth centuries.

In relation to London's West End, for example, the standard account of the transformation of music hall from demotic working-class culture to commercial mass entertainment has been joined by other suggestive narratives. We know how much melodrama, once represented as a small-scale, end-of-pier culture, actually invested in costly spectacle and cultural transfers across European and Atlantic sites. Far from being trivial, it engaged with contemporary issues – typically "questions of race and national origin" in American versions.[6] British melodrama, on the other hand, tended to focus on "condition of England" matters in relation to urbanism, industrialism, and empire. A spate of later Edwardian melodramas – such shows as *The Worst Woman in London* (1901), *A Disgrace to Her Sex* (1904), and *The Girl Who Lost Her Character* (1904), the so called "dangerous woman" melodramas – engaged anxiously with New Woman identities.[7]

Similarly, we know about the displacement of West End burlesque, typically a comic parody of "high" culture interpolated with songs, dance routines, and comic business, by musical comedy. This latter, without doubt the single most popular form of West End theater entertainment between the mid-1890s and 1914, was self-styled as a thoroughly modern commodity, professionalized by impresarios like George Edwardes to attract the broad-based middle classes – men and women, husbands and wives, and seasonally whole families. In stark contrast to melodrama, it celebrated a chirpy version of bright femininity, with shows like *A Gaiety Girl* (1893), *The Geisha* (1896), *Florodora* (1899), *San Toy* (1899), *The Girl From Kay's* (1902), *Our Miss Gibbs* (1909), and *The Arcadians* (1909) dominating popular theater stages through to the end of World War I.[8]

At the same time, competition from continental operetta worried some theater critics, who in the immediate prewar period complained about "foreign invasions."[9] In reality, by the time these exports reached London or New York, they had been thoroughly Anglicized or Americanized. In the process, especially in this early period, the distinctions between operetta and the ascendant form, musical comedy, were often blurred.[10] The huge success of Franz Lehár's *The Merry Widow* in London in 1907 was followed by a string of continental operettas, all, like musical comedy, styled in contemporary ways – Oscar Strauss's *A Waltz Dream* (1908), Leo Fall's *The Dollar Princess* and *The Girl in The Train* (both 1910), and a string of Berlin shows composed by Jean Gilbert – *The Joy Ride Lady* (1912), *The Girl in the Taxi* (1912), and *The Cinema Star* (1914).

As these outlines suggest, popular theater, especially in its musical formations, should be understood as generic to the cosmopolitan metropolis at this early time. A vibrant exchange-and-transfer culture that went back into the nineteenth century was greatly stimulated by the successes of such shows as the 1895 American musical *The Belle of New*

York and, especially, the George Edwardes production *The Geisha* (1896). Prompting an international revival in Japonaiserie, the latter, a show that posited but finally withdrew from interracial romance, played an extraordinary 760 performances on its first London run. It toured the provinces, went to New York, and visited such sites as Johannesburg, Cape Town, Sydney, Melbourne, Adelaide, Dublin, Singapore, Mumbai, and Allabad. Here the best of modern chic, exoticism, and spectacle was sent on a civilizing mission to those administering the far-flung corners of the empire. At the same time, and like many other pre–World War I shows, *The Geisha* was adapted for such urban centers as Paris and Budapest. The German version, *Die Geisha, eine japanische Theehausgeschichte*, adapted by C.M. Röhr and Julius Freund, became a hit in Berlin and subsequently across the whole of Germany and Austria. This was a significant and fashionable culture, then, that crossed what were often seen as traditional national hostilities. In many respects, it could be naïve and repetitive, but, according to William Archer writing in 1908, it was also subtle and "sensitively modern," understanding its significance as "the real New Drama." So much a "sign of the times," it is not surprising at all that this early show, *The Geisha*, should have been paid the compliment of a *Geisha Parodie*, performed at the Alexanderplatz-Theater in June 1897.[11] Nor should it surprise that in the search for modern popular entertainment, traditional boundaries of cultural status and values were often blurred. Writing about the "new spirit in European drama just after the First World War," the theater critic Huntly Carter turned to the popular theater form, revue, to illustrate a contemporary opening up of experimental possibilities and transcultural pilfering. He described a 1921 revue, *The League of Notions*, in which popular entertainment appeared to fuse with art theatre, modern dance, and contemporary art practice:

> [T]here was a "Hell's Kitchen" belonging to the Moscow Art Theatre; a "fete des Mannequins" staged by M. Paul Poiret; "An Episode with Benda Masks" that recalled the modern mask school; and a "Persian Dance" that had stepped out of "The Russian Ballet"; and there were bits of scenery by Marc Henri of the Belgian New Art School.[12]

The transnational dimensions of popular theater, involving both the translation and movement of shows, personnel, performance styles, legal and promotional networks, and so on, is one reason popular theater is significant for understanding modern metropolitan life before World War I. It implies a common culture of material, aesthetic, and intellectual dimensions. Since Peter Bailey's essay "Theatre of Entertainments/ Spaces of Modernity: Rethinking the British Popular Stage, 1890," (1998), contemporary cultural historians have become used to recognizing the role of popular theater in shaping generic urban space at the turn of the century and influencing its characteristic styles and zoning. It impacted on architectures, transport systems, and the development of retail centers in places like Berlin's Friedrichstraße and the redeveloped eastern half of London's West End – around Northumberland Avenue, Charing Cross Road, and Shaftsbury Avenue. Like the department store, theaters such as the Berlin Metropol, the Gaiety, and Daly's in London were signifiers of city style and highly self-conscious of their status in this respect. Indeed, some of the most popular shows of the period – *The Girl from Kay's*, *The Girl Behind the Counter* (1906), *Our Miss Gibbs*, and so on – were nothing less than celebrations of fashionable consumerism. The early Metropol revues – beginning with *Neuestes, Allerneuestes!* in 1903 and ending with *Chauffeu – ins Metropol* (1912) – operated similarly, featuring scenes set in well-known department stores. Here escalators and revolving doors were reproduced as emblems of the modern age; songs applauded the apparently endless diversity and glamour of the modern shopping experience; costume often became product placement in what turned out to be a symbiotic relationship as department stores sold theater tickets, decorated their shop windows like stages, and sometimes bought stocks in theater companies. From this intimate basis, musical theater wrote anthems to the wonder of the consumerist age and one of its most potent emblems, the place where you could buy just about anything you wanted:

> Do you want a hair in curl or switches?
> Mattresses, ladies' riding breeches?
> Pianolas, petticoats,
> Or Quaker Oats?
> Or tennis nets,
> Or cigarettes,
> Enamel chains
> Or aeroplanes?
> Precious stones,
> Gramophones?
> Cauliflowers, paperweights,
> Or bromide plates?
> A telescope,
> A cake of soap?[13]

FIGURE 16 Doing Other cultures. Marie Tempest in *The Geisha* (1896)

Against the complaints of critics of the new department stores who frequently highlighted their corrupting effects – invariably on women – these shows allowed for a celebration of these shopping cathedrals as a "new heterosocial space," a sexualized site offering the opportunity for men and women to mingle relatively freely.[14]

The scale of these shows was often spectacular, involving elaborate efforts to stage the many spectacles of modernity. Racecourses, restaurants, factories, dance halls, fairs, and exhibitions – all were subject to the confident reproductive powers of modern popular theater, as, indeed, were other cultures. *The Geisha* was only one of a string of shows including *The Belle of Cairo* (1896), *A Chinese Honeymoon* (1901), *The Cinglalee* (1904), and *The Blue Moon* (1904), in which places like Japan, India, Ceylon, and Burma were subjected to a confident orientalism often celebrated with what was taken to be anthropological accuracy – although in reality these representations were more pastiche and parody than anything else (Figure 16). Demonstrations of natural power, like the earthquake that erupted twice daily in Robert Courtneidge's production of *The Mousmé* (1911), for example, film sets, ancient Greece, far-away planets, eighteenth-century France – nothing, apparently, was beyond the staging powers of the popular stage as it searched for the latest new craze to bring before urban audiences. The Drury Lane "autumn drama" *The Whip* (1909), for example, famously comprised in a single extravaganza the staging of a horse show, the Chamber of Horrors at Tussaud's waxworks, the pursuit of a train by an automobile, the wrecking of that train as it ploughed into a railway horse van, and a "climactic derby at Newmarket."[15] Not surprisingly perhaps, production costs were so high that a single failure could bring a theater to the brink of bankruptcy, which is why some theater companies were floated on the Stock Exchange. Richard Schultz, manager of the Metropol, spent the fantastic sum of 200,000 Reichmarks on the *mise-en-scène* of a single revue, while the Royal Opera House in Berlin had to make do with 30,000 for a revival of *Aida* in the same year.

There can be little doubt that the popularity of musical theater in such centers reflected booming economies and the conditions that produced a rise in per-capita incomes, in England reaching "a comfortable 150 per cent above subsistence in 1914."[16] Although popular theater has often been associated with aristocratic glamour, its general audience at this time was in fact much more everyday – composed of respectable men and women enjoying institutionalized forms of public performance. The productions to which they flocked were designed as commercial entertainment. Sometimes teasingly associated with the dangerous glamour of the *demimonde*, popular theater was in fact defined much more centrally by its formalizing of the limits of the acceptable. It ceremonialized the shifting boundaries where the urban respectable became manifest, and that is a central part of its fascination and significance.

If popular theater was part of the everyday fabric of mainstream modern urban life, it was also constituent of contemporary *modernisms*, producing fascinating, and often fantasist, interpretations of what the modern world was and how people lived in it. Its authority in this respect was presumably one reason Wyndham Lewis, like many intellectuals from Georg Simmel to a young Aldous Huxley, excoriated popular theater. The first issue of Lewis's iconoclastic *Blast* (1914), for example, took the trouble to get intimate with such phenomena as "Daly's musical comedy," the "Gaiety Chorus Girl," George Edwardes, the musical comedy producer, and Seymour Hicks, the actor, writer, and producer – all being thoroughly "blasted" as products of a bourgeois Victorian Britain.[17] Unlike more intellectual cultures, a popular theater like melodrama dramatized a moral order in which good prevailed, even against the worst dangers and most disruptive changes. While intellectual elites typically mourned what was perceived as a loss of hierarchy and distinction, popular musical theater went even further than melodrama in celebration of the benign order of the modern world. In musicals, the upbeat dispensation of "gaiety" was immanent in the plots of hundreds of shows across the period, which time and again reproduced for their audiences an energizing experience of living in contemporary life, sometimes in ways surprisingly resonant for later generations. Alongside characteristically turn-of-century perspectives on such issues as race, class, gender, and sexuality, there was a strong sensitivity shown to what we might now conceptualize in terms of "hyperrealities" or the "ceremonising of the world."[18] Berlin popular theater, especially the *Jahresrevue* produced between 1903 and 1913, was thematically obsessed with the representation of modern Berlin itself and demonstrated a parallel concern with self-reflection and image generally.[19] Thus in the Kaiserreich musical comedy *Die Kino-Königin* (1913), reproduced in the West End a year later as *The Cinema Star*, film became indistinguishable from real life as actual politics and their film reproduction merged into each other. In a decidedly postmodern moment, a character declares that in her film image, she sees herself "for the first time." Even earlier, the Edwardian hit *The Arcadians* (1909) contains a second act that reproduces the idyll of its first-act Arcadia, cut off by the Gulf Stream at the North Pole and forgotten by time, as a London city restaurant – a Disney-like simulacrum of the real thing complete with waitresses dressed as Arcadians, a vegetarian menu, and copied versions of the key Arcadian equivalent to institutions.

Musical theater reflected the modern urban experience back to its urban and suburban audiences in very particular ways, constructing a version of modernity usually at odds with prestigious intellectual cultures of the day – and with the realities of modern life in many respects. With astonishing consistency, the fantasist narratives of musical shows in particular celebrated a seemingly limitless capacity for assimilation and accommodation, quite contradicted in most respects by urban contemporaneities. A show like *Nelly Neil* (1907), for example, staged socialism in a harmless sing-along version; *The Quaker Girl* (1910) embraced religious dissent by rendering plainness of dress and manner as Parisian haute couture. More than a convenient motif or disposable fashion, this appetite for cohesion was the central organizing principle of popular theater at this time. It was evident in a show like Franz Lehár's *The Merry Widow* (1907), a game-changing operetta which, far from retreating to a fantasy "Ruritania," reconciled traditional aristocracy (Count Danilo) to a version of modernity more conservative and respectable than the decadent hedonism of bohemian Paris, also staged in the show. Agency here is represented by Anna, a figure who makes the transformation from peasant to the engaging and astute widow of a figure most emblematic of the modern world in many of its guises – a powerful banker. Leo Fall's *The Girl in the Train* (1908) was again an operetta styled in modern terms, as was *The Dollar Princess* (1909) set in New York City and "Aliceville," Canada. The latter opens with a chorus of female typists and the narrative challenge in which new money is in the ascendancy and traditional aristocracy reduced to servitude. The gender counterpart to this potentially destabilizing inversion, entirely commonplace in these shows, is that the brains behind the agency are female. Thus it is Alice, the dollar princess, who successfully advises her father on investments, at the same time as making a personal fortune for herself "on the side." The working out of these farce elements into harmonious resolution constitutes the central narrative device of the show around which all its songs and social dances circulate.

Revue in this period, often represented as an outgrowth of music hall and variety, worked similarly, at least before the war and despite the fact that it typically broke with narrative coherency, using other structures to replace the same obsession with happy order. Writing about the 1907 Metropol revue *Das muß man sehn*, Marline Otte shows how conservative and liberal spirits were reconciled through the figures of an agrarian compeer (male host) and the liberal Fräulein Freissinn (the commère or female host). The twinning had racialized dimensions inasmuch as agrarian conservatives were associated with anti-Semitism while liberalism was constructed in terms of a Jewish politics. In the show's version of things, these potentially conflictual forces end up not quite in agreement but at least firmly cemented through matrimony. Children are subsequently produced and the tale concludes with an explicit plea for harmony:

> Commère: Well what do you say about these two fine specimens?
> Compère: I don't find it all that silly. If the exchange continues as it is – between countries and estates – little by little, many prejudices and many barriers have to fall and so it will be just a step toward general understanding, towards world peace.[20]

The suggestion of this framing narrative was clear. As Otte points out, "no antagonism in German society was too great to overcome," at least in theater land – a message repeated over and over in both individual sketches and other more encompassing frameworks in early revue.[21] Here again, the idea of an assimilative modernity was central – just as it was in musical comedy and operetta. A narrative figure often used to structure these same Metropol revues, to take a further example, involved rural visitors coming to town to experience, and be reconciled to, the sophisticated delights of a modern metropolis – the device derived from the travel scheme first used by Jacques Offenbach in *Orphée aux enfers*, in which the gods, bored by the drabness of life on Olympus, visit hell. At the Metropol, traditional deities metamorphosed into country yokels being shown around the dazzling sights and social events of Berlin, thereby becoming familiarized with life in the modern metropolis. Thus in *Neuestes, Allerneuestes* (1903), Serenissimus – a caricature of the perceived self-importance of rulers in the small German principalities then in existence – travels from the country to Berlin, where he is treated like a tourist. Many members in the audience could presumably relate to such experiences – a crucial part of the Metropol's audience was made up of tourists from all over Germany.

Revues in the West End similarly celebrated modernity's powers of national and metropolitan assimilation. *Odds and Ends* (1914) did so in a particularly self-conscious way. This show begins within a "let's make a show" narrative device that welcomes French and Belgium actress refugees; the black-American boxer Jack Johnson; and "Turkish girls from Ispahan" – "We don't want Votes for Women or to be a Suffragette / All we want's one husband for the night" – all to the accommodating world of the modern musical stage.[22] Again, *The Bing Boys Are Here* (1917), billed as a revue, uses that organizing device of country boys coming to London in a show very difficult to distinguish from a musical comedy (Figure 17).

These kinds of devices and narratives again suggested that the popular theaters of places like London, Paris, Berlin, New York, Vienna, and Budapest shared a great deal of common territory, although this often ran alongside the equally determined "local" and "national" dimensions. For popular theater also reproduced strong-spirited nationalist sentiment in city characters and city vernaculars, perhaps especially in the case of a city like Berlin, a relatively new capital and the product of astonishing growth in the late nineteenth and early twentieth centuries – "a growth spurt unprecedented in European urban history."[23] Here popular theater, while underwriting cosmopolitan status, also played

FIGURE 17 The "upbeat dispensation of 'gaiety.'" *The Sunshine Girl* (Paul Rubens, 1912) celebrated factory life

a particular role in the formation of localized urban identities. Highly suggestively, Richard Schultz, manager of the Metropol, took the opportunity of his first revue, *Das Paraidies der Frauen* (1898), to dedicate his theater to the greater glory of the city. He wrote in the program notes for this production that the Metropol "in its dimensions, in the grandeur of its interior decoration" was "a house ... truly worthy of the German Empire's capital. It is a metropolitan establishment in the true sense of the word."[24] The contradictions implied here between the stylish metropolitan melting pot – modern, universalizing, and multiple – and the more conventional attachments to nation, empire, and race go to the heart of musical theater culture as it was constituted at the turn of century and its self-conscious position at a turning point of modernity.

Again, such dimensions became particularly engaged in cultures of translation and adaptation. These transformed Paul Lincke's *Frau Luna* (1899) into a London West End stage show produced at the Scala in 1911. Here a production originally set in the vicinity of Alexanderplatz, a locality with which every Berliner and tourist would be familiar, became reconfigured as *Castles in the Air*, a translation of one of the show's three big hit songs in the original "*Schlösser, die im Monde liege.*" A show that must have once seemed quintessentially "Berlin" – one of its songs, "*Berliner Luft*" ("Berlin Air"), became a great theme song for the city – was in this way newly convened for West End audiences in a Notting Hill setting. On the one hand, the capacity for fluid metamorphosis was part of a generic modernizing world that musical theater represented and in some ways made real. On the other hand, the imperative to construct these shows in "native" terms seemed a reminder of the more fixed dimensions of regional, national, and racial identities.

During World War I, Continental transfer and exchange ceased almost overnight. By the time such interchange resumed in the 1920s, the popular theater landscape had changed in some key respects. The jubilant embracing of contemporaneity as "gaiety," so much the stock in trade of musical comedies and earlier German operettas, appeared no longer viable to the same degree, or, at least, not in the standard West End formulation. The war had rendered their particular variety of naïve and cheerful optimism in the face of the modern world obsolete, not to say tasteless. In terms of the Continental export market, operettas remained popular but in a revisionist form: the once-characteristic mix of localism and cosmopolitanism firmly positioned as a confident negotiation of the modern gave way to spectaculars of a different kind: historical romances such as *Madame Pompadour* and *Die Barry*, both of which were set in prerevolutionary France. Or else, like Lehár's *Die Blaue Mazur* (1920) – which played London in 1927 as *The Blue Mazurka* – or *Wenn Liebe erwacht* (*When Love Awakens*, 1922), they existed in mythic no time and fairy tale no place. In postwar operetta, contemporary complexities were displaced by a return to the safeties and securities of aristocratic order, traditional romance, and waltzes – the standard components of a "Viennese" musical theater now being virtually mass produced in the new center for this kind of product. Berlin became the principal exporter of operetta after World War I, with that form later becoming one of the few versions of popular theater culture to be appropriated by National Socialism.[25]

Play after play in this period followed the same design: after an initial nod to the contemporary condition, they back-pedaled into less controversial territory. *Die Frau im Hermelin* (1919), performed in London as *The Lady of the Rose*, notionally a historical musical, nevertheless pointed to potential contemporary conflict because, produced just a few years after real European revolution, it was set in the days of the Italian *risorgimento*. Within a few pages, however, the show had become a Gothic romance, its terms of reference shifting from revolution to the more domestic domain of a lady's "honour." *Der Vetter aus Dingsda* (*The Cousin from Nowhere*, 1923), on the other hand, began with contemporary dialogue and potential conflict between age and youth. But what starts as the modern story of a young woman coming of age and exerting authority over her guardian quickly shifts gear when a modern house is transformed into a castle in "Faeryland / As in the tales of the days that have been." Here the real 1920s and the notoriously unstable flapper identity were ceremoniously discarded to make way for the return of a traditionalist cousin singing "a yodelling song."

By comparison to the earlier period, the 1920s and 1930s saw a taste developing for a particularly safe version of the romantic. A popular theater that once struggled to embrace the volatility of the modern world seemed now in retreat. Global war, economic upheavals, and social and political bifurcation appeared to have rendered accommodation beyond the bounds of "entertainment." Against this background, it comes as no surprise that adaptation of the cosmopolitan modern gave way to uniform escape into the nonspecific world of "Ruritania" or a snowy "Austria." The dynamic exchange culture of prewar musical theater, in which metropolitan centers competed for authority over the unstable modern, was put firmly back in its box.

In these historiographies, then, popular culture is not part of a progressivist force leading to the flowering of art cultures but rather responds to shifts in the precise historical conditions that surround its formulation. These are never linear, but nor are they simple, and it is, of course, not the suggestion here that by the 1920s popular theater as a vibrant urban culture had lost its force. Clearly it had not. An engaged popular theater entertainment was far from dead and buried. On the contrary, it was becoming more strongly identified with the stylish and sophisticated innovations of an American stage now strongly competing for authority over the modern. At the same time, other forms of popular theater were constructing new versions of contemporary life – new modernisms – sometimes with alarming implications.

Again, it was revue, one of the most underresearched forms of popular theater, that led the way, in this respect constituting, in the postwar period, a new wave that frequently took iconoclastic positions in specific relation to what was now perceived as the established, and tired, conventions of musical comedy. In its postwar West End incarnation, revue was very much a new kind of entertainment that laughed at the passing of the old. Indeed, the revue of the postwar years took the fantasy worlds defined by musical comedy and operetta and turned them upside down. Operating with a new sense of speed and urgency, revue displaced the stately dynamics of the popular theater plot with a wild energy. Far from creating a consistent fabric, whether in terms of narrative or style, the up-and-coming form aimed for bizarre shifts and dramatic transformations at every level. Melodrama could snap into show-time glitz at any minute; film was often interpolated into the performance, implying a multi-media practice that emphasized difference rather than assimilation. The whole production, although written as a single text with songs, dance routines, and sketches, had little interest in narrative coherence. It was not that revue was too unsophisticated to sustain traditional story, as was sometimes argued, but, rather, that it eschewed what it saw as the narrative simplicity and romanticism of the earlier form. Its humor was more abrasive, more risqué, and less stylized than in musical comedy. Routines became parodies of routines; indeed, parody and pastiche became a definite hallmark of revue. More than a simple displacement of one fashion for another, shows like Charlot's *London Calling* (1923), scripted by Nöel Coward and Roland Jeans, exemplified the challenge of revue as a complex expression of the new against the passé.

This dynamic of shift and engagement, far from being alien, was, and is, general to modern commercial culture. It expressed the characteristic imperative for innovation and demonstrated how conceptions of cultural value could change almost overnight in the world of popular entertainment. But more than this, in the London manifestation, revue carried the idea not just that popular theater in its traditional forms had become old hat but that modernity itself had changed in ways that the conventional stage simply could not accommodate. As I have expressed it elsewhere, "in its *most* disruptive, anarchic form, revue represented a kind of *walpurgisnacht* version of modernity, where reality, far from being mediated, contained and generally made safe, was always in danger of running out of control."[26]

Acknowledgment

Research for this chapter has been supported by the Arts and Humanities Research Council and the Deutsche Forschungemeinschaft. My thanks to other members of the research team who worked on this project, especially to Tobias Becker and David Linton.

Notes

1 Gerald M. Berkowitz, *American Drama of the Twentieth Century* (New York: Longman, 1992), 1.

2 Gerald Bordman, *American Musical Theater: A Chronicle*, 2nd edition (Oxford and New York: Oxford University Press, 1992), 58.

3 Thomas Postlewait, "From Melodrama to Realism: The Suspect History of American Drama," in *Melodrama. The Cultural Emergence of a Genre*, eds. Michael Hays, Anastasia Nikolopoulou (Basingstoke: Macmillan, 1996), 47.

4 A brief indicative bibliography might include Michael R. Booth, *Victorian Spectacular Theatre 1850–1910* (London; Routledge and Kegan Paul, 1981); Jacky S. Bratton, *Music Hall: Performance and Style* (Milton Keynes: Open University Press, 1986); Peter Jelavich, *Berlin Cabaret* (Cambridge, MA: Harvard University Press, 1993); and Peter Bailey, "'Naughty but Nice:' Musical Comedy and the Rhetoric of the Girl," in *The Edwardian Theatre*, eds. Michael R. Booth and Joel H. Kaplan (Cambridge: Cambridge University Press, 1998).

5 The Melville brothers (Walter and Frederick) were composers of melodramas in the late nineteenth and early twentieth centuries; Jimmy Davies, who called himself "Owen Hall" because of his notorious financial debts, wrote the librettos for such musical comedies as *A Gaiety Girl* (1893) and *Floradora* (1899); Lionel Monckton was one of the most well-known composers of musical comedy – he worked on the scores of *The Cingalee, The Country Girl* (1902), *Our Miss Gibbs*, and many others. Rubens was a gifted librettist and composer who worked on *The Dairymaids* (1906), *Dear Little Denmark* (1909), *The Balkan Princess* (1910), and so on.

6 David Meyer, "Encountering Melodrama," in *The Cambridge Companion to Victorian and Edwardian Theatre*, ed. Kerry Powell (Cambridge: Cambridge University Press, 2004), 147.

7 See Elaine Aston and Ian Clarke, "The Dangerous Woman of Melvillean Drama," *New Theatre Quarterly* 12 (1996), 30–42. For an outline approach to melodrama, see Meyer, "Encountering Melodrama," 135–63.

8 This was also partly a response to the New Woman. See Len Platt, *Musical Comedy on the West End Stage* (Basingstoke: Palgrave Macmillan, 2004), 130–17.

9 See Frank E. Washburn Freund, "The Theatrical Year in Germany," *The Stage Year Book 1911*, 57–68 (65).

10 The forms were converging in this period, but operetta remained the more serious form in musical terms and musical comedy more disposed toward comic interventions.

11 William Archer, *The Theatrical World of 1896* (London: Walter Scott, 1896), 298–305.

12 Huntly Carter, *The New Spirit in the European Theatre 1914–1924* (London: Ernest Benn Ltd, 1925), 85.

13 James T. Tanner, *Our Miss Gibbs* (British Library: Lord Chamberlain's Plays, 1909), 2.

14 See Judith Walkowitz, *City of Dreadful Delight: Narratives of Sexual Danger in Late-Victorian London* (London: Virago Press, 1994), 45–50.

15 Meyer, "Encountering Melodrama," 160. See also David Meyer, "Changing Horses in Mid-Ocean: *The Whip* in Britain and America," in *The Edwardian Theatre: Essays on Performance and the Stage*, eds. Michael R. Booth and Joel H. Kaplan (Cambridge: Cambridge University Press, 1996), 220–35.

16 Jose Harris, *Private Lives, Public Spirit: A Social History of Britain 1870–1914* (Oxford: Oxford University Press, 1993), 33.

17 Lewis shows a surprising capacity for discrimination in singling out the popular musical actress Gertie Millar for praise. Instead of being "blasted," this particular performer is "blessed," perhaps in acknowledgment of her beauty. Wyndham Lewis, *Blast 1* (1914; London: Thames and Hudson, 2009), 11, 21, 21, 28. While some fin de siècle artists and intellectuals – Rudyard Kipling, F. Anstey, Max Beebohm, Arthur Symons, Arnold Bennett, Walter Sickert, and so on – had a regard for musical hall, few expressed any serious interest in the more bourgeois forms. One exception in this respect was James Joyce, who built the "Sirens" episode of *Ulysses* in part around *Floradora* and incorporated titles of musical comedies into *Finnegans Wake*. See Len Platt, *James Joyce and Finnegans Wake* (Cambridge: Cambridge University Press, 2007), 121–37.

18 Jean Baudrillard, *Fatal Strategies*, trans. Philip Beitchman and W.G.J Niesluchowski, ed. Jim Fleming (London: Semiotext(e)/Pluto, 1990), 166–79.

19 See Jelavich, *Berlin Cabaret*, 104–17. London was a dominant theme in an earlier stage of London drama, as suggested by the titles of plays like *The Heart of London* (1830), *The Scamps of London, or the Crossroads of Life* (1843), *London by Night* (1845), and so on. Later musical theater was differently disposed. See Michael R. Booth, "The Metropolis on the Stage," in *The Victorian City*, vol. 1, eds. H.J. Dyos and Michael Wolff (1973; London: Routledge and Kegan Paul, 1976), 211–24. London returned as the subject of latter revues like *London Calling* (1923) and *The London Revue* (1925).

20 Metropol Theater, *Das muß man sehn!* (1907), 1907, Rep. 30 c/a. Theater Z, Neuir Teil, Landsarchiv, Berlin.

21 Marline Otte, *Jewish Identities in German Popular Entertainment, 1890–1933* (Cambridge: Cambridge University Press, 2006), 265.

22 H. Grattan, *Odds and Ends* (British Library manuscripts: Lord Chamberlain's Plays, 1914, n.p.)

23 Jay Winter and Jean Louis Gordon, *Capital Cities at War: London, Paris, and Berlin 1918–19* (Cambridge: Cambridge University Press, 1997), 26.

24 Quoted in Ines Hahn, "Das Metropol-Theater. Theater als sichere Geldanlage," in *Theater als Geschäft*, ed. Ruth Freydank (Berlin, 1995), 93.

25 See Richard Traubner, *Operetta: A Theatrical History* (New York and Oxford: Oxford University Press, 1983), ix. Traubner's account gives some indication of just how central Berlin was in this respect. The full extent of Berlin's importance in this respect, however, has yet to be fully articulated.

26 Platt, *Musical Comedy on the West End Stage*, 134.

14

Publishing

"Follow me, and take a column, / Even if you have to work free," advised the literary opportunist Mr. Nixon in Ezra Pound's "Hugh Selwyn Mauberley" sequence (1920).[1] Many modernists marketed their own work shrewdly, including Pound himself, the impresario of the movement, who wrote many columns for important little magazines from *The New Age*, *Poetry*, and *The Little Review* onward. So, too, did other modernists, including Marianne Moore, T.S. Eliot, and Ford Madox Ford, along with editing or helping to edit multiple journals. In contrast to the older view of modernism as elite, defining itself against dominant culture, a more recent one sees it with closer ties to that enterprise, alternately resisting and participating in it. A major factor in that revision has been growing awareness of the continuing rise of publishing outlets – including little magazines, bigger-circulation periodicals, and book publishing. As opposed to the well-meaning but ineffectual character Mauberley, modernists quickly recognized and took advantage of new opportunities and new audiences.

The expansion of outlets and of readerships continued trends that had begun in the previous century. In their book *Modernism in the Magazines*, Robert Scholes and Clifford Wulfman identify four factors in particular: the rise of large cities holding masses of people; technological innovations leading to new methods of printing (such as first the rotary press and then the linotype machine); the spread of public education fostering widespread literacy; and commercial interest in stimulating the consumption of consumer goods and services.[2] All these forces combined to create a wider public and mass reading audience than had existed before, on either side of the Atlantic. The linotype machine, for example, was invented in 1886 by German immigrant Ottmar Mergenthaler for the

New York Tribune and in the 1890s was exported to Britain. By allowing an operator to use a keyboard to select a letter rather than doing so by hand, the machine made printing easier and cheaper, as the rotary press had done before it by offering speeds up to ten times the previous rate of hand-setting.

The growing number of magazines and newspapers boosted opportunity for the modernists. Often women played a key role in creating and editing such journals. Founded in 1912 in Chicago by Harriet Monroe, *Poetry: A Magazine of Verse* announced its mission in its subtitle as providing a welcoming outlet for poetry, which was often shunned or minimized by large-circulation periodicals. It published an extraordinary number of modernist writers, including W.B. Yeats as last romantic and first modernist along with Ezra Pound (himself a foreign editor), Robert Frost, Wallace Stevens, Marianne Moore, and H.D., among many others. Eliot's "The Love Song of J. Alfred Prufrock" first appeared there, as did H.D.'s Imagist verse. Two years later in the Chicago Renaissance, along came Margaret Anderson's *The Little Review*, which with the help of Jane Heap and Ezra Pound again as foreign editor published many of the same writers. The magazine scored its greatest coup with the serialization of James Joyce's radically experimental novel *Ulysses*, which it published from 1918 until 1921, when a famous obscenity trial brought by the U.S. Post Office at the instigation of the New York Society for the Suppression of Vice took place. The magazine eventually lost and had to pay a $50 fine but established a reputation as standard-bearer for freedom of artistic expression. Both magazines published artwork, but *Little Review* carried far more, including pieces by Hans Arp, Michelle Duchamp, Max Ernst, and Pablo Picasso among others.

The mastheads of the two magazines embody the Modernist ambivalence toward the surrounding society. On the one hand, *Poetry* sported a quotation from Walt Whitman: "To have great poetry we must have great audiences too." Whitman's remark embodies a radically democratic spirit that assigns the public a collaborative role coequal to that of the artist. In contrast, *Little Review* proclaimed artist and audience oppositional, even antagonistic. "Making No Compromise With the Public Taste," roared its motto, which at least pleased Pound. The duality runs right through modernism, which often saw its own creativity as defying society but at other times took a more cooperative stance. Many writers astutely manipulated public opinion, or at least a portion of it, as in Pound's successful campaign to launch *The Waste Land* and to have it receive the *Dial* Award of $2,000 (comparable to more than ten times that today) in 1922. *The Dial*, of course, was another magazine that featured modernist work during the 1920s before, like *Little Review*, closing in 1929. Slightly larger than the other two, it had a circulation of 9,200 in 1922, the year that it published *The Waste Land*.

Modernist texts also appeared in mid-sized magazines, with circulations in the tens of thousands. Early on, *The Smart Set*, for example, published avant-garde work by W.B. Yeats, Ezra Pound, Joseph Conrad, and D.H. Lawrence. Later it published two stories from James Joyce's *Dubliners* in 1915, their first publication in the United States, and in 1919 introduced F. Scott Fitzgerald. Its pages boasted works by Edna St. Vincent Millay, Theodore Dreiser, Aldous Huxley, Sinclair Lewis, Eugene O'Neill, and Dashiell Hammett among others. Especially under H.L. Mencken and George Jean Nathan, the magazine offered a wider-circulation outlet for modern literature, with average circulation of 50,000 and a high of 75,000 before closing in 1930 under financial pressure from the Depression. So, too, did the longer-lived *Vanity Fair* under the editorship of Frank Crowninshield from 1914 to 1936. Crowninshield had helped organize the Armory Show in 1913, which introduced modernist European art to American audiences, and had a wide range of interests. Under him, *Vanity Fair* included work by Gertrude Stein, Aldous Huxley, D.H. Lawrence, Edmund Wilson, Noël Coward, and E.E. Cummings, along with Dorothy Parker's name on its masthead.

Even large-circulation venues carried some modernist work, more often prose than poetry. F. Scott Fitzgerald's relationship with *The Saturday Evening Post* offers a good example. Best-known today for its Norman Rockwell covers (more than 300 during a fifty-year span), the *Post* offered a range of writing in every issue. Among the more modern fiction contributors were Kay Boyle, William Faulkner, and John Steinbeck, along with poets ranging from Carl Sandburg to Dorothy Parker. Fitzgerald himself never had a blockbuster novel in his lifetime, with works like *The Great Gatsby* initially earning little and selling in large quantities only posthumously. For his living, Fitzgerald depended more on short stories, of which he penned more than 160. Sixty-five of them appeared in the well-paying *Saturday Evening Post*, reaching a high fee of $4,000 in 1929. The magazine could afford such munificence because of its extensive advertising revenue and mass circulation of more than two and a half million copies per week, a long way from the little magazines. Fitzgerald also published in other mass outlets, including *Redbook*, *Collier's*, and *McCall's*.

Modern mass-circulation magazines had arisen in the 1880s and 1890s. *The Saturday Evening Post*, for example, grew from circulation in the thousands to more than three million under the editorship of George Horace Lorimer from 1899 to 1936. Similar growth attended *Collier's*, *Cosmopolitan*, and *Redbook* among others. Mass advertising enabled them to charge low prices of ten or fifteen cents an issue. The resultant large fees affected content as well, especially for short stories and serialized novels, by enticing some writers but repelling others. Authors like Fitzgerald and Hemingway embraced magazine publication anyway. Others, like Ellen Glasgow, resisted it and forbade her agent Paul Revere Reynolds to offer serial rights to mass magazines. By contrast, John P. Marquand responded to an inquiry from England about serial rights with a two-word telegram: "How much?"[3] The "slicks," as they were sometimes called, could also pressure authors to drop language deemed offensive and to write to formulas. After selling "Spotted Horses" to *Scribner's Magazine* in 1931, for instance, William Faulkner had a hard time persuading them to accept anything other than more Flem Snopes stories. After her biography of Lincoln was published, Ida Tarbell suffered continual pressure from magazines for more and more articles about that president. Cautious issues of taste and decorum could also lead to editorial toning down of authorial language, as befell Hemingway and Fitzgerald. Needed income offered a continued temptation for writers to accept such restriction.

Along with expanding media came expanding opportunities for newer groups in authorship and in management. Little magazines, for example, featured determined and talented women at the helm, such as Harriet Monroe and Alice Corbin Henderson at *Poetry* or Margaret Anderson and Jane Heap at *The Little Review*. Equally influential was *The Freewoman*, begun in 1911 by Dora Marsden and first reincarnated as *The New Freewoman* with Rebecca West as assistant editor (along with the ubiquitous Pound as literary editor) and then in 1914 as *The Egoist* under Harriet Shaw Weaver as editor and a succession of Richard Aldington, H.D., and T.S. Eliot as literary editors. That journal counted among its triumphs the influential "Imagist number" in 1915 and serializations of James Joyce's *A Portrait of the Artist as a Young Man* and *Ulysses*, along with a stream of important work by authors including Eliot, Pound, Marianne Moore, Wyndham Lewis, H.D., Amy Lowell, D.H. Lawrence, and William Carlos Williams.

A number of female editors and patrons had enough money to set up their own small publishing houses. Weaver herself established Egoist

Press to publish *Ulysses* in England. That short-lived venture also issued first editions of *Tarr* by Wyndham Lewis, *Prufrock* by T.S. Eliot, and *Quia Pauper Amavi* by Ezra Pound and brought the works of H.D., Robert McAlmon, Dora Marsden, Richard Aldington, and Marianne Moore to the English public, often for the first time. A bewildering and often interconnected web of modernist literature first appeared in other small independent concerns founded or run by women, including those operated by Sylvia Beach (Shakespeare and Company), Gertrude Stein (Plain Editions), Nancy Cunard (The Hours Press), Caresse Crosby (Black Sun Press) and others. First books by Ernest Hemingway, Samuel Beckett, and William Carlos Williams appeared through ventures managed or funded by Winifred Ellerman (better known as Bryher), heiress and companion of H.D. and one of the richest women in England. Taken as a whole, these presses and journals had a massive role in the publication and publicizing of modernism in English, belying their small size.[4]

Among presses run by women promoting modernism, perhaps the Hogarth Press operated by Virginia Woolf and her husband Leonard from 1917 to 1938 stands out. Begun as a therapeutic activity for Virginia and named after their residence at Hogarth House, the Press operated a small hand press bought by the Woolfs and outsourced its larger runs. Output eventually totaled 440 titles, many of them key works of twentieth-century poetry, novels, criticism, translation, politics, and psychology (the Press became the authorized publisher of Sigmund Freud in English, for example). Its first production was *Two Stories*, one by each of the co-owners, along with four woodcuts by Dora Carrington and a geometric cover design. Hogarth went on to publish a variety of important modernist titles, chief among them those by T.S. Eliot and Virginia Woolf herself. The Press issued the first English editions of Eliot's *The Waste Land* and *Poems*, along with his prose *Homage to John Dryden*. It also published all of Virginia Woolf's work after her first two novels. The list of distinguished other writers included Katherine Mansfield, E.M. Forster, and Robert Graves. Yet Virginia's career remained central to its program. Leonard pointed out that "the development of the Hogarth Press was bound up with the development of Virginia as a writer and with her literary or creative psychology." Woolf herself famously declared in 1925 that "what I owe the Hogarth Press is barely paid by the whole of my handwriting.... yes, I'm the only woman in England free to write what I like."[5]

Besides women, another group of new publishers arose in the early twentieth century, particularly on the American side of the market. For the most part, the new publishers were Jewish. Their heads had bumped into glass ceilings in the traditional American publishing industry, as Jews had done in medicine, law, and other endeavors after the large influx of Hebrew immigrants beginning around 1880. Jewish hospitals arose to allow Jews access to hospital affiliations otherwise unavailable; Jewish law firms offered sanctuary to those spurned by white-shoe law firms, and many companies avoided Jews for higher positions. That was true in book publishing, too, where historian Charles A. Madison pointed out, "gentlemen publishers ... would not employ a Jew and made little or no effort to seek out Jewish writers." The new firms often had trouble attracting mainline gentile writers and had to embrace what they could get. As a result, they took up with an assortment of experimental modernists along with authors of Jewish, black, and Irish descent. Alfred Harcourt of Harcourt Brace and one of the rare gentile publishers promoting ethnic literature recalled, "while Boston publishers were bringing out sets of Longfellow and Emerson in new bindings, new publishers sprang up in New York, notably Huebsch, Knopf, and Liveright, who began to publish translations of contemporary foreign authors and books by young American authors who had broken away from the Victorian point of view."[6]

The first to become prominent was B.W. Huebsch, the son of a rabbi. His greatest feat was snaring James Joyce's early works, including in 1916 both the first American edition of *Dubliners*, which fifteen publishers had turned down partly on grounds of obscenity, and the first edition anywhere of *A Portrait of the Artist as a Young Man*. Huebsch published other modernist works, too, including first American editions of D.H. Lawrence and the first edition anywhere of Sherwood Anderson's *Winesburg, Ohio*. Alfred A. Knopf and his wife Blanche published even more modernists, beginning in 1915. In 1920, for example, they brought out both Eliot's *Poems* and the prose collection *The Sacred Wood*. They also published all the major poetry of Wallace Stevens from *Harmonium* (1923) onwards, several D.H. Lawrence titles, and Pound's *Lustra* and *Pavannes and Divisions* among others. The Knopfs welcomed African American writers, too, issuing Nella Larsen's novels *Quicksand* and *Passing*. From 1926 onward, they became the publishers of Langston Hughes, with whom they formed a close relationship as they did with other writers.

In 1917, the brash young bond dealer Horace Liveright came together with the Boni brothers (particularly Albert) to found the pioneering Boni and Liveright, which later separated into two firms, one for the

Boni Brothers and the other for Liveright. The principals were contrasts in many ways. Harvard educated, Albert and his brother Charles had founded an influential Greenwich Village bookshop that had sponsored the avant-garde magazine *The Glebe* and issued the cutting-edge anthology *Des Imagistes* in 1914. In contrast, Liveright had been a hard-drinking paper and bond salesman with little knowledge of the publishing industry but a knack for salesmanship. Together they published avant-garde work by T.S. Eliot (*The Waste Land*), Theodore Dreiser (*An American Tragedy*), and Bertrand Russell (*Marriage and Morals*), along with early books by Ernest Hemingway, William Faulkner, Hart Crane, and Dorothy Parker. As that partial list suggests, Boni and Liveright had a hard time soliciting work by then-established mainstream writers. As a result, they also brought out works by minority writers, especially by blacks, Jews, and Irish. Jean Toomer's *Cane*, Waldo Frank's *Our America*, and Yeats's *Irish Poetry and Folk Tales* all appeared in their catalogues.

Despite issuing titles that made best-seller lists in the 1920s, the firm operated largely on the margins, both because of its cautious Jewish owners and because of Liveright's extravagant lifestyle. Yet the firm continued to take chances on promising young authors. Unfortunately, not all of them escaped the anti-Semitism of the period. The house's Jewish character did not bother Ezra Pound, who published both prose and poetry volumes with Liveright and called him "a pearl among publishers." In contrast, such social concerns did bother William Faulkner, who after doing two books with Boni and Liveright eagerly switched to Harcourt Brace. "I'm going to be published by white folks now," he confided to his great aunt Alabama. "Harcourt Brace & Co. bought me from Liveright. Much nicer there." T.S. Eliot went even further in a virulent epistle to the anti-Semitic modernist patron John Quinn after a dispute with Liveright in 1923 about an advance payment. "I am sick of doing business with Jew publishers who will not carry out their part of the contract unless they are forced to," he complained of the firm that first published *The Waste Land* in book form.[7] Ironically after his flamboyant successes, Liveright's profligate tastes, alcoholism, and expensive theatrical ventures (he cast Bela Lugosi as Dracula on Broadway, for instance) led him to an impoverished early death at the age of forty-nine. Only six people attended his funeral.

Boni and Liveright contributed to modern publishing in two other ways besides its author list. First came invention of its series The Modern Library in 1917. Priced at sixty cents each, its volumes made a variety of avant-garde and traditional writers available to a wide audience at an affordable price. Its early authors included Oscar Wilde, H.G. Wells, and Robert Louis Stevenson along with Continental writers like Friedrich Nietzsche, Guy de Maupassant, and Henrik Ibsen. The success and wide sales of the series helped to fund the firm's riskier ventures. So, too, did the hiring of Austrian-American Edward Bernays in 1919 as publicity consultant. Bernays had worked for the government shaping attitudes during World War I and, after his discharge, founded with his wife a company so influential that he became known as the "father of public relations." The nephew of Sigmund Freud, he combined insights from psychology and marketing to influence public opinion, particularly on then-controversial topics like women smoking in public, for which he designed a campaign for Lucky Strike cigarettes. For Bernays, his role meant using what he thought of as scientific techniques for manipulating public opinion. His influence also led to new publicity of all kinds for books, including greatly increased reliance on advertising. He also published two of his own influential works, *Crystallizing Public Opinion* and *Propaganda*, with Liveright in the 1920s. Under his influence, the firm pioneered advertising methods that quickly became standard, including sending free review copies to newspaper editors along with ready-made reviews. As a result, reviewers across the country often quoted the same few passages.

Modernist authors both shaped and were shaped by their receptions in one other way, namely by getting their work published in multiple forms. To be sure, they had always manipulated new outlets and organizations to their own benefit. So keen an observer as D.H. Lawrence told Amy Lowell that Imagism, which made its debut in *Poetry* magazine in 1913, was "just an advertising scheme." The label first appeared when Pound forwarded some lyrics of H.D. and supplied the signature "H.D., Imagiste." Lowell was accused of trying to usurp the new movement, which Harriet Monroe called "the battle of Imagism" and Pound then derided as "Amygism" sponsored by a "hippopoetess." But modernist efforts encompassed more than single skirmishes. Many of them chose to exploit the new media in magazines, small presses, and larger publishers by publishing the same work (or versions of it) in all three venues. The triple strategy enabled authors both to realize more money for their efforts and to reach varied and hence larger audiences. Two authors – W.B. Yeats on one side of the Atlantic and H.D. on the other – provide contrasting examples of exploiting the new situation.

Yeats rapidly seized on the new opportunities created by twentieth-century publishing, especially after his growing reputation made him a potential money maker. But at first he had to take what he could get. Like many young authors of the time, his first book (the slender verse drama *Mosada*) came out by subscription, in his case organized in 1886 by his father, the painter John Butler Yeats. A reprint issued by the same Dublin firm that published the magazine *Dublin University Review*, in which the work had previously appeared, it attracted only a single review. It did, though, set Yeats's pattern of publishing first in a journal and then collecting the individual works into a volume. That governed his construction of his first real book of verse, *The Wanderings of Oisin and Other Poems*, from the London firm of Kegan Paul in an edition of 500 copies (200 of which went by subscription). Most of the poems had appeared previously, mainly in the *Dublin University Review* again, but also in other Irish journals and even as far afield as *The Boston Pilot*, an Irish-American publication. It attracted thirty-seven reviews, mostly favorable. Yeats's second verse volume, *The Countess Kathleen and other Poems* (1892), appeared from T. Fisher Unwin in London, a house that had been founded ten years earlier. The book was well reviewed, but Fisher Unwin's subsequent publication of Yeats's collected *Poems* (1895) was the book that in its many reissues (with some revisions and additions) shaped Yeats's reception for the next thirty years.

Yeats went on to publish with other English publishers besides Unwin, principally Elkin Matthews and A.H. Bullen, who had strong Irish interests, before settling on the larger Macmillan as his main publisher from 1916 onward. But the founding of an Irish small press in 1903 proved crucial to his usual tripartite strategy of publishing work first in periodicals, then with the Dun Emer (after 1908 Cuala) Press, and finally with Macmillan. The first book offered by Dun Emer was Yeats's *In the Seven Woods* (1903). Dun Emer and later Cuala books carried a dense bibliographic coding. Founded by Evelyn Gleeson as part of Dun Emer Industries to provide training and work for women seeking to escape from the Irish domestic trinity of wife, nun, or service, the Industries offered weaving, embroidery, and printing as alternatives. The last came under the supervision of Yeats's strong-willed sister Lolly, who had studied printing in London under William Morris's collaborator at Kelmscott, Emery Walker. It hired only women, who comprised the entire work force and gave the Press a light feminist overtone. Moreover, the Press highlighted its Irishness as well, not only in its choice of writers but also in its colophons. Most of the women working there ardently supported the nationalist cause, resulting in a submerged but insistent political cast in pre-Independence Ireland. One sees the merging of women and nationalism even in its colophons, printed in red after the manner of Morris and Walker. For example, the one for Yeats's *Responsibilities* volume (1914) reads:

> HERE ENDS RESPONSIBILITIES: POEMS AND A PLAY BY
> WILLIAM BUTLER YEATS, PRINTED AND PUBLISHED
> BY ELIZABETH CORBET YEATS AT THE CUALA PRESS,
> CHURCHTOWN, DUNDRUM IN THE COUNTRY OF DUBLIN,
> IRELAND. FINISHED ON MAY EVE, IN THE YEAR NINETEEN
> HUNDRED AND FOURTEEN.

The naming of the female proprietor and the Irish site of publication in County Dublin all reflect the Press's predilections. Such coding affects interpretation of this volume, which features so many poems on politics and women, including "September 1913," the great elegy on the funeral of Yeats's mentor John O'Leary. In that poem, the Press's imitation of Morris's layout of Kelmscott Press Books, sitting high on the page with larger external than internal margins like medieval and early Renaissance books, itself enacts an alternate economic and social order to that of strife-torn capitalist Dublin. Yeats then went on to publish this volume and most of its successors in a larger edition from Macmillan of London, attracting a wider audience to go with the smaller and wealthier one that could afford books from private presses like Cuala.

In contrast, the American Hilda Dootlittle (H.D.) devised a different strategy, which got her books into the hands of her friends but not into those of a large audience during her lifetime. Launched as an Imagist by her longtime friend and sometime lover Ezra Pound, H.D. saw her reputation first grow and then dwindle, with only four of her many poetry and prose books in print at her death in 1961. After several volumes with commercial presses like Boni and Liveright, Houghton Mifflin, and Constable, she largely withdrew into the world of private-press publishing and even manuscript circulation among her friends. As a result, only three of her completed novels appeared in print during her lifetime. For other work, she published with Darantiere in Lyons (who had set the first edition of Joyce's *Ulysses*) and then Egoist Press before finally finding safe harbor in her longtime friend and lover Bryher's Brendin Press. One of the richest women in England, Bryher (Winifred Ellerman) also provided financial support, which, together with her own inheritance, enabled H.D.'s withdrawal from the world of commercial publishing. The colophons and dedications made her motivation clear: *Kora and Ka* declared that "This edition of one hundred copies has been privately printed for the author's friends," or *Nights* announced, "This edition, of 100 copies, has been printed by friends of the author for private circulation."[8]

H.D.'s decision for limited, coterie publication contrasted with modernists such as Yeats with Dun Emer/Cuala; Joyce, Pound, Williams, and others with Elkin Mathews; or Pound and Eliot with John Rodker's Ovid Press. They used the small presses as way stations en route to broader publication but did so less frequently after the stock market crash and Depression shook the market for luxury editions. H.D. instead became a largely coterie artist with small public outlet. That carried over into her critical prose as well. As Lawrence Rainey has pointed out, from 1916 until her death, she published only forty-three articles, less than one a year. Over similarly long periods, Marianne Moore published more than 400, Eliot more than 500, and the irrepressible Pound more than 1,500 articles. As a result, during her lifetime, H.D. became an increasingly isolated figure, drawn to coterie forms like the *roman à clef*. She felt little need to enter public dialogue with her fellow modernists or to issue critical and theoretic writings arguing for her own experiments. After her death, her work lingered in the obscurity into which it had fallen until the 1980s, when the impact of feminism and other approaches resulted in her recovery and growing fame. Today, there are more editions of her work in print than at any time during her own life.

H.D.'s career and literary fortunes remind us that modernist publishing was not a fixed product but an ongoing process and that physical forms of production play a key role in that process. In assessing the careers of modernist writers, we need to pay attention to their chosen sites of publication. For instance, Yeats's lifelong appearance in nationalist (or at least national) periodicals, his publication of volumes under the feminist-nationalist imprint of Cuala, or his revised and more commercial volumes from Macmillan with their cover designs by T. Sturge Moore all signify different but equally important features of his work. Similarly, H.D.'s withdrawal from commercial publishing into coterie editions published under the Brendin imprint of her life-partner Bryher gesture toward important aspects of hers. That is true across the board and with other writers. The tendency of modernist writers (along with African-American and Jewish ones) to publish at least initially with the new houses that sprang up in New York after the turn of the century indicates the once-marginal status of their writing. So, too, does the work's frequent placement in little magazines like *Poetry* or *The Egoist*. Yet the inclusion of other work, chiefly prose fiction, in larger magazines like *Vanity Fair* or *Saturday Evening Post* signifies the ability of some writers, like Hemingway or Fitzgerald, to attract a wide audience along with a larger income.

If the sites of publication matter, so too does the creation of author-sanctioned variant states of the text that those sites enabled. Yeats and Moore, for example, created multiple versions of some of their best-known works. Which version of Moore's "The Fish," for example, should a contemporary editor publish, the original tidy quatrains of *The Egoist* version (1918), the six-line one in her *Poems* (1921), or the more familiar five-line one of her *Selected Poems* (1935) with its introduction by T.S. Eliot? And what of her famous poem "Poetry," which she approved in forms ranging from forty lines to only three? Such variation extends even to titles. Yeats, for example, published his major poem set during the great Dublin strike and lockout of 1913 first in the newspaper *The Irish Times* under the title "Romance in Ireland: (On Reading Much of the Correspondence against the Art Gallery)," then as "Romantic Ireland/September 1913" in the Cuala Press *Responsibilities* volume, and finally under its present title "September 1913" from the Macmillan *Responsibilities* onward. Recent developments in editorial theory suggest the legitimacy of all those different forms, which are difficult to represent in a codex edition, though Allt and Alspach's *Variorum Edition of the Poems of W.B. Yeats* shows what might be done with older editorial theory while Robin Schulze's *Becoming Marianne Moore* is an advanced effort to apply more recent approaches within print culture. Electronic textuality offers some hope of capturing such information, but so far it too has not produced fully adequate representations. Prolific as ever, modernist works continue to construct and deconstruct themselves in an ongoing enactment of their ongoing nature.

Notes

1 Ezra Pound, *Personae: The Shorter Poems*, ed. Lea Baechler and A. Walton Litz (New York: New Directions, 1990), 191.
2 Robert Scholes and Clifford Wulfman, *Modernism in the Magazines: An Introduction* (New Haven and London: Yale University Press, 2010), 27.
3 James L.W. West III, *American Authors and the Literary Marketplace since 1900* (Philadelphia: University of Pennsylvania Press, 1988), 109.

4 Jayne E. Marek, *Women Editing Modernism* (Lexington: University Press of Kentucky, 1995); George Bornstein, *Material Modernism: The Politics of the Page* (Cambridge and New York: Cambridge University Press, 1991), chapter 5.

5 Mark Hussey, *Virginia Woolf A to Z* (New York: Facts on File, 1995), 118.

6 Charles Madison, *Jewish Publishing in America* (New York: Sanhedrin Press, 1976), 251; and Alfred Harcourt, "Publishing in New York," in *Publishers on Publishing*, ed. Gerald Gross (New York: R.R. Bowker and Grosset and Dunlap, 1961), 255.

7 See Ezra Pound, letter to John Quinn, June 20, 1920; for Faulkner, see *Selected Letters* (New York: Viking, 1978), 41; and for T.S. Eliot, see his letter to John Quinn, March 12, 1923, cited in Tom Dardis, *The Life of Horace Liveright* (New York: Random House, 1995), 97–98.

8 See Lawrence S. Rainey, "Canon, Gender, and Text: The Case of H.D.," in *Representing Modernist Texts*, ed. George Bornstein (Ann Arbor: University of Michigan Press, 1991), 99–124, esp. 105.

Further Reading

Shaping Worldviews

Albright, Daniel. *Quantum Poetics: Yeats, Pound, Eliot, and the Science of Modernism*. Cambridge: Cambridge University Press, 1997.

Armstrong, Tim. *Modernism, Technology and the Body*. Cambridge: Cambridge University Press, 1998.

Berman, Marshall. *All That Is Solid Melts into Air: The Experience of Modernity*. New York: Simon & Schuster, 1982.

Bhabha, Homi. *The Location of Culture*. London: Routledge, 1994.

Bussey, Gertrude, and Margaret Tims. *Pioneers for Peace: Women's International League for Peace and Freedom 1915–1965*, reprint ed. London: WILF, 1980.

Childs, Donald J. *Modernism and Eugenics: Woolf, Eliot, Yeats, and the Culture of Degeneration*. Cambridge: Cambridge University Press, 2001.

Danius, Sara. *The Senses in Modernism: Technology, Perception, and Aesthetics*. Ithaca and London: Cornell University Press, 2002.

Doan, Laura. *Fashioning Sapphism: The Origins of a Modern English Lesbian Culture*. New York: Columbia University Press, 2001.

Eagle, Chris. *Dysfluencies: On Speech Disorders in Modern Literature*. London: Bloomsbury, 2014.

Erikson, Gregory. *The Absence of God in Modernist Literature*. London: Palgrave Macmillan, 2007.

Eysteinsson, Astradur. *The Concept of Modernism*. Ithaca: Cornell University Press, 1990.

Gordon, Craig A. *Literary Modernism, Bioscience, and Community in Early Twentieth-Century Britain*. Basingstoke: Palgrave Macmillan, 2007.

Gottlieb, Julie V. *Feminine Fascism: Women in Britain's Fascist Movement*. London: I.V. Tauris, 2003.

Hammill, Faye. *Sophistication: A Literary and Cultural History*. Liverpool: Liverpool University Press, 2010.

Haslam, Beryl. *Suffrage to Internationalism: The Political Evolution of Three British Feminists, 1908–1939*. New York: Lang, 1999.

Hobson, Suzanne. *Angels of Modernism: Religion, Culture, Aesthetics*. London: Palgrave Macmillan, 2011.

Kittler, Friedrich. *Gramophone, Film, Typewriter*. Stanford: Stanford University Press, 1999.

Lewis, Pericles. *Religious Experience and the Modernist Novel*. Cambridge: Cambridge University Press, 2010.

Maude, Ulrika. *Beckett, Technology and the Body*. Cambridge: Cambridge University Press, 2009.

Miller, Cristanne. "Religion, History, and Modernism's Protest Against the 'Uncompaniable Drawl // of Certitude.'" *Religion and Literature* 41 (2009), 259–69.

Owen, Alex. *The Place of Enchantment: British Occultism and the Culture of the Modern*. Chicago: Chicago University Press, 2004.

Peppis, Paul. *Sciences of Modernism: Ethnography, Sexology, and Psychology*. Cambridge: Cambridge University Press, 2014.

Regan, Lisa. *Winifred Holtby's Social Vision: "Members One of Another."* London: Pickering and Chatto, 2012.

Ronell, Avital. *The Telephone Book: Technology, Schizophrenia, Electric Speech*. Lincoln: University of Nebraska Press, 1989.

Said, Edward, *Culture and Imperialism*. London: Vintage Books, 1993/1994.

Salisbury, Laura, and Andrew Shail. *Neurology and Modernity: A Cultural History of Nervous Systems, 1800–1950*. Basingstoke: Palgrave Macmillan, 2010.

Taylor, Charles. *A Secular Age*. Cambridge, MA: Belknap, 2007.

Tonning, Erik. *Modernism and Christianity*. London: Palgrave Macmillan, 2014.

Weeks, Jeffrey. *Sex, Politics and Society: The Regulation of Sexuality since 1800*. New York: Longman 1981; 2nd edition, 1989.

Visual Culture

Altshuler, Bruce. *Salon to Biennial – Exhibitions That Made Art History*. 2 vols. New York: Phaidon, 2008.

Arnason, H.H., and Elizabeth C. Mansfield. *History of Modern Art*. 7th edition. Boston: Pearson, 2012.

Baudelaire, Charles. *The Painter of Modern Life and Other Essays*. Trans. Jonathan Mayne. London: Phaidon, 1995.

Brown, Judith. *Glamour in Six Dimensions: Modernism and the Radiance of Form*. Ithaca: Cornell University Press, 2009.

Bürger, Peter. *Theory of the Avant-Garde*. Trans. Michael Shaw. Minneapolis: University of Minnesota Press, 1984.

Burstein, Jessica. *Cold Modernism: Literature, Fashion, Art*. University Park: The Pennsylvania State University Press, 2012.

Clark, T.J. *The Painting of Modern Life: Paris in the Art of Manet and His Followers*. Princeton: Princeton University Press, 1984.

Conor, Liz. *The Spectacular Modern Woman: Feminine Visibility in the 1920s*. Bloomington: Indiana University Press, 2004.

Crary, Jonathan. *Suspensions of Perception: Attention, Spectacle, and Modern Culture*. Cambridge, MA: MIT Press, 1999.

Drucker, Johanna. *The Visible Word: Experimental Typography and Modern Art, 1909–1923*. Chicago: University of Chicago Press, 1997.

Ellis, Jack C. *A History of Film*. 2nd edition. Englewood Cliffs: Prentice-Hall, 1985.

Elsaesser, Thomas, ed. *Early Cinema: Space Frame Narrative*. London: British Film Institute, 1990.

Evans, Caroline. *The Mechanical Smile: Modernism and the First Fashion Shows in France and America, 1900–1929*. New Haven: Yale University Press, 2013.

Franko, Mark. *Dancing Modernism/Performing Politics*. Bloomington: Indiana University Press, 1995.

Leach, William. *Land of Desire: Merchants, Power, and the Rise of the New American Culture*. New York: Vintage, 1993.

Leyda, Jay. *Kino: A History of the Russian and Soviet Film*. Berkeley: University of California Press, 1983.

Manning, Susan. *Modern Dance, Negro Dance: Race in Motion*. Minneapolis: University of Minnesota Press, 2004.

McCarren, Felicia. *Dancing Machines: Choreographies of the Age of Mechanical Reproduction*. Stanford: Stanford University Press, 2003.

Nevett, T.R. *Advertising in Britain*. London: William Heinemann Ltd., 1982.

North, Michael. *Machine-Age Comedy*. Oxford: Oxford University Press, 2009.

Outka, Elizabeth. *Consuming Traditions: Modernism, Modernity, and the Commodified Authentic*. Oxford: Oxford University Press, 2009.

Parkinson, David. *History of Film*. London: Thames and Hudson, 1995.

Perloff, Marjorie. *The Futurist Moment: Avant-Garde, Avant Guerre, and the Language of Rupture*. Chicago: University of Chicago Press, 1986.

Pippin, Robert B. *Modernism as a Philosophical Problem: On the Dissatisfactions of European High Culture*. 2nd ed. Oxford: Blackwell Publishers, 1999.

Steele, Valerie. *Fashion and Eroticism: Ideals of Feminine Beauty from the Victorian Era to the Jazz Age*. New York: Oxford University Press, 1985.

Wilson, Elizabeth. *Adorned in Dreams: Fashion and Modernity*. 1985. New Brunswick: Rutgers University Press, 2003.

Entertainments

Balfour, John Patrick Douglas (Baron Kinross). *Society Racket. A Critical Survey of Modern Social Life, Etc.* London: John Long, 1933.

Booth, Howard J., and Nigel Rigby, eds. *Modernism and Empire*. Manchester: Manchester University Press, 2000.

Bornstein, George. *Material Modernism: The Politics of the Page*. Cambridge: Cambridge University Press, 2001.

Friedman, Susan Stanford. "Periodizing Modernism: Postcolonial Modernities and the Space/Time Borders of Modernist Studies." *Modernism/Modernity* 13.3 (2006), 425–33.

Gems, Gerald, Linda Borish, and Gertrud Pfister. *Sports in American History*. Champaign: University of Illinois Press, 2008.

Gordon, Beverly. *The Saturated World: Aesthetic Meaning, Intimate Objects, Women's Lives, 1890–1940*. Knoxville: University of Tennessee Press, 2006.

Graves, Charles. *Champagne and Chandeliers: The Story of the Café de Paris*. London: Odhams and Long Acre, 1958.

Graves, Robert, and Alan Hodge. *The Long Week-End: A Social History of Great Britain 1918–1939*. New York: W.W. Norton, 1994.

Guttmann, Allen. *From Ritual to Record: The Nature of Modern Sports*. New York: Columbia University Press, 1978. Revised 2001.

A Whole New Ball Game. Chapel Hill: University of North Carolina Press, 1988.

Heap, Chad. *Slumming: Sexual and Racial Encounters in American Nightlife, 1885–1940.* Chicago: University of Chicago Press, 2008.

Holt, Richard. *Sport and Society in Modern France.* London: Macmillan, 1981.

Sport and the British. London: Oxford University Press, 1989.

Kern, Stephen. *The Culture of Time and Space, 1880–1918.* Cambridge, MA: Harvard University Press, 1983/2003.

Marek, Jayne E. *Women Editing Modernism: "Little" Magazines and Literary History.* Lexington: The University Press of Kentucky, 1995.

Miller, Monica. "The Black Dandy as Bad Modernist." In Douglas Mao and Rebecca L. Walkowitz, eds., *Bad Modernisms.* Durham: Duke University Press, 2006, 179–205.

Otte, Marline. *Jewish Identities in German Popular Entertainment, 1890–1933.* Cambridge: Cambridge University Press, 2006.

Pennybacker, Susan Dabney. *From Scottsboro to Munich: Race and Political Culture in 1930s Britain.* Princeton: Princeton University Press, 2009.

Platt, Len. *Musical Comedy on the West End Stage, 1890–1939.* Basingstoke: Palgrave, 2004.

Rainey, Lawrence. *Institutions of Modernism: Literary Elites and Public Culture.* New Haven: Yale University Press, 1998.

Simon, Andy. "Black British Swing: The African Diaspora's Contribution to England's Own Jazz of the 1930s and 1940s." http://blackbritishswing.wordpress.com/. Dec. 22, 2012.

Taylor, D.J. *Bright Young People: The Lost Generation of London's Jazz Age.* New York: Farrar, Straus, and Giroux, 2009.

Walkowitz, Judith R. *Nights Out: Life in Cosmopolitan London.* New Haven: Yale University Press, 2012.

Weinbaum, Alys Eve, Modern Girl Around the World Research Group, ed. *The Modern Girl around the World: Consumption, Modernity, and Globalization.* Durham: Duke University Press, 2008.

White, Jerry. *London in the Twentieth Century: A City and Its People.* London, New York: Viking, 2001.

Index